The 89

Acknowl

Thanks to the people below wh(
construct these seventeen years ~. ... ...,
Mum and Dad for funding the early years and picking me up from the Haymarket at the dead of night while my sister Sue and the rest of my family have put up with years of devotion to the cause.
Bryan Thorley, for being the best headteacher you could hope to have (despite his Manchester allegiances).
Sheila Stonehouse for her research.
Paul Samber for enabling me to despise and envy Arsenal. His wife Claire for putting up with endless phone calls.
Charlie Kelly and Andy Griffin for their constructive criticism and input.
My grandad Lawrence Flynn, who though unfortunately is no longer with us, did so much to encourage my enthusiasm.
David White, my Manchester United supporting friend, who also sadly passed away but provided me with endless chances for mickey-taking but never ever bit back. RIP David.
Gillian, my wife, for putting up with my hours spent locked away in various libraries and programmes and giving me the belief in myself to attempt this.
Finally Holly and Jasmine who have had to put up with my football obsessions ever since!
Thanks everyone!

If I had known at the age of thirteen the torment they would put me through, would I have still set off down this road?

Richard Stephenson's growing up in Tynemouth didn't exactly fulfil the country's stereotype view of the average Newcastle United fan of the 1980s. Living in the sleepy, historic seaside town held little of the traditional industrial image of the North-East. The shipyards were just an outline on the up-river horizon while the nearest coalmines existed beyond the Blyth power station to the North.

His background wasn't working class enough, or his accent strong enough, to really be a Newcastle fan so both had to be disguised. The first visit to St James' Park when he was thirteen proved to be the turning point in his life.

Teaching college in southwest London lead to two years of educating London children who'd never heard of Newcastle. He moved back to the North-East in 1993 after completing six years of exile. His marriage to Gillian, a Middlesbrough fan, in 1996 was followed by the arrival of two daughters... Holly and Jasmine.

From oddball to football

The date was June 11th 1969, Newcastle United heroically recovered from 2-0 down to beat Upjest Dozsa 3-2 and in so doing won the Inter City Fairs Cup (the old UEFA Cup). Two months and seven days later, I was born. The timing of my birth became an unhappy part of my supporting career as Newcastle has failed to win a major trophy in my lifetime. They had come close a few times but they seemed destined never to reach the top; to promise the Earth... but deliver nothing.

If I had known at the age of thirteen the torment they would put me through, would I have still supported them?

In November 1983, my sister, Sue, braved her first football match. Her boyfriend Chris was taking her to the Newcastle v Cambridge United match.

None of our close family liked football; my uncles did, and my grandad did, but not us. It was a stupid game in which twenty-two men kicked a pig's bladder around for ninety minutes as far as we were concerned.

Why would anybody be interested in that?

Predictably, she hated it.... the cold, the drink (how anyone could honestly enjoy Bovril was beyond her), the game, the people, the noise, the language.... the very things (except the Bovril) that would eventually attract me to the game. She gave me her programme and gradually I started to take an interest in football on TV. I also listened to the conversations going on at school and began to think maybe there was something to this game after all. I wanted to know what the lads at school were getting excited about, and be a part of it. Here was a group who had their own credibility and place to belong. There were: the Newcastle Fans, the Sunderland Fans and the Manchester United fan. There were even the teachers who could be counted upon to forget about a lesson and join in the ritual abuse of whose team had performed the worst that weekend.

At school I was labelled an oddball. As a member of the school choir, my credibility was zero. I was an easy target for anybody who fancied having a go. One of the smallest in the year, my best form of defence was my speed which served me well throughout my school life and beyond.

I had no interest in sport and but was fascinated by Science Fiction. Any other world to escape the one I was in. Dr Who, Star Wars, Space 1999, the list was endless. My ability to quote large sections of films didn't win me many admirers. Not interested in pop music and with few friends, I became branded as weird by most and sad by the rest.

There were about four people that I could call friends and we were drawn together by the very fact that the rest of the school thought we were misfits.

One of these friends introduced me to Ice Hockey at Whitley Bay. Suddenly, sport wasn't that bad after all.

The crowds at Whitley tended to be dominated by women, presumably because the men had been to the football match the day before and took their wives or girlfriends along to "keep them sweet", after all they'd had their freedom yesterday. The men would usually keep quiet and let the women shout the insults and abuse.

I wanted to shout and scream but since the men around me kept things mostly to themselves, my friend would tell me to sit down and stop being so embarrassing. I needed somewhere I could vent my frustrations without any inhibitions.

The more my sister went on about how she couldn't see Chris thanks to 'another football match' and the more my mum and dad questioned his priorities the more I felt he had them just right.

Not coming from a sporty family meant I'd never seen Newcastle United's ground, never mind gone to a match, I was clue-less. The more I asked my sister if I could go with Chris, the less he seemed to come around.

One day, in May all that changed...

May 5th 1984 - Derby County (h)

'.....but you don't even like football.'

Those immortal words signalled the start of my new devotion. I'd only been to one match before this day (North Shields v Walsall in the F.A. Cup) and now two lads from school had said I could go with them, daring me more than anything, but I jumped at the chance.

In preparation, I rushed from school to the town on the Friday night to buy, in true football tradition, a programme, scarf and cloth cap. I had to look the part and not reveal that this was my first match. The flat cap was a must (I thought), an essential part of my supporting uniform. I bought them in the Supporters Shop in Haymarket.

It was one of a row of dingy ramshackle shops in the shadow of Marks and Spencer, run by a great set of old dears who could tell you Jackie Milburn's inside leg measurement or the favourite drinks of the 1950's Robledo brothers. If you'd pushed them they might have known someone who had seen Hughie Gallacher walking in a strange fashion near the Newcastle to London express line. Over the next few years this place became my Mecca.

That night I poured over the programme, remembering none of it the next day, shoving it in my back pocket to give the impression I'd just bought it.

We were to meet outside Haymarket at 2:30pm, but this was my first 'date'. I tried to be casual - get the last possible train, not look bothered if I was late, but I was far too excited for that.

The Metro station at Tynemouth was inhabited by one solitary fan but as I got nearer to Newcastle, each station platform seemed to be more tightly packed, inflating my sense of occasion.

Three-quarters of an hour early I bounded upstairs that led to the surface, ignoring the calmly lumbering escalators, hoping the others were going to be early, to no avail. As Metro after Metro arrived, the sheer volume of fans coming out of the station sent my pulse racing. I wasn't going to get in. The gates would be shut five minutes before we got there.

All this stress...for nothing!

By the time they arrived I had started to lose my cool and my hands were drenched in sweat.

"Been here long?" they casually enquired.

"Nah, just got here," I lied coolly, but nobody believed me, thanks to sweat-stained T-shirt and dripping face.

Walking through the streets towards the ground, I wanted to sprint ahead but didn't dare appear too eager. After all, I didn't want to ignite that sign above my head that announced to the world that I was a "match virgin". I had to act like *a* veteran, chat casually and stroll with the rest of the crowd.

The ground came into sight as we turned into a packed Strawberry Place. It was 2:40 by now and sure enough, outside the turnstiles long queues snaked back along the road. My worst fear was to be realised, my day in tatters. Some queues seemed to have hardly anybody outside them. I suggested joining a shorter queue. "Don't be stupid, man. I'm not paying three quid." We joined what seemed to be the longest queue and it was now I realised why. The shorter queue was for the adult price. We had attached ourselves to the juvenile one. I looked around at the fans waiting alongside me, it seemed that if you were under the age of twenty-four, you could try and pass for under sixteen. There were men with full beards dragging screaming kids behind them, all trying to save themselves £1.50, the price, I imagine of a couple of pints.

The police would saunter up and down the line turfing them out, every time a 'copper' came along there would be a mass effaces buried in programmes or tying shoelaces.

To take my mind off the time and the slowness of our line I watched the thousands of black and white (and grey) bodies streaming past, their pace quickening every time they glanced at their watches. I was trying my best to remain calm and failing miserably. After what seemed hours, but was in fact ten minutes, I was in. £1.50 to the gate-man before tackling the endless steps that twined their way up the grassy bank.

We fought our way past men and boys queuing for burgers, pies, crisps and toilets then came to an abrupt stop. The pitch was nowhere in sight, but there was a mass of bodies in front of us. As small fourteen year-olds we hadn't a cat-in hell's chance of seeing anything from amongst the army of fans who had just left the pub at 2:45, so it was a case of pushing to get further into the heaving scrum. At that moment the team emerged, led by Kevin Keegan. The fleeting glimpse I'd had of the pitch was squeezed out of me. I became moulded around a thick and immovable concrete barrier.

The match started with Newcastle attacking the far end (simply called *'the* Leeezas"). This meant that I would be able to see what was happening, or so I thought. Wrong! Every time we looked like getting anywhere near Derby's penalty area the crowd surged forward welding me to the barrier even further, I fought to stay upright as thousands of pints of Exhibition, Newcastle Brown and McEwan's lager pressed down on me.

This was bad enough - then we scored! As far as I could tell the little man at the far end of the ground put the round white thing that was the centre of attention into the big bag. This action resulted in my position being shifted ten metres to the right as I was flung from one jubilant body to another. I tried to keep on my feet while looking as if I had never been happier (which of course, I hadn't). This happened four times, and by the last I had become a veritable expert, even managing to have a glimpse of some of the action. This made it all that much sweeter!

We left the ground to the strains of Buster singing 'Goin' Up' with its inspirational chorus of 'Coin' Up, Coin' Up Goin' Up, Up, Up, Up, Up.' The fact that Newcastle had won 4-0 didn't have much bearing on me because I'd hardly seen any of it.

The whole experience had me buzzing as we walked away from the ground to the Metro station at Haymarket. I joined in with the shouting/ singing voices as they dispersed in every direction, all with the same delighted expression.

I'd at last joined a group where I didn't have to prove anything to anybody. I was happy to be a faceless individual, eager to prove my loyalty to my new found cause.

May 17th 1984 Liverpool (h)

Ever since a young and emerging Mark Lawrenson outpaced Kevin Keegan in an F. A. cup match at Anfield, he had made it known that he would retire at the end of season 1983-84. This gave me my second taste of St James' Park. I had been disappointed that the last game of the season against Brighton had long since been sold out, so when the lads told me that they were going to get tickets a few days after the Derby match I knew what I had to do.

The problem was that tickets went on sale at 10am on the Tuesday and stopped selling at 4pm. Exactly the time I should have been at school. We worked out that in our lunch break we could get up to the ground and back in time for English. Everything went to plan-

> 12pm - race for the metro.
> 12:30pm - reach the ground.
> 12:31pm - pick ourselves up from the

ground where we had just sunk after seeing the size of the queue as it wound itself out of the ground and along Barrack Road. We hadn't thought of that one! Oops. We were here now so we had no alternative - Kev expects!

We waited, glancing at our watches every time the line stopped. There were a lot of schoolboys there with the same bright idea as us (we'll be back before we're missed seemed a common misconception). It wasn't surprising to hear when we arrived back at school, having missed English and dived into a just-beginning Maths that a register had been taken in English. The proverbial shit was going to hit the fan for us. There were a lot of parents who had written letters of excuse for their sons (dentists, doctors, funerals...) but a few of us had no such notes (or wanted them). Were we going to stand up and take our punishment like suckers? No! Like men (or 14 year olds who had just spent £1.50 of their hard-earned pocket money on the best ticket of the year). Our punishment was an hour in detention (my only ever), a serious talking to about suspension for a week and disgrace to our parents and finally an 'enjoy the match' dismissal.

I remembered my dad's immortal words six days earlier, I did like football but I was in love with Newcastle United and everything that went with it.

I felt vindicated when I looked in the match programme to see Lord Kitchener staring, with his finger pointed directly at me and the immortal words....**YOUR CLUB NEEDS YOU!**

We arrived earlier for the game that night (ten minutes). I looked at the barrier with knowing eyes and this time, I levered my way under and in front of it. I could see not only the goal at the far end - but also the top of the goal at our end - success. For the first time I had a chance to glance round the ground. It was a warm night and the grass glowed in the beam of the floodlights. The rest of the ground was in black compared to the glow of the pitch. The game got under way and my satisfaction at my positioning barely lasted as a silence hit the ground - Liverpool had scored. This was obviously not supposed to happen, even the starlings above settled glumly on the roof of the West Stand. The atmosphere picked up once more after the initial shock had subsided. Newcastle responded. As the ball bounced around in the Liverpool penalty area, the crowd shouted the same unrecognisable phrase. The next thing I knew I was flung from my vantage point and carried down and off to my right amid a sea of ecstatic faces. I had been prepared for a goal but not this! From my new perch, sandwiched between two lager bellies and holding on to the bodies in front of me, I tried to steady myself. We all swayed with the repercussions from further up the terracing and watched as Keegan placed the ball in front of the goal, took two steps back before blasting a shot. As the ball squirmed in the net, I was again flung forward, further from my place of safety.

The match ended 2-2, Terry McDermott equalising a second Liverpool goal. At the final whistle, Keegan walked around the ground, as if applauding each and every member of the crowd. I felt like I was gate-crashing a party but felt the overwhelming power of the evening. The stadium was alive as he climbed emotionally into a waiting helicopter and ascended as if to the waiting gods as fireworks lit up the sky and the sprawling city. Tonight, I had been a part of history, I would be able to tell my children and grandchildren that I'd been a part of it all.

Once the sky had returned to its normal black with an orange glow, it was time for the serious business of getting out. I decided to avoid the crush as the occupants of the Gallowgate tried to shoe-horn themselves through a gap three metres wide. For them, the added incentive of extra time available to drink the evening away if they could only push their way past everybody else with the same idea. For me as a fourteen-year-old it was back home to bed, to reflect upon the evening. So I waited.

I looked around me as the floodlights beamed down, and I was able to take in the sheer size of the concrete shapes which rose up around me. The old wooden West Stand which looked like the bridge of a battleship, seemed out of place, a relic from a glorious past. Every other part was grey and functional with an imposing aspect that reflected an area grown up with mining and shipbuilding. More spaces appeared as the crowd gradually thinned, taking with it all the energy and passion of the evening, I listened to the buzz of animated conversations taking place, and realised that I was about to change. The boy who had enjoyed long hours hidden away in his room playing with plastic soldiers before developing on to Star Wars figures (Princess Leia in her various outfits) was being replaced. The ability to make a machine gun or laser noise wasn't important any more. What was? The next match, the feeling of belonging, the thrill and sound of the ground as the ball hit the back of the net, the faces around me and the joy that we all shared - that's what was important.

1984-1985 Season

The Summer, after those two games, went slowly. Musically, the country seemed to split into two camps as Frankie Goes to Hollywood battled it out in the charts with Neil from The Young Ones. One half was worried about being wiped out in a Nuclear Holocaust while the other half was more worried about the hole in their shoe which was tragically "letting in water...". I had much more important things to worry about, namely the newly acquired problem of holidays and the beginning of the football season. After all what self-respecting fan would be on holiday for the big kick off?

We went with some friends to the furthest part of France, as far away from the impending football season as you could get (it seemed to me... although I think the Arctic is further). Before this, I had become obsessed with anything Newcastle which could be gleaned from the press. I read about Sheffield Wednesday and Chelsea (the teams promoted with us) buying players with first division experience and longed for an article linking United with .... well, anybody. Then came the news that Arthur Cox had resigned because the board wouldn't give him money to buy players. I feigned the despair that I knew everybody else was feeling (after all I'd only been supporting three months), which wasn't lifted when Jack Charlton became the manager and announced that he would 'not be panicked into buying players...' which basically meant 'I've got nowt to spend.' This certainly didn't satisfy my need for big spending and star players.

When the time had come to depart for France, there had been no new signings, which made me even more desperate for news. The sun shone down each and every day, but all I wanted to do was play football, acting out what I imagined might happen in the season to come. I was absolutely hopeless but, as with a lot of crap players, enjoyed running around a lot. My friend in France was a boy called James who was also a Newcastle fan. He was a decent player, had very blonde hair and seemed to have no problem with girls, who thought he was drop dead gorgeous, whereas I resembled a rather awkward runner bean, especially in shorts. It was at this point that I realised I wasn't going to be a hit with the ladies just yet, so football would give me my sense of pride.

My parents had noticed this new turn in my life and for my birthday they bought me the Newcastle away shirt. It was silvery grey (just grey really) with black pinstripes and the all-important club badge - NUFC written in a circle so that the other letters sat upon the C. It was an incredibly dull badge but it was what it stood for that was all important. 'Fifteen pounds was a lot to spend on just one shirt,' my dad would say and although I never said it to him it was exactly what I'd wanted.

To make things worse I was going to be stuck in France while Newcastle started their first season in the First Division in six years. On the Saturday Newcastle was due to play Leicester I started feeling itchy. Saying things to James like They'll be coming out the tunnel now', or That'll do for half time' and then 'It's all over bar the shouting!' These phrases rolled off the tongue along with many others, but it didn't help me know the score. There was nothing for it but to ring home. The nearest phone being five miles up a mountain road it meant I had to suggest that 'it would be nice to see how grandad was doing.' After an hour pleading a Grandson's concern, they gave in and grandad was indeed able to inform me that we had beaten them -nothing to do with me but I had been with the lads in spirit and that must have counted for something.

I couldn't find anything out about the home game against Sheffield Wednesday. All the English papers I bought said nothing and it was when we were driving back across France that I managed to buy a paper which said ' ...after Newcastle's 2-1 victory over Sheff Wed ....'. This prompted celebrations on the back seat of the car, which my dad had been driving for four hours and I was told by everybody else to shut up otherwise they would leave me in France and then I'd never to get another game. In my mind I was crushed against a barrier again, couldn't see a thing and was happy.

The journey continued into England and much to my protestations we were going to stop off in Cambridge to see my sister's new University. I did point out that if we drove non-stop at an average speed of 60 miles an hour and didn't go to Cambridge we could reach Newcastle by 2:30, they could drop me off in Newcastle and I'd go to the match and meet them back at home. After all, I argued it wasn't every day that your team could go top of the league. I can't think why, but my idea wasn't even given any consideration, it would have to be Radio 2 Medium Wave. What chance Newcastle v Aston Villa being the second half commentary game?

It was 0-0 at half time I'd missed nothing. Three minutes into the second half Chris Waddle scored as I leapt about in the car, somewhere on the fast lane of the M1. The game finished 3-0 and although my dad threatened to turn the radio off at various points during the game, it stayed on as it was announced that Newcastle were top. My career had started with an unbeaten run, but as I was soon to find out, it wasn't a frequent occurrence and I should enjoy it while it lasted because the only way was down.

September 8th 1984 Manchester United (a)

The next couple of games had shown me the down side of my new passion. Away to Arsenal we had been beaten 2-0. It even made the News at Ten headlines -'....and the leaders are beaten for the first time.' This was no real surprise to me but worse was to follow. At Manchester United we were beaten 5-0. It had been 0-0 approaching half time but with Man United not looking like scoring, John Ryan passed the ball back to Kevin Carr and it was intercepted by Jesper Olsen who latched onto it and scored. After that Newcastle fell apart like the proverbial pack of cards. I still remember Ryan's name and can't help but spit it out in the same sentence as the word 'Donkey' and 'What was he thinking of?' What made it worse was that his piece of lunacy was repeated over and over again because ours was the featured match that Sunday on The Big Match. Each time I kept on hoping that Carr would save or Olsen would send it shooting into the back row of the seats behind... but he never did. Listening to the match on the radio had been hard enough without the persecution that Ryan and myself received. Of course, I didn't have to watch it the next day... or did I?

September 15th Everton (h)

This was my first visit to St James' Park since the Liverpool game. James was going to come too and I intended to get to the ground early. I decided it might be a good idea if we could see the goals go in. The best place to do that was from the front. We arrived at 2pm and made our way down a virtually empty Gallowgate end. Once at the bottom the view was completely different. I looked up at the goal through the standard ten-foot high fence that encircled nearly every ground. Of course I now wore my away shirt along with the cap and scarf from the previous matches but now to finish off the image of a dedicated supporter- I had an extra scarf tied around my wrist. A throwback from the seventies this final piece of supporting apparel may have seemed excessive but I didn't want anyone to be in any doubt as to who I supported. A shirt could go under a jacket, a cap could be knocked off but you could guard your wrist scarf with your life, making use of when it came to singing 'You'll Never Walk Alone', raising it aloft as you joined thousands of others swaying together, honouring your heroes.

We were also able to take advantage of the lads and (occasionally) lasses who wandered around the cinder track selling plastic bottles of pop, crisps and previously unheard-of chewing gum-cum-mint called Klix.

This mobile sweet shop proved too much for my itching fingers (especially when I noticed the size of the crisps - giant, with a price to more than match it).

With crisps and unexpectedly explosive Klix resting in my trembling hands, I could soak up the atmosphere in the same way children's trips out weren't complete until they bought something...anything.

My decision to stand at the front was justified as, in the thirteenth minute Chris Waddle was tripped. I knew what to do because I'd seen this one before.

'Penalty!' I shouted and pointed in the direction of the penalty spot.

Sure enough the referee pointed to the spot too. Peter Beardsley stepped up to score as I grabbed hold of James, who was somewhat taken aback and along with an assortment of young boys and old men we pogoed in celebration.

Thirteen minutes later we were stopped by an Everton goal. After half time Kenny Wharton restored the lead thanks to a sloppy back pass by Derek Mountfield. That was to be the last time we were jubilant as Trevor Steven (born in Berwick - you thought he'd have known better) and Andy Gray in the last minute quelled our enthusiasm. This was the first defeat I had been to. A great game it had been but what was the point of that - we had lost. Why couldn't dad have driven faster so I could have gone to The Aston Villa match? Why did we have to go to France at all? The kind of thoughts only a depressed fourteen-year old would have thought raced through my head. Was I a jinx?

September 22nd 1984 Queens Park Rangers (a)

On the Saturday Nigel (a Newcastle fan) and Jon (a Manchester United fan) came down to Tynemouth for a 'kick-about'. This meant that we would spend a couple of hours trying to outdo each other in a completely crap way to score with shots from the edge of the penalty area. We would spend five minutes lining up a fantastic shot, thinking of Waddle charge in from the wing to unleash an unstoppable shot before being mobbed by his grateful team-mates. In reality, when the shot was ready to be taken it either rolled limply along the ground (and if it resulted in a goal claim that it was all part of the trickery), or it soared skywards, over the fence and onto the main road behind the goal.

Jon was a Manchester United fan but, contrary to the popular rumour that Man U fans come from anywhere but, he actually came from Manchester and had just moved to our school. Since they weren't a very successful team at the time it meant we had some grounds to take the mickey out of him. In fairness to him, he always knew who they were playing, which was more than some.

This particular day we decided that we'd listen to the radio before embarking on our 'match', also Manchester were playing Liverpool that day so there was a good chance we could rib Jon if Newcastle weren't doing well. As the first half wore on Newcastle kept on scoring goals. Neil McDonald started the ball rolling then Chris Waddle knocked in his hat trick. Nigel and I greeted each goal with astonished delight while for once Jon couldn't say a thing. It was made all the sweeter because in those days the radio commentary was in the form of the 'It's a goal' show. There was an introductory shout with music which interrupted an interview or a quiz then; "It's a goal", the reporter would act 'surprised'.

He'd say "Let's go straight to Loftus road where we understand there's been a goal..." the tension would mount as the reporter at the ground would say; "Hello, can you hear me?"

"Yes, we bloody well can..." Each time we heard the shout and accompanying music all conversation trailed away, "Is it our game or Sunderland's?"

"It's ours, we're bound to be losing, I can't listen..." but we always did.

On this occasion, each time they went to Loftus Road it was another Newcastle goal. We were all happy by half time because Man United was beating Liverpool 1-0 but we were winning 4-0. What a team we had...no-one could stop us ...we'd soon be top again. Confident about the result we decided it would be the right time to re-enact those precious forty-five minutes on the field. So we set off.

Typically we were in inspired form, lifting shots over the bar from two yards, missing the ball when it was "...easier to score..." and generally playing as we and many thousands of football fans could. From time to time we'd mutter things like "...and Beardsley makes it 8-0, what a team..."

But Jon started chipping away at this new found confidence.

"What would you do if..." Various scenarios were presented, 4-3, 5-4.

"Would you cry if..." The scenarios included were 4-4, 5-5. "I would laugh if..."

The final options were 5-4 and 6-5 to QPR.

The confidence was teetering inside us...surely they couldn't...could they?

That was it, game ended - we had to know. As we charged back to my house our moods had changed. Jon was cheerfully predicting all manner of unthinkable situations, and we tried to laugh them off, all the time trying to push such ideas from our own minds.

The walk was quicker on the way back and we were greeted by my dad. Although he'd no interest in football he would dutifully turn on the radio or teletext to find out the score, if only just to predict what sort of mood I would be in when I returned. His face was grave. We knew it was bad when he uttered the words "I think you should sit down, Richard...".

Jon was overjoyed, "You lost, the only team in history (probably) to lose after leading 4-0!"

"What happened, dad - tell us the worst."

"It was five all." He then left us... in silence. Jon exploded... there was nothing we could say after Man United's 1-1 draw with Liverpool.

September 29th 1984 West Ham (h)

In the week leading up to the game, one of my wishes came true. At school, someone had heard that the signing of a new player was imminent. So at four o'clock I raced to the paper shop, and there on the billboard that advertised the Chronicle was the headline - 'United's new signing - Latest'. It *was* true. The names of top players bounded around my head - Craig Johnston, (Nick said he wasn't happy at Liverpool) or Sammy Lee to bolster up the mid-field. The suspense was mounting as I opened the newly purchased newspaper. There he was...Pat Heard. Who?

The news wasn't exactly the major signing I had hoped for. Was he the man with the sole responsibility for re-starting the season? I didn't have a clue who he was. Charlton told the press, "he is not a spectacular player but he would definitely strengthen the team." Who was I to criticise him? The most enjoyable part of it for me was that in exchange went John Ryan and £50,000 pounds, which bearing in mind my memories of that back-pass at Old Trafford seemed pretty good business, especially if, in exchange, we got a mid-field player, a position we weren't exactly abundant in.

A 1-1 draw was notable for the treatment of Bobby Barnes, West Ham's black number seven. During the game a succession of bananas was thrown at him by a number of idiots. This was my first direct experience of racism towards a black person. The first time I remember seeing black people in the flesh was when I was on holiday in London at the age often. In Newcastle at the time you never met black people on the street. There was a healthy Asian community but that was it. Racism against Asians was widespread and unfortunately accepted in Newcastle but there were no black people to abuse. Football gave these idiots that opportunity. I wasn't aware of the problems faced by those of a different racial background and it wasn't until I moved to London to go to college that I was able to appreciate the diversity of cultures within our society.

Sadly, the pattern I observed that day became a pattern whenever black players played against Newcastle and continued well after players like Cole, Ferdinand and Asprilla had been hailed as Newcastle 'greats'. It seemed that if they played for us they received honorary Geordie status.

Afterwards, Charlton and the board of Newcastle apologised to Barnes and said that anybody caught chanting racist abuse would be ejected from the ground. But it was the lack of respect that some of these 'people' had for such players that came across clearly in conversations I overheard on the terraces. Later that season Newcastle signed Tony Cunningham, not a brilliant player but a real trier, who won over a lot of Newcastle fans but his 'tune' went along the lines of -

"He's black, he's broon, he's playing for the toon, Cunningham, Cunningham." He took it in the spirit that it was meant, understanding the fondness that the fans had for him. Nonetheless, however well meaning, it was still insulting and summed up the lack of understanding that prevailed.

My first teaching post was in Greenford, West London where there is a large Asian community. There were a great number of talented Asian footballers on my school team but sadly this wealth of talent would not be seen on the professional football field. I hope there will come a time, when the game is fully multicultural but it seems there is still so much to be done.

January 1st 1985 Sunderland (h)

After the Bobby Barnes incident the furore over Newcastle fans and their racist tendencies died down. Newcastle stumbled along in the league, slipping towards the bottom. Christmas had been and gone, including the heartache of missing my first home game of the season against Arsenal because we were going to go to my cousins for Boxing Day." It's only one game" they said, "You're not going and that's that" and finally I had to admit defeat. I made them suffer though as I sat with my new radio which I got for

Christmas (nice one Mum) tuned into the "It's a Goal" show and headphones pinned over one ear. After all I didn't want to be anti-social, did I? Maybe it was fate because I didn't have much to shout about as Newcastle lost 3-1.

Strangely, since that day I have never been made to go to a family meal when there's been a match on, I wonder why?

We had also signed a player, during November, I had actually heard of (sorry Pat). Gary Megson was signed from Sheff Wed for £165,000 and it was a sign of my further development as a football fan that I was able to give my opinion of him, "...he's a good player" I would tell the other lads.

The most eagerly awaited game of the season had arrived. Sunderland on New Year's Day was going to be my first taste of the rivalry that existed in a Tyne-Wear derby. Demand had been so great for this match that the only tickets we could get were in the Paddocks, a narrow strip of terracing below the West Stand. There were no child reductions so we had to pay the scandalous sum of £3.50- to see a football match! My friend Burg (who had no interest in football whatsoever) came and so did Will who had started coming along with me and James to the matches and soon got hooked. Burg came so he could take the mickey out of all the Sunderland fans at school and this was his first ever game. We took our places early, in order to soak up the atmosphere. The Leazes end which normally only had fifteen hundred away supporters in one exposed corner was full of Sunderland fans and there promised to be quite an atmosphere as the Gallowgate filled up after the pubs had shut. This was the first time I had an opportunity to watch it in full flow. The surges created as more people piled forward made me think of ripples after a stone has been thrown into a pond. One bellyful of lager would push a couple of others and before you knew it nearly a hundred bodies were struggling to stay upright with the familiar cry of "Hey man, ho'man". I could even make out faces being squeezed against the barriers with the same agonised joy I had shown barely eight months earlier. Our view of the pitch was obscured somewhat by the barrier fence that circled three sides of the ground. We would have our own mini-surges whenever play disappeared into the top left corner as we strained to follow it. Generally, though life was more sedate as we all had a fair bit of room to move around in.

The away end burst into life half an hour before kick off with the predictable, "We hate the Mags and we hate the Mags..." (to be repeated until opposition is bored or you've been struck by a bottle). This signalled an instant response of anti-Sunderland venom from the Gallowgate as the whole ground joined in with various tunes being sung independently of each other. The effect of all this was just a wall of sound, which rose into the air to disappear in the rain that had been falling all day. People from Newcastle refer to anybody from Sunderland as Mackems because of the difference in the two accents. While we say make and take, Wearsiders say mack and tack. I had never heard this said until I started work in a Sunderland school and the children would always fight over who was going to 'tack' any corners or free-kicks. Before this I had always known that they talked differently but when I heard it for the first time on a Wearside football pitch it was like having a door opened. It was true after all and I had a satisfied glow around me for weeks, like the glow children used to get from eating Ready Brek on the adverts from the 80's, only it was the glow of knowledge.

On the other side of the argument, Sunderland couldn't shout about hating Geordies (unlike the rest of the foot-balling community doon Sooth) because a lot of Sunderland fans were Geordies as well. This was because they came from South Shields and Gateshead which were within the smell of the Tyne - the definition I use of a Geordie. (I am saying this and completely ignoring the outdated theory that you had to be born within the sound of St Nicholas' bells). Most Sunderland fans come from Sunderland and its surrounding villages whereas Newcastle had a larger conurbation to draw from - including Tynemouth through to Blyth, South Shields in the East and out to Hexham in the West. I never had any alternative but support Newcastle whereas if I had lived South of the River Tyne I could have supported either.

Today though, both sets of supporters were making the most of the first derby for five years. When the teams came out the atmosphere was turned up another notch. The rain made the game even more exciting as tackles slid in whenever either team got the ball. We feared the worst as Sunderland had the upper hand, taking advantage of the fact that we were without Waddle, mid-field battler David McCreery and also club captain Glen Roeder. Roeder was the owner of the legendary (at least in

Newcastle) Roeder shuffle which he used to great effect when bringing the ball away from the United defence. He would go towards an opponent and then at the last minute shuffle his feet and magically he would be away, charging onto the attack - brilliant! Well we didn't have them so that was that - no hope. But, in the fifteenth minute, Beardsley drilled a shot goal-wards in typical fashion. Burg celebrated by grabbing hold of me and shaking me, all around us bonding was taking place on a grand scale on three sides of the ground. There then followed the joy of a sending off as Howard Gayle brought down Wes Saunders for a penalty (more shaking from Burg once I had explained what was happening) and Peter Beardsley scored his second. The rest of the game followed in the same amazing style, as Peter Beardsley missed a second penalty before scoring a third to complete his hat-trick, while Gary Bennett was sent off for good measure.

    The feeling when we left the ground was one of relief because Sunderland had been tipped as favourites. Their team was in the quarter- finals of the Milk Cup and higher in the league but we were the better team today. Going back to school we could hold our heads up high, scribble "There's only one Peter Beardsley," on our rough books and then wave them under the nose of a Mackem. We could also 'cough' 3-1 when we walked past them and generally rub it in that we were the best, forget Liverpool or Man United - Newcastle were the ones!

    I also saw my first (but not last) piece of football hooliganism as some yobs set about first rocking, then turning over, a transit van they obviously thought was from Sunderland. I stood there watching for about five minutes, waiting to see whether the owner was actually from Sunderland or not. If he was... what then? Was I about to rush across and tell him who did it? I think that my curiosity was an example of what made football hooliganism such a popular thing for the TV and newspapers to cover. I didn't know why they turned the van over but I wanted to find out. I didn't know whose van it was but I wanted to find out. Similarly, people say it's disgusting and they just make up their own theories as to who football hooligans are and why they do it. A living soap opera, but by focusing on the misery of it all they were giving it life, allowing something that should have died out in the seventies to breath well into the eighties and beyond. The news doesn't spend the same time looking at violence when people get drunk and get into fights on holiday because that's just down to too much drink. Football hooligans should just be arrested and left to serve their sentences without their crimes being publicised. Some children at school are constantly in trouble because they have worked out that is the way to get some attention.

Being good doesn't put them in the spotlight... but hit somebody and it does.

January 9th 1985 Nottingham Forest (h)

My first ever match was in the FA Cup 2nd round in 1982. It was North Shields against Walsall. Shields played at Appleby Park (now, sadly knocked down and replaced by housing -a waste.) It was 50p to get in and I went with Andy who had got me into ice hockey at Whitley Bay. The only thing I remembered was that there was an amazing amount of violence at the game. We had got a good spot on the home terracing behind the goal when everybody pushed our way and there was a sudden roar as half a dozen spotty Shields 'lads' pushed their way through muttering things like "We can take them there's only a few of them." Only for these self-same boys to push their way back past us muttering "We'll have to get reinforcements..." My days of playing with toy soldiers and watching any old war films told me that they weren't comparing thoughts on the ongoing match, which Shields were losing 1-0. The scoring of the goal coincided with the start of all the pushing...how strange. The pushing subsided as a ring seemed to be formed with two particularly hard looking Walsall fans standing on their own on a section of recently emptied terrace.

"There's plenty of room over there" I mentioned naively," Let's go and stand there." This was an idea Andy and his Dad were not in favour of. For the second half we moved to the side of the pitch as the action began to unfold. The game continued to go badly for Shields as two more goals were scored but my interest had long since gone as far as football was concerned. The cause of this was the two Walsall fans from the first half who had now been joined by a few friends and a crowd of young lads from Shields. We had a great view. I remember vividly, as the final whistle went, the Walsall fans being thrown over the back fence of the ground and into someone's garden. It was done in the same way we used to give each other the bumps, but I had a feeling that it was nobody's birthday.

In my pre-supporting days, because of my sister's involvement with Duncan, whose Grandad was on the board of directors, we both watched Newcastle's 1984 third round cup game at Liverpool on TV. She wanted to spot him in the crowd (fat chance I told her, as I had become an expert on televised football). I was interested so I could take the piss out of him next time I saw him. Needless to say she didn't spot him in the crowd and I'd plenty ready to say for our next meeting... but I didn't. Newcastle had lost 4-0 but when I got to school, ready with all my carefully prepared quips, the mood of optimism took me aback. These people cared so much about Newcastle and they all felt the same way... Liverpool were miles better but next year Newcastle would get revenge, (and they weren't so bad in the first half).

After that I watched my first F.A. Cup final in 1984... Watford v Everton. I had been to precisely two Newcastle games by now and sat and watched the whole of the coverage on BBC1. My dad couldn't understand what had happened to me. Here I was watching two teams I hadn't heard of getting on to their respective buses, I had bought the match programme the night before and was telling him about all the players, information I had diligently swotted up on. I watched the interview with Elton John who was chairman of Watford, listened to him singing about the blues and didn't say anything about hair pieces or crap records. I was besotted by the idea of the FA Cup. Every year I have looked forward to watching the moment when the teams leave their hotels for Wembley, and the send-off by the few dedicated fans who follow after them. Every year since that first final I longed to see the Newcastle players board one of those buses, and every year I've been disappointed.

This was my first experience of the FA Cup. I soon learnt a few facts that every self- respecting fan must know.

1. Every year be prepared for BBC's showing of Ronnie Radford scoring for Hereford in 1972, accompanied by the inevitable commentary by John Motson: "...now Tudor's gone down for Newcastle...Radford again.., oh, what a goal, WHAT A GOAL! Radford the scorer, Ronnie Radford."

2. Newcastle won three FA Cups in 1951, '52 and '55. In '55 Jackie Milburn scored the quickest goal in a cup final.
3. Newcastle last appeared in the final in 1974 and were humiliated by Liverpool.
4. Trelford Mills had single-handedly knocked Newcastle out of the cup the previous season when he refereed the game against Brighton, and when you mentioned his name you had to spit violently upon the ground.
5. It had been X years since that final in 74 and we were due a change in luck.

The first week in each year you could guarantee hearing all these facts at least twice, on the TV, radio or from the bloke next to you on the terrace. It was part of Cup football on Tyneside...and tradition.

That night we were playing Notts Forest, 7th in the first division and "a good bet for the cup". We had drawn at the City ground and now were going to "finish the job off". Yeah, as if! To add extra spice, there was the added attraction of a midweek match.

As you approached the ground the smell of hot-dogs and burgers greeted you. Your breath met the cold air like fumes from a pyre, twining into the blackness as it did and all thoughts of the day at work or school drifted away with it. The stadium took on a different personality under the glare of the lights. The unfriendly character of the ground along with any gaps in the crowd disappeared in the dark. The pitch looked greener and lusher and the shouts of the crowd seemed to drift across the stadium easier.

Three minutes into the game and we had hit the post twice and had one shot cleared off the line. We were watching eleven men on heat...Chris Waddle scored to send us into delirium but gradually our bright start faded as Peter Davenport equalised for Forest, despite a snowball launched at him as he shot. Newcastle were out of gas and although the match went into extra time there was an inevitability about the outcome as the final score was 3-1 to Forest. I remembered how I hadn't been too upset when Forest equalised in the first game when we were playing so well because it meant I would be able to go to my first FA Cup game. I looked forward to singing all the Wembley chants I'd heard on TV, but there'd been none of that. The Newcastle fans were far too superstitious for that...not until we reached the quarter finals at least. I blamed myself, I shouldn't have assumed we would win the replay. I would learn the hard way that Wembley was an elusive prize everybody sought but few won. It was back to school, knowing that the Sunderland fans were ready with their taunts and jibes. They were through to the quarter-finals of the Milk Cup and a potential trip to Wembley and we'd nothing but a victory on New Year's Day. Words couldn't describe how we felt, but in the end we'd have the last laugh.

Monday April 8th 1985 - Sunderland (a)

This was it - my first away match! I had joined the big boys! I would be at one end of the ground, surrounded by a partisan crowd, baying for blood. I'd thought about how I'd feel when we scored... the whole ground silent except us. Everybody would be looking at us, thinking "If only those fences weren't there..." in that fearless way football supporters think when they are on the other side of the ground, shouting obscenities at a target who can't hear and therefore doesn't care what you think... At the same time they would have that feeling deep down as the opposition celebrated -that someone had got one over you, not only that but they'd done it in your house... but that they were sitting in your bedroom laughing at you.

There wasn't any better place to do it than at the home of the local enemy.

Nige's dad gave me, Nige and Will a lift to Seaburn that morning and at 10:45 we left the car and began the walk to the ground. An eerie atmosphere surrounded Seaburn. You couldn't see anybody in the houses, nobody standing chatting, everybody was heading for the same place. Even the bricks of the houses were redder than Newcastle bricks. From time to time I could see glimpses of floodlights, hear patches of noise...which only got me more nervous. Had the game kicked off already? Did I have my ticket? Was there a bunch of mad Mackems around the corner? I kept on trying to walk faster, urging the others on then stopping to let them catch up. Then...there it was... and I relaxed as I saw the queues of Newcastle fans waiting to get in. I was amongst friends.

In contrast to the relative drab newness of St James', Roker Park was a feast of red-painted wood and steel. It seemed the ground hadn't been changed since the 1930's. There was a worn, well-used look to the ground which made me think I was stepping back in time. I expected the players to come out with baggy shorts as if in a black and white newsreel... with straight backs and Brylcreemed hair. History seemed to spring out from every corner, almost making you forget the cold blowing in from the North Sea.

As we took our positions, I wished we had set off earlier, there was the barrier, the big bugger behind me... and survival was once again the name of the game. I would have the upper hand because this was my territory. Nigel and his dad were from the seats and not used to it. I just had to make sure I didn't lose sight of my lift out of here.

Sunderland had made it to the Milk Cup final and took great delight in reminding us of the fact. Unfortunately for them they'd lost to Norwich with an own goal scored by Gordon Chisholm. The return of "One Gordon Chisholm" seemed to stop their joy quite swiftly.

The game kicked off and the noise we generated seemed to echo off the far end. Maybe it was my imagination but could I hear Newcastle fans in the Fulwell end opposite? There followed, twenty minutes into the game, a parting of the Sunderland fans as the source of the Newcastle "echo" was discovered. The Newcastle fans in the Roker end realised what was going on and began to cheer, singing about "Geordie aggro". Suddenly the match was a side-show as hundreds of Newcastle fans were led from the Fulwell end, along the side of the pitch and put into our enclosure. Each of them was received as a hero and suitably raised their hands to acknowledge this praise. I didn't even think of them as hooligans because I hadn't seen any violence. The Sunderland fans had just parted on discovering who these imposters were.

Attention returned to the match, which was a shame because it was crap and non-eventful but every so often whenever there was some more action in the crowd the atmosphere picked up. Again, it just seemed to be a lot of pushing and jostling before the invaders were taken out but I know it would have been different if it had happened near me. As the final whistle blew we were happy with a point from a goalless draw and could taunt the Sunderland fans about their imminent relegation. The Newcastle fans were kept in for twenty or so minutes as the Sunderland fans dispersed and then we were released into the by now empty streets of Seaburn.

As we left, conversation was kept to a minimum. We walked quietly back to tie car, still keeping a look out for angry Sunderland fans. It wasn't how I'd imagined an away match to be but it was only my first. I hadn't experienced what it was like to 3e a jubilant interloper or part of the miserable minority. All that was still to come.

Saturday 4th May 1985 - Tottenham Hotspur (h)

For the Spurs game my Grandad bought seat tickets in the West Stand. As we took our positions I was amazed at how much more you could see from there. For starters you didn't have to peer through a fence and you weren't getting pulled everywhere by the bloke behind you. I could actually see the players clearly, even their faces. They looked different when they weren't behind a wire fence.

With Newcastle needing a draw against Tottenham to be certain of staying up and with the scores locked at 1-1, a certain Glen Hoddle hit a thirty yard shot. As it hit both posts I (fatally) relaxed... only to watch it drop in for the winner. Although Newcastle equalised, Spurs scored again. This late strike meant that we could still be relegated! In only my first full season! There was one game left - away to Norwich and I had to be there. It wasn't the fact that Newcastle still needed a point to stay up that drove me on...it had nothing to do with the team, it was an entirely selfish desire to prove my loyalty.

Saturday May 11th 1985 - Norwich City (a)

The season had reached its final day. Newcastle had won six out of the last fifteen games and were still not safe.

Since I'd been going to the matches I'd finally found a place where it didn't matter that I wasn't popular in school. It didn't matter that I'd had no success in asking girls out (no matter how hard I tried) or that according to my teachers I always "could do better". All my anxieties were irrelevant when I passed through the turnstile.

The lads who'd first introduced me to Newcastle carried on their own match day routine but I now had my own. James had stopped going to matches with me at Christmas and, though he was more popular with the girls, I felt justified in saying that I was the more dedicated fan. I now had to prove I was better than all the others from my school who talked about the matches each week - it was a social thing for them. Anyone could go to the home matches and the trips to Sunderland... but to go to Norwich, that was the action of the true football fan! Newcastle and I needed each other. They performed on the pitch and I did the business from the Gallowgate. I had also found out that I could start chants in my section of the ground. I would hear a shout of "United" from the back and I had the right timing, pitch and rhythm that encouraged those around me to join in. Some people tried and got one or the other wrong and they ended up singing an embarrassing solo but I seemed to have a gift. Not many people could (or wanted to) do this but it was important to me...it meant that I was an essential part of the crowd. Here I was, a 14 year old, and a small one at that, able to encourage a crowd that was mostly older and bigger. They wouldn't have taken any notice of me or what I said normally and that made the match all the sweeter.

I knew that The Supporters Club organised buses to every away match. I also knew that the trip to Norwich was going to cost £3 for the match and £8 for the coach. Money wasn't the problem because each month I got £20 to buy clothes, thanks to my sister demanding the right to buy what she wanted to wear without my mum's approval (seventeen year olds, honestly). I already had a Newcastle shirt so had all the clothes I needed. My Mum and Dad were not going to be in favour of my trip, however. I decided that my best bet was to just book the bus and then see their reaction. The worst objection was from my grandad who used to have a season ticket but stopped the season before Keegan arrived. He just looked at me and said "...why on Earth do you want to go to Norwich?" I didn't really know myself. I mumbled something about Milk Cup winners but I desperately needed to go. After plugging my grandad on Norwich's record on hooliganism they decided that I was old enough to make my own mistakes and so began the next phase of my life - the travelling supporter.

The bus left at 8am from outside the "Supporters Hut" which meant that I had to get up at 6:30am. The night before I'd made a packed lunch and tea to last me the day (I wasn't rich enough to buy anything). So complete with Walkman, egg sandwiches, drink, fruit and crisps (a balanced diet) I caught the metro at 7am. I felt like a man with a mission on that overcast morning and when I reached the pickup point I saw a collection of the young, the old and the in between waiting to accompany me on my milestone journey.

There were two buses going down and everybody on the bus carried a copy of the morning's Journal, complete with team news and the story of Newcastle's 4-1 youth cup win the previous night at Watford. Our bus was packed, with the elderly and women at the front and from the middle to the back filled with various ages of young men and lads, a real assortment. There was a group of three 'girls' who I would see at every away match afterwards and they took great pride in telling everybody that they'd been to Watford and got back at 2:30am only to be up four hours later. They raved about a young mid-field player called Paul Gascoigne who had shared all the goals that season with the horse-like Joe Allen (who later played for Chelsea and then sank without trace). Understandably their enthusiasm waned as the journey wore on and eventually they slipped into exhaustion - induced 'comas'. Next to me was a man called Andy. We talked about the season for a while but as the country whizzed past us, I retreated into my Walkman.

As we drove through the streets of Norwich, I remembered my thoughts about Sunderland and its cold and empty streets. Now we passed through streets filled with yellow and green supporters who just stared at the bus and waved. In return we flicked the V's and reminded them of their looming relegation. I'd eaten my packed lunch and was looking for somewhere to channel my nervous energy. Nobody was interested in the famous cathedral (not that I could see it) or the city's architecture... all we were interested in was watching out for the floodlights. Everyone had the same idea and when they were spotted there were the calls of "What a dump" or "Looks like a good second division ground" or the ultimate "It's worse than

Joker Park". There were still two hours to kick off so most headed for the pub. I'd money enough for a programme and didn't have any inkling of going to a pub so I wandered off on my own to take in the ground. I enjoyed the feeling of isolation, I felt special because here I was more than two hundred miles from home yet I was at home with football. I was aware of the glances of the Norwich fans, most, I imagined wondering what I was doing there alone. I headed for our turnstile where I started talking to an elderly couple called Mr and Mrs Brown who had been on my bus. They'd been following Newcastle together for years - home and away. As we stood on the steadily filling terrace they told me about their trips to Wembley in the 50's and 70's, getting their bus stoned in Leeds in 1974 coming back from the FA Cup Semi-final at Hillsborough and I was enthralled. He talked to me without patronising me for two hours and the time flew by.

    Three o'clock finally arrived and by now the small corner of terrace we had was heaving. The atmosphere was made more intense by a corrugated roof that ran around in a horseshoe shape, the sound from both sets of supporters rebounded about us. The closeness was a complete contrast to the relative distance of Roker Park. Everything was that much nearer and louder. We had stood in front of a metal barrier and it turned out to be a wise move indeed. The view for away fans was terrible as a giant net hung from the roof of the rugged steel stand down to the fence and managed to block any sight of the goal at our end. Every time there was any action the away fans would desperately lean forward in order to see, and so we spent the whole game trying to see the unseeable. The atmosphere in our corner was fantastic and as there were only 1500 of us. I felt like I was one of the elite, die-hard fans and thus shouted even louder. The mood between the opposing fans was good humoured despite the precariousness of Norwich's position. This contrasted with the Sunderland atmosphere which bordered on near hatred.

    Norwich were desperately fighting for the win which never came thanks to backs to the wall defending from Newcastle, which provided a boring match. The only highlight was in the last minute when Peter Beardsley raced clear but his shot bounced off the crossbar. Minutes later the final whistle went... we were safe and Norwich were looking very dodgy with a game still to play and were eventually relegated.

We walked joyfully back to the buses, our voices hoarse but, as we settled onto the bus, the atmosphere changed. There had been a fire at Bradford and fifty three people had died. Everything we'd gone through that afternoon was forgotten. We'd all joked about Norwich's ground being in keeping with supporting tradition. Perhaps, many miles away, Lincoln fans had begun the afternoon good-humouredly baiting the Bradford supporters. They could not have imagined how the afternoon would end. As we left Norwich, we sat silently listening to Sport on Two, everyone lost in their own thoughts.

We sped up the A1 and the news became worse. Fifty-three had died and one hundred and fifty gone to hospital. As if to add more misery to the day there'd been trouble at Birmingham v Leeds game and a supporter had died. The blackness outside the bus only seemed to heighten our gloom. I started thinking of my parents sitting at home, listening to this, wondering "Why did he have to get involved in all this?" "Why didn't he listen to us?" "Is he alright?"

I suddenly felt guilty for being on the bus, putting them through this anguish and so as we pulled into the services, I ran to the phone. My dad answered and seemed unconcerned, he knew that there had been nothing at Norwich, but then again he doesn't give much away. The male code of emotional conduct restricted any shows of emotion or weakness, but at least now I'd ensured he would be waiting for me at 11 pm. As I stepped off the bus at Newcastle it was as if everybody on the bus had shared a significant moment in their lives. We hadn't said anything to each other, only shaken heads in disbelief, but somehow we knew we shared a sense of grief for fellow fans, guilt that we were coming home that night but also relief that nothing had happened to us. The sight of my dad waiting for me at the Haymarket, amidst the revellers leaving the pubs, was one of the most welcome sights I can remember. He watched as the bus emptied of young boys and OAPs and he laughed. Were they part of the British disease?

We walked back to the car as the rain started to fall. Neither of us said much...that night there wasn't anything you could say. Enjoyment wasn't exactly a word that could describe the day but I knew, and so did he, that my experiences today had only strengthened my resolve to travel the country with Newcastle.

Summer in France - again

This time I had it all planned. There was no missing the beginning of the new season. We were going to be back in time this year. We were going camping in France. I would even be back before the pre-season friendly against Sheffield United...yes!

Things had not gone well for football in the close season. There had been the tragedy at Heysel; English teams were banned from playing in Europe indefinitely; Margaret Thatcher thought we should all carry identity cards and that there should be **no away fans.** No sooner had I found my devotion in life and someone was trying to take it away. I hadn't caused any trouble so why should I be stopped?, I'd no fears it could happen to me, I always kept my wits about me to avoid the thugs at school... wasn't this the same?

On the Newcastle front, Chris Waddle had gone to Spurs for £590,000. My favourite had always been Peter Beardsley and Waddle's form had dipped in the second half of the season so we wouldn't really miss him. Besides we'd just won the FA Youth Cup, Gascoigne and Allen were supposed to be promising. No, we'd be alright. I had a feeling that Waddle was going to Spurs mostly because he scored against them just before Christmas and the goal was replayed over and over again on Match of the Day. What wasn't replayed was the fact that we bloody lost 3-1 after leading at half time. If we hadn't lost then I would have been ecstatic about the goal but we had. We'd stuffed up on the big stage, again. Newcastle seemed destined to be second rate for ever. Whenever one of our players did something special he was immediately linked with one or more of the big clubs.

So here we were, camping in France. First job when we arrived was to check the site for any entertainment. I was delighted to see there was a football tournament organised on the camp-site... yes and double yes! What was even better was that all the other competitors were younger and probably smaller than me, I might not look as crap as I normally did!

The day of the tournament arrived and I was appalled to see two lads wearing Tottenham strips. In my silvery grey away shirt I sauntered over to them and said "Alright..." then I launched in with, "Waddle's shit you know!" They took it in the spirit it was meant and we soon became good friends. They were called Mark and Jeremy and both were season ticket holders at White Hart Lane. We formed a team for the tournament and swept our way through into the final. In the final we found ourselves 2-0 down but I am delighted to say I led our fight-back. I laid on one and then ran clear to score past a very frightened French nine-year-old goalkeeper (he never stood a chance!) This led to a penalty shoot-out...sudden death. The score was 1-1, Mark had scored for us and it was down to me. As I steadied myself to take it, Patrick (the organiser) whispered not to hit it too hard. I didn't, but nerves got the better of me and in true Chris Waddle fashion, spoofed it (I claimed that it had hit the post and gone in but to no avail).

That holiday was the best I'd had and we all exchanged addresses and arranged to go and stay when Newcastle and Tottenham played each other. What was even better was that I had found a girl who liked me, called Claire...yes! Everything was looking up! She was part of our group on the campsite and it also turned out that she lived only a mile away from me at home. We promised to get together when we got back home. So while we were out bike riding in Holywell Dene in Whitley Bay I asked her if she would go out with me, she said she'd think about it but, later on, said yes, to add to my excitement. I thought of all the times I'd watched Newcastle players score great goals and the feeling that gave me ranked up there.

Not only was she a girl who didn't just want to be friends, she was actually good looking to go with it...what a bonus! She knew nothing about what people thought of me at school and my garden was suddenly rosy.

Saturday August 10th 1985 - Sheffield United (h)

The game itself was terrible. After a goal-less first half, Tony Cunningham scored but the lead didn't last. As the game ground out to a completely dull stalemate, the small crowd in the Gallowgate started singing about Jack Charlton. Songs such as "If you think Charlton's shit... clap your hands..." did not go down too well. It was a small group singing because they were bored and I never thought any more of it. When I arrived home, my dad said.

"You've done it now haven't you?"

I naturally didn't know what he was on about but when he said Jack had quit Newcastle I wasn't exactly upset. True, he was a great manager but Waddle had said he'd have stayed if Jack had gone and Beardsley had hinted he might have been next. The team had just avoided relegation and there was little sign of any new players coming to Newcastle (apart from Alan Davies... a Man United reserve). The fans had had enough of the lack of ambition at the club and felt something had to be done, but the actions at the game weren't organised in any way, and nobody thought it would have the effect it did.

On the Monday morning, I went up to the ground to buy a ticket for the first game of the season (at Southampton) and it led to my first appearance on national television. I saw a crowd gathered around the club offices opposite the ground and decided to have a look. When I arrived there was Jack Charlton getting into his car being watched by a silent crowd of fans.

Unwittingly, I had positioned myself next to his car and as he drove off, I did what any fifteen-year-old lad would do and banged on the top of his car. I hadn't noticed the TV cameras watching the incident and when I watched the news that night was amazed to see the whole sorry episode replayed back to me. I jumped around the room shouting that I had been on TV. The whole family sat ready when the next news broadcast was on, but at the crucial moment I ran and pointed to the screen and in a blink of an eye they had missed my moment of glory.

Jack's departure led to Willie McFaul, the club coach, taking over and how different the next few seasons turned out to be.

Saturday 17th August 1985 - Southampton (a)

After missing the start of last season, I was determined not to miss the beginning of this one. The first game was at Southampton, not exactly a local derby... but a must all the same. There was a resigned look about my dad when I asked if I could go and so I booked to go on the bus with a friend called Nick. The bus left at midnight on the Friday and as I boarded it, there were the same faces looking as sleepy as I'd left them in May. Here we were again, I hadn't any idea who they were. I'd never talked to them but it felt as if we were lost souls once more thrown together. Or were we the fans that time forgot? Whatever we were, I took comfort in being on this bus, staring into the night, watching the lights speed by and catching the odd bit of sleep as the lads at the back slept off Friday night's excesses.

At about four-ish we pulled into Trowell services (I think), near Nottingham. We looked a real state as we stepped off the bus... dishevelled and resembling a group of zombies on their way to a wake. There were only two things to do... eat or toilet. Most chose both. The food on offer was an early breakfast fry up - too early and tender for that - or tea and a sticky bun (the cheaper alternative). Nick and I had been talking to two lads from our bus (not exactly lads as they were probably nearly twice our age). One called himself (and everybody else) John. He was fat, balding and had an Evening Chronicle still stuffed in the back pocket of his jeans, the ultimate in style. The other was tall, thin and a dead ringer for Jack Charlton. He wore a suit which he must have had for twenty years and a 70s silk Newcastle scarf. Nick loved talking to John about the violence from that period and I think held him in great admiration as a fellow voyeur of football thuggery. Peter (the Jack Charlton look-alike) had a very soft voice and spoke with a stutter. I decided he was definitely only interested in the football played, a man after my own heart. We chatted over four over-priced cups of tea until it was time to go back to the bus. We set off for our next stop in London and the atmosphere became a bit stale to say the least, as fifty bodies, sweated, farted and snored their way through the rest of the night.

When we arrived in London at about nine o'clock, the sun was shining from an incredibly blue sky and for the first time since we had set off, talk drifted to the day's match. We stopped near Kings Cross and were given an hour to explore. Unlike the service station in the small hours of the morning there was plenty to see. Around the corner at the British Rail station Chelsea fans were setting off for their match at Sheff Wed and at St Pancras, further along the road, West Ham fans were on their way to Birmingham. Newcastle had poor relations with both sets of fans. We had been promoted behind Chelsea in '84 and there had been trouble at the two games against them and in the seventies there had been a firebomb thrown into the West Ham fans' section at St James'. The latter had resulted in tension between the fans which had been made worse by a song sung by the Newcastle fans every time we played which immortalised the incident. We expected trouble but only saw a surprised group of young lads and pensioners, the London equivalents of ourselves.

They wondered what a group of over a hundred Newcastle fans was doing in London so early in the morning. We told them where we going to which they replied, "Suppose you do live miles away from everybody else..." and out came the quips about cloth caps, whippets, coal bunkers and had we discovered household electricity yet. (Never mind the fact that we invented it, mate! Still, it didn't do to show you were too clever!)

From that moment on I loved any interaction with opposition fans, which always gave you a new view on your own small world. The rest of the world believed the stereotypes but that only made us that much prouder of the North East.

We made a strange quartet as we wandered down Marylebone Road passing the early-rising tourists queuing outside Madam Tussauds waxworks. We all looked dishevelled and made our accents broader in order to put across the idea of incomprehensible Geordies. I loved being an oddity, having people wonder who we were and why we were enjoying ourselves so much. It was at that point that John (or Carl as we had now discovered he was called) started reading a card on the phone box entitled Sexy Suzy. It had a phone number on it and invited interested readers to ring up and find out more. So he did just that. As he listened, he started jumping up and down, making his belly quiver. He then read us a long list of her favoured sexual activities at which we all fell about laughing in the style of two teenagers and two wannabe teenagers. It was even more exciting for me because we were three hundred miles away from home and I was acting like a "lad". I was no longer a boy, I had a girlfriend at home to disapprove of my actions and we could do anything we wanted (not that there was that much I felt like doing except going to a football match). I was miles away from the bullies at school and I was going to a place nobody sane would dream of going to for just two hours.

This made our London adventure all the sweeter.

At ten-thirty we continued the journey from one end of England to the other and arrived a couple of hours before kick-off in a warm Southampton. After an hour looking around the ground it was through the turnstile to find a spot for the match. We were stunned to see a terrace that reached barely higher than the regulation seven-foot fence I was accustomed to. Not only that but the size of the ground which held less than half the number St James' could. The wooden stands at the sides made me think of Sunderland, complete with the original wooden bench seats that made your bum numb - no expense spared. At the far end was the bizarre sight of a steeply banked triangular terracing that hung over the one below with only a bar at the front to stop someone plummeting to their deaths. Never one to be keen on heights, I was convinced that it was only a question of time before some poor sod did just that. I tried not to think about it and just hoped Southampton didn't score to avoid putting my theory to the test.

As kick-off approached, the talk was that Paul Gascoigne was going to make his first full debut. We had positioned ourselves as far away from the one entrance as possible and at 2.50 pm I noticed the terrace we'd avoided was jammed to bursting... but nobody seemed to mind. I was just glad I could feel the ground beneath my feet.

Although I had been to the Sheffield game the week before, the small stadium meant that the atmosphere reached the level I had remembered for the first time since the previous May. The Red Devils parachuted in, and a kazoo band assaulted our ears, as the sun beat down. This was what football was about, it was better than Roker on a cold April morning. As the teams came out red and white balloons floated up from the home end and three quarters of the crowd was engulfed by ripped up newspaper to add to the effect. Newcastle were wearing their grey away strip and so was I - how could we fail.

After a hundred and eighty minutes of away football I'd yet to see a goal and in the third minute a cross by Alan Davies was met by Gascoigne. Peter Shilton produced a fantastic save as a reply. I'd become complacent because, at that moment, I was flung forward as three months without football, coupled with the length of the journey, resulted in an over-exuberant set of Newcastle fans. The volume on the terrace easily drowned out the home fans but this was silenced just before half time as David Puckett (an apt name for a footballer?) put Southampton ahead. Despite that, for the first time since Keegan, we'd seen Newcastle committed to attack and we were also amazed at the tricks

Gascoigne had performed. Life was still hopeful! I knew the team would give me that elusive first away goal. Four minutes into the second half, a jinking run from Beardsley (he only ever did jinking ones, according to the papers) was cut short by Southampton's Holmes and to our delight a penalty awarded. Coolly, Beardsley scored. In my mind it was as if Peter had done it just for me and he was trying to spot me in the crowd as we all danced about.

That goal had rounded off a perfect trip. To see your team score a goal at home was one thing, but to see it scored miles away from St James' on a hot August day was something else. I floated onto the coach and dreamed the next seven and a half hours away. The bus pulled into a very empty Haymarket at two o'clock in the morning. There was my dad, overjoyed to be meeting us. In all the excitement I had forgotten all about my sixteenth birthday, which I was now enjoying, happy birthday from Peter Beardsley.

The next day I made my public radio debut as I rang up a Metro Sport radio phone in to enthuse to the North East. I felt a sense of pride in saying I was there as Gascoigne had made his debut and predicted that he would play for England. The presenter told me not to get too carried away by one performance but I knew I was right because I'd seen it with my own eyes!

Saturday 24th August - Liverpool (h)

I had learnt to dread matches against the big clubs like Liverpool, Man Utd, Arsenal and, in those days, Everton and Tottenham. In these games you knew that you hadn't beaten them since nineteen seventy something and they would score early and then dominate for the rest of the game. If you were lucky you might only be 1-0 down and there was a chance that you could grab an equaliser, but that was the best to hope for. The Chronicle would start the match preview saying Newcastle had a good record at home to whoever we were playing but then added that all the victories were before the war. By the time you got to the game you were resigned to defeat.

You also knew that the game would attract one of the biggest crowds of the season and these extra people would be the ones who stood next to you telling how crap the team were and how much better they were in 1965. Why did they bother? Because they enjoyed a good match! To add insult to injury, it would usually be on Match of the Day and the TV pundits would spend the whole game destroying every aspect of Newcastle's play, as if your Saturday had not been bad to start off with!

For this game I had been lent a season ticket in the East stand at the Gallowgate end. I settled into my seat and waited for the expected early goal...but it didn't come. In fact, Newcastle were playing well. Newcastle were fielding Ian Stewart, Willie McFaul's first signing and both he and Beardsley tore Liverpool apart. In the Liverpool defence were a certain Messrs Hansen and Lawrenson, a pair whose ability to stifle attacks made them the most unpopular footballers in the country (excepting at Anfield). In the sixty-eighth minute the unbelievable happened. Neil McDonald (affectionately known as Spotty more for his tender years if not his reliance on acne cream) chased a lost ball. He then looped it into the middle and, right below me, the towering beanstalk George Reilly headed the ball past Grobelaar for the winner. Revenge was ours! This would make the world sit up and take notice...are you watching Sunderland? Well, actually, 'no' was the answer. As the euphoria slowly ebbed away you suddenly realised why we had won - the TV cameras hadn't been there. It all started to make sense. We were bound to win all along so why did we worry? A great moment in our season, ignored by the rest of the country... absolutely typical!

At home my dad was washing the car.

"You'll never guess what we've just done!" I spouted.

"You won, didn't you?" he answered.

"Yes, but who did we beat?"

"Liverpool?" I knew the point was lost on him, but at least he took an interest.

My mum said, "That's nice dear."

What I needed to do was go to the nearest Scottish and Newcastle pub and celebrate with the punters there, but unfortunately I was sixteen just) and looked fourteen. I'd just have to be content knowing that I'd been there, with the best possible view from my seat. If only someone would come down to the park to recreate it!

Saturday 7th September 1985 - Tottenham Hotspur (a)

Newcastle were sixth in the first division, despite a 0-3 defeat at Manchester United. The team were playing exciting football and Jack Charlton had been forgotten - Willie McFaul was the man.

This was the first opportunity I'd had to visit the friends I'd met on holiday. I booked myself on the non-stop Clipper setting off at midnight and arriving in London at 5:45am on the Saturday morning.

The trip to Southampton had proved to me that overnight travel was a good way of extending my time in London. The bus had cost me the princely sum of £10 (the alternative to buying some new trousers). I'd so much to talk to my friends about - Claire and the fact that Newcastle were four points above Spurs in the league (they'd been warned about Waddle). The trip down passed and at six in the morning I arrived at Victoria, making my way down to the underground station. I then had my first glimpse of the capital's homeless population who spread along each part of the station. I had never thought about homelessness in Newcastle because I had only been there during the day. They were just tramps who usually smelt of booze and were to be given a wide berth but here, you couldn't avoid them. I had to step over bodies just to get to my train. Here I was, a boy from a reasonably well off family who had not really seen poverty to such an extent as this and instead of caring, I stepped over them, held my nose and turned Nick Kershaw up on my Walkman. He was a nice clean cut singer, much beloved by teenage girls and not the type of singer I admitted to liking to anyone at school where AC/DC was the cool thing to like. At that time he was far removed enough from the bodies that littered the ground about me to make his mention acceptable.

Once on the tube I thought that I'd have to tell Mark and Jeremy of my underground adventures, with added details for excitement and then didn't think about it again.

Everything about London became a case of one-upmanship. The metro is cleaner and quicker than the tube. We have fresher air, cleaner water than you. Newcastle is better than Tottenham...but all the while I felt strangely attracted to London and the excitement that offered a teenage boy. Of course I didn't mention this to my London friends.

Their dad had got us all seats next to the Newcastle fans but amongst the Spurs fans. I took great delight in revealing my silver (alright shiny grey) shirt complete with black and white scarf and cap... I was from the North and I wanted everyone to know it. My accent thickened as I realised that there were some fellow Newcastle fans behind us. The thrill at being amongst "the enemy"! I could go to school on Monday bragging how I had been in the Tottenham end and survived. I didn't care what happened that afternoon, my week was already made. I shouted "Judas" at Waddle, along with the other supporters as the teams came out then settled down, my confidence was high...too high!

An accident that morning hindered my enjoyment of the game. The boys' sister had broken one of the lenses in my glasses so I could only see with one eye closed. This meant that I missed a brilliant diving header from new boy Alan Davies. The lads behind me were up in an instant but I couldn't believe our start and it took a quick look at a chaotic away end to confirm my suspicions. A little late, I started throwing myself about with my hands in the air, pausing only to affectionately whack my friends on the head. -

The joy I had experienced was short lived as Tottenham poured towards the goal at our end as if to punish Newcastle for having the audacity to score. The inevitable happened as Falco scored the equaliser. I sunk into my seat as my friends returned the compliment. The roar of the crowd combined with the sickening feeling of having lost something precious made me shiver. Everywhere I looked people were dancing jubilantly, hanging from every available vantage-point hugging the stranger next to them and pointing at the silent and motionless group at one end. We responded with a rousing chorus of "Newcastle, Newcastle..." (those being the only lyrics- to be repeated ad infinitum) in order to lift the team but Tottenham walked all over us and a few minutes later we were behind. John Chiedozie tapping into an empty net after goalkeeper Martin Thomas had saved a Danny Thomas shot. I was gobsmacked. How could they do this? The answer was — easily. The second half was even worse and after George Reilly missed a good chance which I had tried to will into the net the score became 3-1. By the time the final whistle went the score was 5-1. By that time, though we had accepted our fate and were trying to win the Noisiest Supporters Award - which we usually did - and we were contented with that. We'd been humiliated on the field but won gloriously off it so the final score was 1-1, really. The lads behind me had long since given up and headed off to drown their sorrows so I was left to the gloating shouts of the Spurs fans and the din of "Glory, glory Tottenham Hotspur" blasting out not from the Spurs supporters but from the PA speakers. Mark and Jeremy were remarkably restrained, maybe because they had expected it — it was only New-carrstle after all.

The bus journey home next morning was a subdued one but I'd nevertheless enjoyed my weekend in The Smoke and was determined to make the most of my smashed glasses. "It was a Spurs fan..." I would say and miss out the fact that it was a five-year-old girl. Nobody really needed to know, did they?

Saturday 14th September 1985 - West Bromwich Albion (h)

The match whizzed by for one reason only... Claire was meeting me in town after the match. Newcastle won 4-1 which added to the day's thrills but it was the after match activities that were dominating my mind.

We had been out once since I had asked her out - a trip to the cinema in Monkseaton. I had been terrified of making a fool of myself. I'd seen all the films where women slapped men who even tried to put their arms around them - would I risk it? I didn't. What about kissing? Where would I start? Coming from an all-boys school hadn't helped my knowledge of females. I'd asked plenty of girls out without success and then Claire had said yes. Everything was a potential pitfall. Football supporting was a doddle compared to this - the match was the five a side game on the pitch before the real event. At the match Will hadn't a clue what I should do so I was on my own as I left him to meet her.

I kept on imagining Metro Radio commentating on our date, "...it's a good start from young Stephenson, a jubilant hug after a great result - good start. Off to the Wimpy for a casual burger - not one of your flair players, Stephenson, but this build-up's looking promising. Good technique as he confidently orders two meals -still going well under tricky conditions. Oh no!

Disaster...where did that post come from? He's walked slap bang into a pillar - what an own goal! There's nothing the keeper can do! He started off so well! Is there any way back for him?"

I had to calmly pick up the remains of our meals, trying to retain any remaining shred of dignity before searching out a deeply traumatised girlfriend.

Needless to say Claire was completely embarrassed and disappeared upstairs without uttering a word. I caught up with her but didn't know what to say. There was no little clump of away fans cheering me on -just a stony silence.

I managed to recover from this shaky start, but only after countless apologies and my confidence had been severely dented. I doubted if she would walk out of the restaurant at the same time as me, never mind any chance of a goodbye kiss.

I sheepishly walked her home and was overjoyed when she agreed to go out with me again.

"...despite that dreadful lapse in concentration Stephenson has scraped a replay. He'll have to do better if he wants to progress to the next round."

In the end our relationship went to several replays but I never did get to the next round; fear of defeat blunting any attacks that I managed to muster.

Saturday 26th October - Aston Villa (a)

After about a month of our relationship, Claire decided she'd had enough and called full time. She gave me the old "We can still be friends," routine but, even though we were still friends that wasn't enough for me. I no longer had the social standing of having a girlfriend - I had a girl who was a friend but what was important was the order of the two phrases. One was more sought after than the other.

I decided that since there was money there I needed to get away - where better than Birmingham, Villa Park to be precise. While I had been happy in love, some of my glow seemed to have rubbed off on Newcastle. They had only lost two games (although they'd only won one) but they had gone to Arsenal and come back with a surprising 0-0 draw. The match before we had lost to Notts Forest 3-0 so I felt we both needed a lift - was today to be the day?

After a £6 trip on the Armstrong Galley buses we arrived at the inevitable snarl up at Spaghetti Junction and our first glimpse of the ground. I had remembered seeing the ground on FA cup semi-finals day, balloons and confetti filling the air as the teams came out on a warm, sunny Spring day. I hoped that there might be a similar atmosphere today. I was to be disappointed because not only was it foggy and damp when we arrived but the ground was barely a quarter full. Only 12,000 people could be bothered to watch this match. Villa were seventh from bottom and, to add insult to their injury, were below local rivals Coventry and Birmingham... while Newcastle were in the middle of the table, having faded after their bright start. Hardly a fixture to whet the appetite of any neutrals.

I'd still to see my first away win, despite imagining over and over the jubilant chanting of the score as we swarmed into the streets, buses buzzing as we made the long journey home. Discussing Beardsley's amazing hat-trick or the brilliant saves made by Martin Thomas. I could almost taste victory.

The ground was exactly as I remembered it from television, except it was empty and cold. I'd decided to splash out £5 on a seat behind one of the goals and the view was impressive (despite the fog which cleared later to just overcast). The goal at the Holte end opposite looked a long way away but that didn't matter, we'd score all the goals at this end. There was also a big cheer when it was announced that Gascoigne was to start only his first game since Southampton and when the game started he picked up from that game. Newcastle made a great start but couldn't score so the few hundred fans who had come down were jubilant when, at last, Gascoigne popped up in the penalty area to grab a goal. He ran to the fans like a man possessed not that we had time to take too much notice, we had our own celebrating to do. Half time came and the score was 1-1. The ground was like a morgue as the PA announcer tried to lift the home fans but *we* didn't need lifting. The second half seemed to drag on until thirteen minutes before the end, Beardsley popped up with the winner. Because the other end of the pitch was so far away, I could only see him charging down the left wing and then cutting into the penalty area. A small white object shooting from his boot and the unbelievable happened... it screamed past the Villa keeper and bounced around in the net. All around me was silent, as Beardsley's actions registered, then, it was like opening time at a jumble sale. Arms and legs were everywhere. Nobody had really thought we could actually win. A forty-year hoodoo, gone in an instant, or so we hoped. For the first time in the game we were anxious, screaming for the final whistle, Villa had no answer and, as the match ended I had a smug glow of satisfaction. This was nothing like I had imagined... sure we were shouting and singing, but there was hardly anybody to listen to us or many of us to be heard. The streets were empty as we set off back to the buses and, for me a celebratory sandwich and Mars Bar. We cheered every time our score was read out on the radio as if we'd just heard it for the first time and then gradually the bus settled down. I plugged into my Walkman and Madness surrounded me as I stared once more out of the window watching time and my thoughts disappear.

I expected there to be a welcoming committee out to meet me, but there was only the usual bunch of Saturday night revellers ambling around the Haymarket pubs. They were oblivious to my achievement and as I got onto the nine o'clock metro back home, I was back in the real world where nobody was bothered about the landmark I had just reached in my supporting career. Still, at least I could say I was there and it meant something to me.

Saturday 2nd November 1985 - Watford (h)

Will now went to most home games with me and for this match we decided to go to a different part of the ground. All the seats were sold out so we decided to go into the paddocks next to the half way line. There were no reductions for juniors or people who still looked like juniors so we had to pay £3.50 for this new position. Before the game started the mascot provided the entertainment. Not being content to kick the ball at the Martin Thomas in goal, he decided to run up the field to score past the Watford keeper. He ran as fast as his little legs could carry him, unopposed towards the unsuspecting keeper. Once the crowd realised what was going on the noise picked up. The little lad was, unknown to him, acting out everybody's fantasy – to score at St James' and as such gained the support of the crowd once his intention was clear. He got to within a yard of Tony Coton and slipped the ball through his legs into the net - instigating cheers and celebrations. Disaster followed as he received the ball from Coton and started back towards Thomas' goal. Despite the cries for him to turn round he carried on, ignoring the crowd completely as he repeated the trick at the opposite end. Obviously we wanted him to score again and he duly obliged. After completing the victory single-handedly he was picked up and whisked away to the centre circle for his photograph.

The crowd hoped this would be a guide to the real final score, but this wasn't to be and by the end of the match, the humour had left the ground, to be replaced by hatred. The subject of this loathing... public enemy number one, referee Trelford Mills. Not content with knocking Newcastle out of the FA cup a few years earlier he denied us a winner on the stroke of full time.

We were terrible and Watford deservedly went ahead through Luther Blissett in the twenty-ninth minute. After that Newcastle twice hit the bar and then Beardsley put a penalty wide of the right hand post. Gascoigne was the only player with any imagination but Newcastle couldn't score. Then, with the floodlights beaming down onto a freezing evening, Gascoigne curled the equaliser past Coton. Suddenly the ground woke up from its slumber. The crowd responded immediately cheering the players on and for the next few minutes the Watford goal was under siege. Just when it looked like there was not going to be a spectacular ending, George Reilly (now nicknamed Rambo due to his now-customary Sylvester Stallone-style headband) hurled himself at the ball to head it into the net. The crowd had been building up their frustrations throughout the game and finally it looked as though everything had come good. Trelford had other ideas and stopped the crescendo of noise dead. First he disallowed the goal for a push by Reilly then blew the full time whistle. The crowd wasn't stunned for long as a torrent of abuse and missiles showered down on the sprinting figure of Mills, who had decided that he would like to fight another day. It had all gone too well for us, so he decided that we couldn't have a happy ending. He was able to stop a speeding juggernaut, seemingly for the fun of it. Was it my imagination, but was he laughing as he ran off?

Will and I left the ground cursing our luck. If that had been Liverpool, Man United, Spurs or Everton the goal would have stood, but no, this was Newcastle. Poor old Newcastle, just an ordinary team with a couple of stars. They should be thankful with a draw instead of moaning about the ref.

We knew, however that it was just another in a long line of matches where we had thrown points away or suffered refereeing injustices. It didn't feel like it at the time but we were just like every other club in the league, never quite reaching the top but expecting the team to deliver regardless. Trelford Mills probably didn't have a vendetta against us but he had become a scapegoat for two terrible performances and many seasons of frustration. Still there was always next week - perhaps we'd do better then.

Saturday 7 December - Sunderland v Portsmouth

I've no idea why I ended up at this game. Newcastle were away at Luton and I fancied watching a game. The only option, apart from going to a non-league match, was Sunderland. Portsmouth were top of the Second Division and Sunderland were mid-table, a good chance of an away win and an opportunity to laugh at the Mackems. I went on my own as Will didn't find the idea of freezing at Roker the least bit enticing. As I stepped off the train at Seaburn station I suddenly realised I had slipped into away fan mode - scanning everyone around me, trying not to stick out and acting natural, even though I was churning inside. It felt unnatural to be going to a football match without any colours; like going out the of the house naked. I felt the whole train knew I was a Mag and were preparing to run ahead of me, hide behind a wall and then jump on me when I wasn't suspecting anything. There was also the chance that someone from school would recognise me and expose me; just like the scene from Invasion of the Body Snatchers when the aliens all pointed at the remaining humans whilst letting out high-pitched squeals. A throwback to my science fiction days.

At the exit from the station was a set of welcoming policemen. They were ushering Portsmouth fans to one side. I decided this seemed more relaxing than mingling in the Sunderland end so I swooped amongst them and safety. Even then I was waiting for the lunging fist or kick, just to teach me a lesson but it never came. To my delight we were all shepherded into a transit van and driven to the ground -brill! On the way I started talking to the others in the van. It turned out they all lived in London and were members of the Portsmouth London supporters club. I latched onto a young couple called Lynne and Duncan. We spent the next hour chatting about my dislike for Sunderland (I wasn't that bothered really but it was more manly to say I was). In turn they told me how they disliked Southampton, and gave them the name 'Scummers'. I realised that such intense hatred could only come from years of being second best to them. They had been following Pompey (Portsmouth) for about fifteen years and hadn't seen them beat Southampton (or Scumhampton whichever you prefer). They listed all the heartaches suffered and recounted the jibes from work mates when Pompey (inevitably) came off worst. I was lucky. Okay, so Sunderland had been to the Milk Cup Final and we hadn't, but we had beaten them and then seen them relegated. Surely that had made up for their moment of glory? Of course it had! I was still looked forward to Mackem misery. To add spice to the game, Lawrie McMenemy (Sunderland's manager) used to be manager of Southampton and every time he popped his head out he might just have heard faint cries of "Scummer, scummer..." from a few hundred fans in the corner of the Roker end.

The game started at a fast pace with Portsmouth doing most of the attacking. There was an extremely big bloke wearing the Pompey equivalent of my Newcastle Utd cloth cap who spent the whole of the first half constantly shouting "Play Up Pompey" and encouraging everybody else to join in. The little group around me went crazy when Tommy Christensen put them 1-0 up and the big man in the cap grew even more animated when Kevin O'Callaghan put them 2-0 up. As the half time whistle blew, there was a deathly hush around the ground as all eyes focused on a metal construction next to our corner with most of the letters of the alphabet on it. Gradually the boxes below the letters started to fill up with numbers - 1... .2, 0... 1. It suddenly dawned on me that this was their Scoreboard. I was used to the scores whizzing past on the electronic board at the back of the Gallowgate, but this was like something from the dark ages. A quick check of the programme also reminded me that I had forgotten all about Newcastle. We were away to Luton - on an artificial pitch and therefore bound to lose. As score 'R' was put in I held my breath - first the number 1. There was a rumble around the ground. Then the number 0. The crowd was instantly revitalised. The Fulwell end swung into action and people in the seats were leaping up and down to the cries of "We hate the Mags..." I suddenly thought what it would be like for a Sunderland fan doing the opposite journey to me -watching Newcastle when Sunderland were away. They would experience the same feeling... misery because your own team were losing balanced up with joy at the enemy losing... at least nobody could gloat on Monday was a good reason to be thankful.

As the second half kicked off the big bloke started up again. He seemed to be swaying in a manner I'd seen from quite a few Gallowgate regulars - I recognised the symptoms and knew the cause was alcohol. Duncan told me about how this bloke was a Portsmouth nut. He was called John and went to every game they played - home and away along with all the reserve games he could manage. He lived in a massive house and had a caravan full of Pompey videos he wasn't allowed to keep n the house. I was also told that John's girlfriend was gorgeous, at which point Lynne gave him a dig in the side but his hands had painted a good enough picture. Our conversation was cut short abruptly when Paul Wood made it 3-0 and the festivities resumed in the Pompey ranks.

By the time the final whistle went Portsmouth had won 3-1. Eric Gates pulling one back late in the game. The others soon nominated me their lucky Geordie mascot and I was offered numerous season tickets and places to stay so that I could help them achieve promotion. I was introduced to John the big bloke as the reason for the success and I was invited to stay in his caravan whenever I was down on the South coast. I felt very pleased with my afternoon, for once I had been the centre of attention, even leading a chorus of "Newcastle...". This prompted a predictable reply from the Sunderland fans. The only sore point was the result from Luton... we had lost 2-0.I put it down to that plastic pitch and called Luton cheats and received a round of applause. After being held in the ground for half-an-hour the away fans split into two groups - those who were travelling by train and those who had come by bus. The latter group looked strangely familiar and it was only later that night that I realised how. It was me and the others from the Newcastle supporters' buses. Sure, they were wearing blue instead of black and white but there they were congratulating each other as they got on the warm bus, listening to Sports Report and cheering when their score was read out. They were tucking into their sandwiches they'd made or bought without a care in the world and reading the match programme before the bus set off for the long journey home. They would be squashed together for seven hours in silence after conversation had dried up after half an hour. I had somehow expected different fans to act differently, it was bizarre to think of all the identical groups all over the country carrying out the same rituals.

Our train-bound group was different. We had to walk back to the station, no transit van this time. The streets were empty as the police walked us along, occasionally shouting for us to keep together. By now the black sky glowed orange from the streetlights. The houses lining the route looked welcoming, filled with people sitting down to a cosy night in front of the TV. Here we were, still miles from the sanctuary of our homes (ten, in my case but the others a damn sight more). Along the way individuals would dive into off licences and emerge with bags filled with cans. After all it was going to be a long trip back. Their conversations would last longer -fuelled by alcohol. Everyone seemed to know each other due to countless trips away and there was a great sense of togetherness. Not to attack anybody else but just to make sure each and every one of them felt a part of the group and that included me. "Come back to London with us..." they offered but I had to decline. I took Lynne and Duncan's phone number; said I'd come to visit them when Newcastle were in London, then I left them waiting for their train home.

I hadn't known such warmth from complete strangers and looked forward to our next meeting. As I walked away I wished I was going with them. No hassles from school bullies who had known your weaknesses since you were seven and no chance to dwell on what might have been with Claire. I walked into the bright glare of the Metro station and back to the real world. I'd see them again - I'd make sure of it.

Saturday 21st December - Liverpool (a)

It was Christmas time and what better way to avoid trailing around the shops looking for presents than booking a trip to Liverpool. I always enjoyed the last Saturday before Christmas for precisely this reason. A chance to escape from arguments and festive apathy (on my part). My mum couldn't find me to tell me to tidy my room, put cards up in the living room or any of the other little jobs that I'd be found whenever I happened to sit in front of the TV. Being absent suited me down to the ground. Will obviously had the same idea as we booked our places on the supporters' buses.

    The game against Liverpool was a daunting one but I wanted to experience the atmosphere of the Kop first hand, to put my chanting skills to the ultimate test. We were also one of only three teams to have beaten Liverpool that season, the others being Arsenal and Queens Park Rangers. Since our draw with Watford our form hadn't been too good. Wins away at Birmingham (1-0) and at home to Southampton (2-1) (that one obviously for my new found friends) were the only highlights as we lost the other three games. No-one travelling expected anything better than escaping a pasting. Liverpool were, after all second in the table and unbeaten since the beginning of October - what chance could we honestly have. It was the usual group on the bus and after a few hours were on the lookout for the ground as we travelled through Liverpool. The first thing that struck you was how much football obviously meant to the people of Liverpool. There was no Sharon loves Terry plastered on the wall (unless it was Terry McDermott and if it was - poor Sharon). Every bit of graffiti was related to Liverpool or Everton (usually with the word shit scrawled after it in a different hand). There were references to the Munich air disaster of 1958 when eight of Man Utd's Busby Babes were tragically cut down in their prime. The children all around wore either blue or red and when our bus was spotted they turned and flicked the V's, shook their fist or made signs questioning our success with the opposite sex. In most towns you would have had the odd group of kids doing this but here every corner had them. It seemed to be a regular event for Saturdays and the bigger the team the more supporters they could abuse. There was nothing thrown, no danger of any trouble and we responded in kind with the odd moonie from the boys at the back. This seemed to make their day. The worst thing for them would have been to be ignored. They might then have had to look for a bus full of pensioners to offend instead.

Inside Anfield, a multitude of coloured plastic seats made parts of the ground look like they were constructed from giant Lego bricks. Although our corner expected nothing but defeat we weren't going to let that little detail spoil our day. We sang from half-an-hour before the kick off until long after it.

There was the usual song about Liverpool slums, then the songs declaring our allegiance to Newcastle and our hatred of Sunderland. Out of tradition I joined in the Sunderland songs but really all I felt was a patronising pity - they were in the second division after all.

Every mistake that had been made by the team was forgotten as each one received a hero's welcome - we'd slag them off at St James' but we didn't want to wash our linen outside of Newcastle. The team, in turn, would respond by raising their hands and applauding us while they exaggerated their warm up exercises. They would look as if they valued the warm up but deep down we knew they wanted to try and hit thirty yarders against their mates.

The game kicked off and we waited for the Liverpool goals but Newcastle hadn't read the same script and they attacked the Liverpool goal. Paul Stephenson, a product of the youth team was in inspired form, as was Paul Gascoigne and in the second minute he went down in the penalty area and the referee awarded a penalty. We were shocked and stunned for a fraction of a second and then started the celebrations in earnest. This joy was cut short as the referee saw the linesman had flagged for offside and felt relieved not to have to give a penalty against the home team. There was silence in our part of the Anfield Road stand. Our spirits, lifted by the initial decision started to take a battering as Ian Rush twice forced great saves from Thomas. Had we stung Liverpool into action? What made us think we could take the lead against them? Now we were going to pay! But, no the lads weren't lying down as they launched attacks of their own and we roared them on. Every missed chance brought exaggerated "Ooooohhhs" from us, maybe there was a chance. There was, and when it came the strangest feeling came over me.

It all came about when frizzy-headed fullback John Bailey cleared the ball out of defence and Beardsley chased after it. He beat Hansen and Beglin and lobbed the ball goal-wards. The scene that followed always comes back to me in slow motion, as if I was watching from the opposite end of the ground, watching the away end. The ball looped over Bruce Grobelaar's head and looked to be going wide. It spun as it moved through the air and as it hit the far post we all cursed our luck. But no! It was squirming on the goal line. Liverpool defenders were rushing back but, at the last moment and with three thousand fans trying to half suck/ half wish it into the net, it duly obliged.

There was unprecedented chaos as bodies were flung forward and legs emerged from the crowd. After leaping on a delighted Will, I was content just to stand and scream at the top of my voice until I was grabbed and embraced by a bloke with a moustache. We became part of a screaming mass of limbs which lasted an age (it seemed) to be replaced by the triumphant shouts of a jubilant army. In all this the person we had noticed the least was the goal scorer who had stood triumphantly waiting for us to pay him some attention but we'd been too busy to notice.

True to form Liverpool equalised twelve minutes later but that couldn't take the shine off some monumental celebrations and a great goal. The rest of the game passed in a blur - all I wanted was for the whistle to blow. Liverpool had most of the chances, falling predominantly to Ian Rush who hadn't scored for five games and didn't look likely to today - thank goodness. The previous disappointments were forgotten about when the game finished.

We had again stopped Liverpool from winning and just as enjoyable we'd out sung the Kop (in our opinion). We had beaten and drawn with the Mighty Reds in the league. Suddenly, we had become a force to be reckoned with. Perhaps we could get to Wembley in the FA Cup I dreamed on the way back. One thing was for sure, we had to do better than last year, didn't we?

Saturday 4th January - Brighton and Hove Albion (h)

Here it was again - the FA Cup. I had been dreaming about a trip to Wembley and being able to say "...it started against Brighton in the third round..." when I was summing up for my eager children and grandchildren in years to come. I watched all the Cup previews on the local news programmes and rubbed my hands with glee as experts appeared and predicted great things from Newcastle. We'd an exciting team - full of potential and brimming with confidence. Draws away to Liverpool and Sheff Wed and at home to Everton had raised everyone's expectations. Even one of the pundits on football focus had tipped us to win the cup. An easy home game... Gascoigne and Beardsley in sparkling form... it was music to my ears. Somehow, although I wanted to believe all they said, I couldn't. Something was going to go wrong - it always did. That something was my dad. I should have told him how important today was. If I had done, he would have realised the stress I was under and not shouted at me for something or other (I can't remember what) but shout he did and an argument swiftly followed. I realised then that my FA Cup dream was to end that day. The team would surely pick up on these bad vibes and lose.

    The pitch was frozen solid and there was a layer of snow on it. My sense of foreboding was justified as Brighton of the second division scored after fifty seconds through Eric Young. Newcastle attacked for the rest of the game but never looked like scoring. They forced twenty-six corners but couldn't make any count. Every time we got anywhere near their goal, Young, their large headband-wearing centre back cleared. As so often happened five minutes from time the mop-headed Dean Saunders scored from long range to seal the tie. They'd had virtually two shots all game and scored from both - thanks to my argument that morning.

    I was sickened. It was freezing and we were out of the cup without a whimper. What made everything worse was that school re-started on Monday, back to a cocky bunch of Mackems revelling in another Newcastle Cup shocker. This usually led to attacks on my diminutive stature and physique. A girlfriend would have given me some degree of respectability, at least then I couldn't be accused of being a poof. Still, there was fat chance of that. I was doomed to the drudgery of a mid-table football team, misery at school and a non-existent love life.

Saturday 18th January 1986 - QPR (a)

I have no idea why but a trip to the West End of London seemed a good idea. We'd drawn away to West Bromwich Albion 1-1 but I can't think that would have motivated me to forget my Cup woes and travel three hundred odd miles. It was the call of the day tripping Supporters' Buses which beckoned and I answered. The trip down was non-eventful. People were still talking about the Brighton game and how we had managed to lose it (I didn't mention my argument with dad, fearing recriminations). Everyone seemed to be wondering why they were here but no answer could be found... beyond calls of insanity that is. The match itself passed by. QPR scored twice then Gascoigne pulled one back and after a few minutes of Newcastle pressure they scored to finish the game. We trooped back onto the bus and longed for the next few hours to zip by so we could get back home but that was not going to be the case.

All was fine until we reached the Woodall services, near Rotherham. The two buses, filled with the usual bunch of the elderly, young and wannabe young, pulled in to the services at about eight or nine o'clock. It was now dramatically colder thanks to a clear winter sky. Night was firmly upon us as we walked from the bus to the services. On the way down to London we had walked past some Millwall fans, who were on their way to Sunderland. We'd said "Alright...", got very little response from them, muttered "Miserable buggers," under our breaths and thought no more of it. Meeting fans from other clubs, there was usually the usual "Where are you off to?", and "How's your season going" and then comparing notes on how dire our respective teams were (not possible with Liverpool fans). After that we'd wish each other well... but not today. As we walked from the buses the fans we had seen that morning appeared out of nowhere and ran, shouting, past us. They lashed out and spat as they went and then disappeared. I rang dad to tell him that we'd be in at about 11pm, confident that was the extent to their attempt to add to our misery. It was just a show of bravado - the sort I'd seen at school when trouble broke out. A lot of facing off, exchanged insults and then the fight was broken up. As I got out of the phone box there was a young man in his 20s waiting to go in, I held the door open for him and thought nothing more about him. As I walked back to the bus, the Millwall louts (they certainly weren't fans) came running back and I was barged off the path and into the bushes. Before I could react (probably by curling into the smallest ball I could and rolling into any available hole) they had gone. I didn't think about the man in the phone box or any of the other fans still in the services but walked gingerly back to the safety of the buses.

As I turned around the corner I saw our buses. The other bus was awash with glass and the coach's curtains billowed out into the night air. The shock was evident on the faces of the supporters who'd witnessed it. The senselessness of it screamed out at us. Most of the occupants had been the older members, too tired or too sleepy to walk to the services. They'd hurt nobody so why had this happened to them? More people came back to the coach to see the carnage with news that fans had been attacked and robbed. The loneliness of the long distance fan suddenly struck me. We were in the middle of nowhere. There were only a few people serving in the various shops on the site. There was no sign of any police and our mixed bunch was wondering if there would be a repeat attack. Everybody wanted to be safely at home but that was hours away and there was the small matter of the smashed bus. We weren't going to leave anybody behind so we would just wait for help. Eerily the louts had disappeared as quickly as they'd appeared, but we'd no idea whether they would return. Everywhere I looked was black, except for the services. The harsh lights beckoned but only to lure us into a further trap. There was probably an ambush waiting for us, perhaps reinforcements had arrived to launch another attack. My imagination was on overdrive. I remained in the relative safety of the coach, listening to all the tales of fights and finally the news that one of our number had been stabbed. He was just an innocent man who came from the wrong end of the country as far as they had been concerned. I remembered cheering when we heard that Sunderland had lost, if I'd known now what I knew then I'd have reacted differently, how I could I cheer when these animals had won? It left a bad taste.

For what seemed an age we sat there quietly listening to the emerging stories, everything had happened in slow motion, like a nightmare but the problem was that we weren't asleep and it wasn't going to end when we woke up. The man who had been stabbed had been ringing home (just like me) and when he came out of the phone box he had been attacked. He had fought back and in the process been stabbed. We had no idea whether he was dead or alive, but it could so easily have been me. I doubt I would have fought back, it wasn't in my nature... I didn't know how to, which was probably why I was an easy target for anybody who fancied having a go. I couldn't help myself being frightened, I had been close to a man who might die from his knife wounds - I was scared and wanted to be anywhere but here. Nobody wanted anyone to see they were shaken and so, apart from a few voices recounting their experiences there was nothing. We just listened.

Eventually an ambulance came and the nightmare started to end. The police arrived and took statements... and then left. While they were there they told us that it was safe to go into the services and so I rang home to tell them I would be late but that I was alright. The people from the other bus were transferred to ours and we set off, squashed but relieved. We got back at two in the morning, a very tired and relieved group. Maybe I'd been lucky, or the man who had been stabbed unlucky but there was always a risk - it was all about surviving; by riding your luck. I didn't like to admit it but it was probably what added the edge to away travel.

Watching the local news two days later, one of the headlines was about the man who had been stabbed. I was horrified when I recognised him as the man who I had held the phone box door open for. He had been coming out when he was set upon and his wallet was taken. In the ensuing struggle he was stabbed and lost consciousness. He vowed never to go on an away match again for the sake of his family who worried about him. I imagine a few people questioned whether it was all worth it - the risk of attack, never mind the time and money spent but most came to the same conclusion.

Watching Newcastle was a dedication and though there were bound to be times when you put yourself on the line for them, you couldn't stop going because...the lads needed you. We had all been lucky to avoid being stabbed or severely beaten up, while the man who was knifed had been lucky to come out alive. The fact that we had been lucky just meant we would be more careful in future, but would be there next week because it was a way of life that only a select few shared (or probably would want to have).

In nearly three years of following Newcastle this was my first close encounter with hooliganism - which meant that if I was careful I could last another three years without meeting violence. Mum and Dad would obviously not have agreed but they knew how involved I was and wouldn't have been able to dissuade me. They trusted me to look after myself and to keep my wits about me, and hoped it would be enough.

Saturday 22nd **March 1986 - Tottenham (h)**

This was Mark and Jeremy's first visit to Tyneside. It was the return leg of our visits to each other's houses. They expected to see all the stereotypical streets - terraced with cobbles, with washing hanging in the back yard and dogs running up and down the streets. They expected to see a coal mine nearby or a factory and we of course all wore cloth caps. These scenes out of a Catherine Cookson novel seemed to be popular myths among people who were from "the South" and it was very satisfying showing my guests the coast at Tynemouth and Whitley Bay. The streets weren't filled with coal dust and each wasn't part of a long terrace. There were even green spaces to play football on and the sea air to breathe. To make things all the sweeter; it wasn't raining and was warm. So much for the bleak and cold North East coast.

The match itself was a cracker 2-2 after Tottenham had twice taken the lead, Billy Whitehurst and John Anderson the scorers. It wasn't revenge enough for the defeat in September but it was a result. At least we were still higher than them in the league. My parents said it was the best result to keep the peace but that was an entirely neutral opinion and therefore completely wrong. I had been denied the chance to gloat, something that I was never able to do when it came to Newcastle scores. Just once would have been nice!

Saturday 29th March 1986 - Everton (a)

This was my first away match since the QPR game but I knew that I would be safe. There were over six thousand other fans going to Liverpool, besides me. There seemed to be nearly fifty coaches lined up along Barrack Road. Everyone seemed to be going to Everton. Since the QPR game Newcastle had drawn one (Tottenham) and won five - beating Nottingham Forest 2-1 away and Arsenal 1-0 at home among others. Everton were the league champions and with our last visit to Liverpool on our minds, expectations were high. I also recognised the man who'd been stabbed at Woodall services. Just like the others that night he had put his experience behind him (which must have been hard) and was here amongst this immense crowd.
This was also Easter Saturday and a good excuse for many to escape their families. The route to Everton was the same as that to Liverpool only parking on a different side of Stanley Park. There were groups of kids shouting abuse from the street corners, I couldn't be sure but they might have been the same as in December, the sentiment surely was. A sea of black and white took over one end of the ground. We were in the terracing at the bottom of the Park End Stand and although we had got there early to get a seat, once again we were separated from our position by the sheer number of people in that section. We were crushed against the back as the teams came out. John Bailey, who we had signed from Everton that season, was given a tremendous reception - a bit different from our treatment of Waddle. The difference here was that Bailey was on the way down in his career whereas Waddle had been sold prematurely.

Despite playing well we fell behind in the twenty-ninth minute - Newcastle-born Kevin Richardson doing the damage. In the second half we tore into Everton and in true Newcastle tradition fluffed every opportunity. Gascoigne hit the post with a twenty-five-yarder, and the rebound fell to Ian Stewart who missed an open goal from ten yards.

Ian Stewart always appeared in the papers as Northern Ireland international Stewart or some variation on that theme.

This was done to make us feel we had such a great player, but the way he missed chances always proved this wasn't the case. However, Billy Whitehurst (always referred to as a bustling centre forward - which really meant he was a big clod) missed more chances more regularly and today was no exception. We just couldn't score for the toffees that had been thrown into the fans at half time. Our luck seemed to change when Roeder did his shuffle into the penalty box and was brought down - a penalty! Unfortunately, Peter Beardsley had missed his last two penalties and he didn't look too certain as he stepped up for this one. Surely today would be different! We watched the usual careful laying of the ball on the spot and the measured steps back. There was then the careful glance to a corner of the net and run up... and a hopeless shot which sailed high over the bar into the delighted Everton fans behind the goal and their not-so careful celebrations.

We knew that was it... we had played well but got nothing. The away fans sang throughout the match with no reward. We didn't expect anything different, after all this was Newcastle and we were devoted to cheering them on to endless gallant defeats - it gave us something to moan about anyway and we came across as good humoured and a threat to nobody who had a decent team. We were like the Liverpool fans - only they had success on the field - not just a decent position in the top half of the table, but in terms of winning trophies. That was the hard part and we didn't seem to have a clue how to do it. We always travelled with hope and great history, but that gave little substance to the efforts on the pitch.

Monday 31st March 1986 - Sheffield Wednesday (h)

I was very superstitious from the off. Everything from socks to my scarf had special significance. Defeat meant I was wearing the wrong socks or underpants. By now I had a home and away shirt so losing when I was wearing one, meant relegation to the subs bench and the other one worn in its place. Playing well and losing, might earn it a reprieve but there were no second chances. Sometimes, underpants and socks would have to be changed the minute I returned home, in readiness for a midweek match. My clothes would be laid out lovingly on a chair, ready for the next day's action.

Today, however, I had played my trump card. Even better than newly washed socks and underpants - my mum was coming to the match with me! In true teenage tradition I wouldn't have been seen dead with her in the Gallowgate but the offer of seat tickets meant that none of the Gallowgate faithful need ever know.

The family who had given me their season tickets for the Liverpool game couldn't go so they gave them to their grandad, called Mr Collins who went to the same church as my mum. He, mum and I went in their place. It was her first football match (my dad once went to an ice hockey match at Whitley and was bored (and frozen) rigid by it. I hadn't thought about the difficulties that might arise if she was going with me - the main one being that I wasn't allowed to swear at anybody, not the referee, linesmen, opposition players or fans. I hoped that it wouldn't be a tense match otherwise my silence would tell a tale. There was also the language of all the other supporters around us. What would she make of that? I could stop myself swearing but not anybody else. She might ban me from going ever$_4$again (not that it would work or that she would want me moping around the house anyway).

Would I feel duty bound to explain everything to her - the offside rule, penalties and free kicks? No, should just have to muddle through it. I'd give her a crash course in the rules on the way up and that would have to do her! What happens if it was cold or a boring game? Would she want to go early? If she did...tough!

All my worries seemed to evaporate as the day went on. Newcastle were playing brilliant football (couldn't hit a barn door from two yards but playing nice football all the same) and, (more importantly) it was a gloriously hot bank holiday Monday. Everyone was in short sleeves and there was a reasonable crowd. The view was excellent and she seemed to be enjoying herself. All that was needed now was a good start.

I couldn't have dreamed a better first half. After nine minutes of reminding my mum how many chances we'd missed against Everton, Paul Stephenson turned and smashed a shot into the roof of the net. Billy Whitehurst then rounded the keeper only to have his goal disallowed for offside. Gascoigne headed in and just two minutes later Beardsley scored from the edge of the box to make it 3-0. Sheff Wed were sixth at the start of the game but we had torn them apart.

My face and the faces of everybody around us were ecstatic. My mum had seen the best finishing all season and seemed to understand why the team took up so much of my time and accounted for many of my moods. In the second half, things calmed down after the fourth and final goal a minute into the half. This time it was Billy Whitehurst who I had called every name under the sun after the Everton game but was now back in my good books after sweeping home a Beardsley cross.

The party started after that goal and the match became an exhibition with Wednesday gaining a consolation in the sixty-eighth minute. We had nothing to fight for from the season but with football like this to watch, who cared. The smiles around the ground said it all at the final whistle. Even better was the news that Sunderland had been beaten by Sheffield United and were slipping towards Division Three. There's nothing like kicking a horse when it's down! Unfortunately mum never came to another game so I never got to test the lucky charm theory. I thought that if we ever needed a win then I could recruit her as a lucky mascot. The cost of a ticket for her would have been more than worth it if we won the Championship or a Cup.

Somehow I doubted I would need her for some time to come.

Saturday 3rd May 1986 - Leicester (a)

This time last year I'd been a novice away traveller but now I was a veritable expert. I had been to nine away matches (and all the home matches) and experienced my first (and only) victory, three draws and five defeats. I'd experienced football hooliganism first hand and come back unscathed. I'd out sung the Kop (in my opinion) and seen us put both Mersey giants under the cosh for long periods on their own turf. Most important I discovered a way of escaping from the everyday worries of a teenage boy - school and girls (or the lack of interested ones). Worrying about football meant I couldn't blame myself for their failures (apart from my socks and underpants). I could be a different person from the one at home and school. I kept my travels to myself, apart from my closest friends, and that suited me. When things were against me, I would remember all the times I'd escaped - the feeling of watching Beardsley score at Southampton, my friends from Portsmouth, the Liverpool game. Everything had been so new to me. I couldn't imagine any of the others who taunted and picked on me at school doing the things I'd done that year. The best bit of it all was that there were more delights in store next season. Perhaps a Cup run...that would be nice, carrying on the way we finished this season...challenging for the title perhaps...I couldn't wait.

Today, though was the last game of the season. Leicester needed to win in order to stay up, we needed to win just to amuse ourselves. There was a carnival atmosphere in the away corner. There was a great big fence between us and the Leicester fans which made the nearest goal hard to see (a now-familiar experience). Unlike Norwich, Leicester got the victory they needed. They had young Alan Smith and Gary McAllistar playing for them, pulling the strings to secure victory and when the final whistle went, the Leicester fans partied and we applauded an enjoyable season. On the way out some Newcastle fans decided that they would play target practise with the surrounding factory windows. It was the small minority who felt it their duty to spoil our good name. They didn't care about the repercussions for future Newcastle fans coming here, or perhaps they were hoping for a response and a chance to start some trouble. The truth of it all was that no-one was around to care and so they left unfulfilled. The large number of away fans were marched away from the ground and another season. But the problem now was - what was I to do each Saturday without a weekly dose of Newcastle? Standing by in the wings - the World Cup! Thank goodness.

The World Cup and 'Our Peter'

I hadn't been dreading the Summer break from football this year quite as much as I had the previous years. My parents were even surprised when I was not moping around in the house in the manner sixteen year olds were supposed to. Household chores were carried out on request without the usual moaning or pulling of pained expression. Hoovering, washing up and tidying away were all swiftly dealt with. They knew that something was up...but what?

The answer was simple - it was the World Cup and I had worked out that for the duration of it there was a lot of football to be watched. It was my duty to do just that job. Unfortunately, while I was doing my duty there were other programmes, on other channels that mum and dad might like to watch thanks to their complete indifference to the beautiful game. I was going to have to walk a tight rope in order to achieve my aims. I could not have any arguments with them because the only thing that would suffer was the World Cup through losing my patronage. To make matters more enticing for me, Peter Beardsley had become a prominent member of the England squad. I felt this was in some small way down to my efforts (and the rest of the St James' faithful of course). We had stood in all manner of atrocious weather, cheering the little genius on, chanting his name when he missed the penalty against Everton (...and the others he missed) and making him feel secure to weave his magic and perform his miracles. We had raised him - given him the confidence to achieve (the man himself, coaches and managers throughout his life had had some hand in his success too, but that didn't matter to me). Now the world was to see him blossom into a world class player. The icing on the cake was that, after the world cup, he was still going to be a Newcastle player. I wouldn't be any help to him if my dad insisted on watching the Money Programme or my mum wanted Gardeners World instead of England v Poland. Therefore I had to be careful.

When England played Mexico in a friendly in Los Angeles, it was late at night, our house was silent and I'd gingerly crept downstairs to watch the match, avoiding the stairs that I knew creaked, anxious to see my mate Pete. Mum and dad were safely asleep and oblivious to my nocturnal wanderings. I had the volume turned down so that I could just make out the commentary. England went 2-0 up, two goals from Mark Hately. Each goal was greeted by a silent celebration - clenched fists punching the air emphatically and a carefully mimed "Yes!" The second goal had sent me into inaudible raptures because Pete had sent in the cross for Hately to head. All my careful planning and control went up in smoke eight minutes before half time, however. Glenn Hoddle hastily took a free kick. The Mexican defence was static as the next few seconds slowly ticked by. The pictures seemed to come, frame by frame...Beardsley expertly controlled the ball on his chest...

There wasn't a defender near... I rose expectantly from my seat unable to breathe... the ball was on the end of his foot... my arms started to rise up... the Mexican goalkeeper started to react with flapping, grasping fingers... but the ball eased itself past him... all self-control I had was gone...

"Yeeeeeeeeeees...!"

I screamed at match volume. The only difference was that it was half past twelve in the morning and I wasn't in the middle of thirty thousand rejoicing fans, I was in muted and sleepy Tynemouth, on my own, in a hushed front room.

There was a crash upstairs, then the sound of thudding footsteps.

"What the bloody hell's going on?" my Dad managed to spit out at me. I was oblivious to the time in the morning or the affect I'd had on two peacefully slumbering parents. The only thing that mattered was my boy, our boy, the whole of Newcastle's boy had scored in an England shirt.

"Beardsley's scored...!" I replied enthusiastically.

"What do you think you're playing at..." my mum pleaded, her eyes little more than cracks. She knew it was useless after taking one look at my beaming face. I was beyond reason and she just looked at me and, shaking her head, went back to bed muttering something about keeping the noise down or there'd be no World Cup. After that the rest of the match was plain sailing for England and there was no repeat performance. I returned to bed, *a* satisfied and tired individual, confident that at seven o'clock, my mum and dad would make a point of waking me up and returning the compliment.

The World Cup proper started a week later and despite my early morning outburst, I was granted exclusive use of the television (anything for an easy life). Beardsley wasn't picked to start the first England game against Portugal, and Bobby Robson's boys lost a pretty boring game 1-0. They never looked like scoring. The next game was another bore... a draw against Morocco. The first four games in the group had resulted in only two goals scored and it had been nicknamed The Group of The Sleeping for obvious reasons. Bobby Robson had persisted with the old favourites of Bryan Robson and Ray Wilkins affectionately known by some commentators as Captain Marvel and Butch respectively. Unfortunately they were no longer the super-heroes they'd once been and should've hung up their international caps long ago. The good thing to come from the Morocco game was that Captain Marvel had injured his arm (as he was prone to do to various parts of his body) and was out for the rest of the tournament. Butch had been sent off for getting stroppy with the referee (nobody told him that even supermen weren't allowed to throw footballs at the referee).

The whole of Newcastle screamed for Beardsley to play in the final game against Poland and for once Bobby did something that everyone agreed with. Sure enough England won 3-0 thanks to a Gary Lineker hat trick and Beardsley had a hand in the first two goals. What was even more satisfying was that Beardsley had taken Chris Waddle's place in the England team. He had shown Waddle that the real class was still at Newcastle and happy to be there, unlike Waddle and his Diamond Lights (see 1987) down south.

In the next round, it was Paraguay and once again, Beardsley was playing. This was also the first time mum and dad decided to watch any of the games. Suddenly the front room was no longer my own special reserve. I'd been allowed to shout, scream at whoever I wanted to and nobody heard me. But now I'd to share my room.

I was suddenly tossed out of the comfortable reclining chairs and made to sit on the sofa with my bottle of Coca Cola and large bowl of crisps. This was the equivalent of the people who only came to the Newcastle games against Man United or Liverpool. They weren't interested when it was Charlton Athletic or Watford, but when the big boys came so did they. The queues to get in would be greater, you might not get your favourite spot on the terraces and you couldn't see because they *Mere* all eight-foot-tall and wanted to stand in front of you and anybody who was with you. England was one step away from the World Cup Quarter Finals and suddenly there they were - pushing me from my World Cup seat and onto the not so comfortable sofa. What right had they to do this? (Apart from the fact that they paid for everything in the house, including me). I had to just be thankful that they were letting me watch it because there might be something more interesting to them Dn... Yes, I was in their debt. They didn't seem that bothered about the score, but I /vas. For them it was an interesting diversion...to me it was my national duty as a football supporter, and my duty to Peter as a Newcastle fan to be with him, in spirit watching his every action. It was the difference between The Oxford-Cambridge Boat Race and a Newcastle match. I couldn't give a toss about one but was passionate about the other. They (and a lot of the country) were interested in both but not passionate about either. So why was it that I ended up in the cheap seats? It was all town to money - I had none.

The game kicked off and I was trying to get myself into match mode but knew would look daft in their eyes. My mum had been to the Sheff Wed game and knew he drill but dad wasn't aware of the effect football had on people. He'd picked me up rom away trips and seen the others meekly getting off the bus. What he had seen however, was the aftermath of football battle. He'd missed the moment when the two armies faced and taunted each other and battle had been joined. He told me to sit down when Terry Butcher made *a* suicidal back-pass, leaving Mendoza of Paraguay free to beat Peter Shilton at will. He frowned when I jumped and cheered wildly as Shilton saved the eventual shot. The next minute England went ahead through Lineker and I leapt into the air, prompting the call "Careful of your drink. You nearly stained the carpet." I was the jubilant minority now. Ten minutes into the second half, my efforts to cheer on the boys despite the barracking and barrage of abuse ("You're not having any more crisps because you're getting crumbs everywhere.") was rewarded in the best possible way - a Beardsley goal. It wasn't a screamer from outside the penalty area, more a rebound from six yards but it was done with a shuffle as only Peter could. I immediately ran around the room, my wish fulfilled and then rolled on the carpet kicking my legs in the air, like a fly, dying but who has just seen how exciting a place heaven was really going to be for him. My mum just smiled at me, as if to say I don't know what you're doing but stop it, while my dad just told me to stop being so bloody silly and to get up. Somehow I don't think they understood my delight.

The final score was 3-0 and I started to think about the Quarter-Final against Argentina. I wonder what the crowd control in our house would be like for that game?

The security was pretty tight especially around the comfortable reclining chairs. Those seats had been booked long before the tie had been announced, I don't even think that they were ever open to the general public (me) and so once again I took my place on the sofa with my refreshments - wagon wheels and Coke. There was an air of suppressed anticipation from a third of the crowd in our house, mixed with a sense of dread. England and our Peter were going to play against one of the big boys of international football. Did they have what it takes to win? There was optimism in abundance but this was only skin deep. Underneath, it was the same feeling you got when Newcastle were playing Liverpool, a sense of why are we turning up? There was not even the chance to try and outsing the opposition fans. It was a home supporters only match as far as that went and the dire atmosphere to go with it. Perhaps a couple of Argentineans, passing, would ask to watch the match to raise the atmosphere but I doubted it would happen due to the lack of Argentineans in Tynemouth.

England looked a bit shaky and as Argentina took control of the game through the skills of Diego Maradona, my nerves started to show. I never touched any of the available refreshments and the sense of foreboding grew. It started in my knotted stomach and seemed to creep upwards through my veins, taking hold of my shoulders, making them move involuntarily, hunching them made a loud cracking sound akin to the sound of a fire cracker exploding. The England team was chasing shadows that were quicker and more imaginative than they were and I was getting more and more twisted inside. I was trying to keep my increasing frustrations to myself, cursing mentally while all the while praying that Peter could conjure up some piece of magic. I had been calm and relaxed in the previous two games due to the relative ease of each win but now I was being made to suffer in silence and in agony. Half time arrived and it was still 0-0. My dad's only comment was that they weren't playing very well and he went to make the tea. I sat listening to all the pundits at half time confirming my dad's synopsis only in more detail. We'd turn it around in the second half and then I could start enjoying the game. We settled down for the second half (I hadn't budged an inch anyway - it was my duty to stay focused on the job of beating the Argies).

Six minutes after half time my frustration erupted from within me and like lava freeing itself from a volcano, so did I as Diego Maradona rose to fist the ball into the net. I stood up outraged, and completely oblivious to the fact that my mum and dad were sitting quite serenely in comfort next to me and shouted;

"You fucking cheating little Argentinian bastard."

As soon as I had uttered those immortal words I realised where I was. I wasn't in the middle of thousands of snarling, irate and vengeful fans, I was sitting at home next to my mum and dad who had never uttered an expletive in their lives. They stared at me, aghast and agog. Where had I learned such language and what had happened to their little boy? I was horror-stricken at my lapse and stared back, trying to show them I was sorry but instead I tried to justify myself...

"He handled it..." I began, but I realised it was too late for that. This wasn't what they wanted to hear and my justification was weak as far as they were concerned. I feared the worst...the red card. I was ordered to my room and told not to come out until they told me. I told them I was glad I wouldn't have to watch that lot and ran out.

I rushed up to my room to my old portable black and white TV. I furiously tried to tune it in, waving the aerial frantically to get a decent picture from the fuzziness that I had picked up. The picture came into view just as Diego Maradona skipped past Peters Reid and Beardsley, then glided inside Terry Butcher and then Fenwick... before embarrassing Shilton to score the goal of the tournament. My outburst had left me beaten and subdued, I lay on my bed, down and out. Downstairs was silent as well. The fight was lost, I became an impassive observer like my parents. I had accepted mine and England's fate...for us the World Cup was over, no more favours for either of us.

But then the unthinkable started to happen, England started to fight back. Chris Waddle and John Barnes came on and suddenly Argentina was desperately trying to defend against renewed English vigour. Barnes crossed and Lineker headed in. My subservient state had gone as I leapt about on my bed, cheering. The goal seemed to have compelled dad to have a change of heart and he shouted I could come back as long as I kept my opinions to myself, which I promised to do. Suddenly everything seemed rosy, England was only a goal behind, had the South Americans rocking and I had served my time in the sin bin (twenty-five minutes for un-gentlemanly conduct). Even my parents seemed to be getting excited, especially mum. We watched spellbound as England swarmed around Argentina. We all breathed huge sighs of relief when Argentina hit the post. The whole room was absorbed for the final ten minutes or so. My dad seemed to have an inkling of what watching football was all about and my mum was as gripped as I was. Despite the pressure, it was not to be and the game finished in defeat and so too did our shared love of football.

We were all subdued at the final whistle, I returned defeated to my room in self-imposed exile and mum and dad read the papers downstairs as if nothing had happened. They had seen the way football could affect their son and preferred not to think about it. As long as I didn't bring that side of me back after matches then they would turn a blind eye, continue to pick me up at stupid times at night and in the morning while pretending to be interested in the fortunes of eleven men.

The World Cup had provided a stopgap between seasons and the next day I was dreaming about how well we'd do with Peter, our little world beater (almost) and Paul Gascoigne back together. In between I spent two weeks away from parents in London with the National Youth Theatre. I was away from them for the first time and I met new people who knew nothing about me. I was starting a new chapter in my life, as the two weeks passed I grew in confidence. London, and all its attractions, was calling out to me, beckoning me towards this new part of my life. I was going to have to choose where I wanted to go to University and all paths seemed to lead there. I didn't want to stay in Newcastle, despite the draw of United, I wanted to explore foreign parts, away travel having whetted my appetite. There were eight clubs in the first division from London which made up for the loss of home games. There were also the holidays when I could go to home matches. Portsmouth wasn't too far and all my new found friends from the South coast would be nearby, along with those from Tottenham so I couldn't have gone to any other part of the country. Over the next year I had to get into a London University or College, but to study what, I didn't know or really care.

Tuesday 4th August - Heart of Midlothian (a)

After I returned from London there was a lull. There was not much to do, just visit Surge and wander around Tynemouth with him, trying to think of things to do. There was an extremely brief romantic fling with a girl from round the corner, which was a sign of my new found confidence but lasted only two days. It was a case of waiting for the football season to start again. The trip to Edinburgh for a pre-season friendly seemed to me a beacon in the distance. I borrowed the money from loyal parents and then set off, complete with egg sandwiches, Walkman and the Eurythmics to listen to, taking my place, in time honoured tradition near the front of the bus. During my stay in London, I had been introduced to a large number of people who considered themselves to be cool and who was I to disagree but it was during my stay I had been introduced to the spiky sounds of Annie Lennox. I consider this to be the start of my journey towards musical education and coolness.

    I hadn't been to Scotland since the family had sat and shivered in a tent at the age of ten, watching the rain pour down while mum mentioned something about camping having limited attractions and my sister and I moaned incessantly about being bored. I was looking forward to the trip up the A1 as a pleasant change. It wasn't raining as we entered Edinburgh. There was no time for sightseeing as we went straight into the ground.

    I expected there to be some difference between English and Scottish grounds but there was the same collection of terracing and corrugate-roofed seating that was common. There was terracing at each end of the ground which seemed tailor made for sending abuse across the expanse of grass that held so much interest for us all. Everything was painted maroon and white which seemed to lift the drabness of the concrete and steel.

Friendly matches provided an opportunity to prove, once again that you were a fanatical supporter due to the small numbers that attended them. We didn't care what the game was like, it was another notch on the bedpost that said "I was there... and you weren't." Our terrace was nearly as big as the Gallowgate and was surrounded by dark-red brick houses that looked like something from Charles Dickens but gave an excellent view down onto the pitch and thanks to the favourable slope of the terrace, residents had a good view of both goals. There was the obvious banter with residents who were leaning out of their windows but eventually the fans grew tired of this. Instead they took to looking around the ground to see the Hearts fans trickling in, the next victims for our taunts. Our section was populated by about two hundred supporters, all positioned in groups of one or two (or even three) at available barriers. The people on their own (me) made a beeline for these metal constructions in order to have something to lean casually upon. They would try to look as if they did have lots of friends who hadn't arrived yet, then would swing on them when they gave up trying to look cool and popular and were just bored. Of course it wouldn't matter when the match got going because after months without football we'd have been happy just to stand on the terrace and watch the grass grow. Unfortunately we weren't. The match was slow and lacking passion, while we over emphasised every attack to convince ourselves it was a good idea coming. Entering the final minutes the score was still 0-0 and only a few chances to get excited about. This all changed when Gascoigne scored and our little band of two hundred made good use of the extra room on the terrace as we leapt about, amazed more than anything else to the obvious annoyance of our Scottish hosts. At this point the ground emptied considerably, which only added to our delight as we chimed " We can see you sneaking out!" This was one occasion when actions spoke louder than words because as we left the ground to make our way home, we spotted young Hearts fans forming regimented rows in the distance. We stopped, unsure of what was going on. I was certain what was going on and started easing myself to the back while the head-cases pushed their way to the front, hoping for a re-run of Culloden. For a brief tense moment the two groups eyed each other up and then the Scots charged down, row by row towards our small group. Never one to fight when I could run faster (never one to fight, anyway) I turned round and along with a few dozen similarly brave souls ran back into the ground from which we had come. Some bright spark had the idea of closing the large wooden doors through which we had just ran and so we blockaded ourselves in the silent and empty ground. The scene resembled a medieval siege as we ran to the top of the terrace to see any potential attackers before they arrived, we would have been ready with the boiling oil or large boulders if it had been from the twelfth century... .it wasn't and we weren't. We were just a bunch of football fans who didn't fancy getting lynched. Nobody followed us or was even bothered about us so after about five minutes we emerged, sheepishly into the empty street. There were no bodies, no police or anybody for that matter and the only thing that was left to do was to make our way sheepishly back to the buses... after all they could come back. As we boarded the bus it turned out once they had charged down the hill, their momentum carried them away from the site, perhaps ready for a surprise attack further away from the ground for supporters making their way to the train station. Although our small group had taken drastic steps to avoid violence, we had come through unscathed. Some people enjoyed the clash to show how hard they were and to brag about it later. I enjoyed the element of danger but without the desire to prove myself against anybody else. It was safety first. That was the way I had learnt to survive and it came naturally to me. I enjoyed being part of the self-preservation society.

Saturday 23rd August 1986 - Liverpool (h)

My high hopes after the Hearts game combined with last year's brilliant performances against today's visitors convinced me that we had turned the corner. Liverpool had won the league last year but they hadn't managed to beat us. Our good form from last season was to be the building block for greatness this year. Everything was going to be great... I could feel it.

These high hopes lasted five glorious minutes, after Ian Rush had scored it was back to reality. Liverpool, sat back and let Newcastle huff and puff for the rest of the game and just when I thought things were looking up, Ian Rush gave us a lesson from the school of life. The moment you think you have achieved something, some bugger (called Rush) comes along and spoils everything. It was the perfect opportunity to show everyone that last season wasn't a fluke, we *were* one of the big boys and we blew it. For years Newcastle had been known for its passionate fans who would turn up to watch the grass grow, but this image disguised the heartache that seemed to follow us each year.

Monday 25th August 1986 - Tottenham Hotspur (a)

My trip to see the lads from Tottenham saw me travelling down on the non-stop Clipper with every chance of being publicly humiliated again. There was as much chance of us avoiding defeat as there was of Chris Waddle having a hit single... but stranger things have happened.

Once again, Mark's dad had got us tickets in the seats to one side of the away fans. On my previous journey I hadn't had a chance to take in my surroundings and despite suffering the biggest humiliation of my footballing career twelve months before, this had to be the best ground I had been to. Sitting below two levels of executive boxes made me feel like the coyote staring up at the cliff, thinking what wasn't going to hit him next. Opposite was the Shelf, not one but two pieces of terrace with seats on top of that. Wherever I looked, the stands seemed to tower above me. St James' was more open and although it was dark and imposing, didn't seem as imposing as this. It was like comparing a Victorian terrace house to a modern detached.

There was to be no repeat of our great start of the previous season and it was no surprise to be 1-0 down when Clive Allen scored. What was surprising was that we were only one down. I knew the script, however - a repeat of Everton last season if we were lucky (or is that unlucky) i.e. constant pressure with no penetration or the previous game against Liverpool (for Ian Rush read Clive Allen). The game died after that and neither team seemed to have any chances and struggled to do anything more than pass the ball to each other. Most football fans are pessimists presumably because the defeats stand out more than the victories. Monumental victories become flukes after a while and in all the possible permutations I had worked out for the game, each ended in defeat. To find an optimistic fan was a miracle. Even when we went to Anfield, the Liverpool fans remembered the fact that we had beaten them in August, and forgot the fact that since that game they had won eighteen and lost only two (both away). That's why it was so easy for fans to compare their life to the fortunes of their football teams. The highs in both are quickly forgotten and the lows remembered and later dwelt on. I didn't know it but this was what I was starting to do. Newcastle needed a bit of luck, I hadn't had much recently - therefore no hope for this to be reversed. Just when we looked like scoring last time - what happened? Rush scored. I wriggled my way through the first half. I was frustrated and unable to share it with my neighbours. The Spurs fans seemed to be comatose by the match and the only life seemed to come from the small band of Newcastle fans that jeered every time Waddle got the ball. Mark and Jeremy didn't know what to say to me, maybe it seemed unfair that here I was again and Newcastle were losing again. They seemed as embarrassed as I was with Newcastle's ineptness and so at half time I decided it would be best for all of us if I went and stood in the away fans' 'cage'. This would allow both of us to go back to our natural state - I wouldn't have to keep quiet and they could relax and enjoy their victory without any misgivings.

  The stewards let me take the short walk around the pitch to the away supporters' end. I felt like one of the fans at Sunderland when they were marched away from the Fulwell End, proclaiming themselves as heroes as they saluted the crowd. But this wasn't Sunderland, there were only a few hundred fans, we were 1-0 down and nobody noticed me. I saw Mr and Mrs Brown and stood next to them telling them all about my nightmare with the Spurs fans. They nodded politely and offered me a mint. I instantly felt amongst friends and it was now us against them. We were in our cage and could call them anything we wanted to... safe behind steel bars, police and stewards. We applauded the team as they come out and tried to lift their spirits. There was a slight improvement but the game still dragged on. The brief glimmer of hope had gone again. We sang because that's what we did - "Sing when we're losing..."

The piece of luck I was hoping for suddenly appeared. Beardsley scored late in the game to reward our efforts. By now drizzle had set in around the ground and the sky cast a dull shade of grey that made the Victorian terraces seem incredibly dull and dingy. The goal was at the far end of the ground and we couldn't even see it but that didn't matter. What did was the fact that at the end of the match we were on the up. We wouldn't have to listen to the crowing of the address system or the fans outside. We'd spoilt their party (such that it was) and would let them know about it for the next few minutes. We probably couldn't even be heard on the other side of the ground but that was just a technicality.
      As we said goodbye to our afternoon cage, that candle of hope for the season was lit once more. My mind was whizzing with a mild attack of euphoria. It was an amazing fight-back, not a lucky escape. We'd achieved more than this time last year...it had to count for something. We had played badly and for the only time I could remember scored in the last few minutes. This would turn a few heads. Liverpool was history, we'd build upon today, challenge for the top...I shouted loudly as I left... "Newcastle, Newcastle..." this time it was a victory song, not one to encourage a flagging team.
      I met the others outside the ground, filled with excitement. I couldn't wait for the chance to rub it in but they weren't that bothered about the result.
      "We've still got four points from two games," they mumbled. They were more bothered about the cold and rain! Robbed of my moment of glory. This was the ultimate put down.
      If it had been sunny would I have rubbed it in more enthusiastically? It certainly took a shine off it all.
      It all left me wondering why we didn't win on sunny days?

Saturday 20th September 1986 -Wimbledon (h)

I had a friend called Hassan who was of Arabic descent. He supported Sunderland and at school, most break times were spent telling him how crap his team were. After heavy defeats he would usually agree with me despondently but would also give as good as he got when needed. A few weeks earlier I had travelled to Roker to watch Sunderland beat Brighton 2-0 and he returned the compliment this week. Whenever we went to each other's matches the rules were that no mention would be made of the other's allegiances. We would support the other's team in return. It was easier for me because I knew Newcastle was the more successful team out of the two and could be condescending in my support for Sunderland.

We stood in the Gallowgate but not in my usual spot just below the Scoreboard, instead we went to the front in one of the quieter sections of the ground. I thought it would be fine standing there, remembering that Newcastle fans still had a reputation to be racist at times. We would stand with the middle-aged supporters and their children, it'd be okay there.

The match itself represented a tough game, Newcastle had lost their last three matches and Beardsley had been injured for all of them. To make matters worse we had Gary Kelly making his debut because Martin Thomas was injured. We were bottom of the league and desperate for our first win of the season. Wimbledon started well and Kelly had to make some great saves, but at this point I started to notice Hassan getting uncomfortable. I didn't know why so I tried to listen to what was being said around me. The conversations all revolved around John Fashanu, who had missed a hat-full of chances. They were ordinary fans with children but every time they talked about him, he was referred to as "That monkey...", "...nigger..." or "The darky..." It wasn't said with any malice but Hassan was frightened they would turn round and see him. He had heard it all before but he knew that to them, if he was on the street, he would be referred to in the same way. Never mind the fact that he came from a different continent to Fashanu, he was still one of 'them'. If I hadn't been standing with him I wouldn't have noticed but throughout his life he'd obviously become accustomed to it and had to desensitise himself from it. To them, it was just like calling someone fat or thin (except in most cases you can put on weight or lose it) but to Hassan, he saw it as something that wasn't desirable in their eyes. We moved at half time but he was still nervous and felt like he stuck out like a sore thumb. He couldn't help having darker skin (nor should have had to mind) just as much as I couldn't help the colour of mine. The difference was most people from the North East had the same coloured skin - my colour. For years I never saw any blacks or Asians at Newcastle matches and looking back, if there had been more, then maybe people would have thought about how insulting some of the things that they were saying were. If they had turned around they'd have been embarrassed but Hassan would have been even more so. The racism that day wasn't as bad as the banana throwing aimed at Bobby Barnes of West Ham two seasons before, people had realised that that wasn't funny. This represented an improvement. But it would be a long time before fans of different cultures would be able to go to a Newcastle match and feel comfortable. The only thing I could do was apologise to Hassan but it left a sick feeling that Paul Gascoigne's winning strike couldn't come close to removing.

Tuesday 21st October - Portsmouth v Derby County

Life wasn't going too well - Newcastle was still bottom and the pressure was on to knuckle down to work towards my mock A level exams and to earn a place at a College or University somewhere. I knew I wanted to go to University in London and had now decided to do a teaching degree, mainly because I couldn't see myself sitting at a desk, working in an office all day and my mum was a teacher. I also seemed to enjoy being with children, probably because I was never destined to grow up. Me, Burge and another of our gang called John decided to go down to London for a few days. The main reason I wanted to go was to see my friends in Portsmouth. It just so happened, amazingly that Portsmouth had a home game against Derby County so it was all set that we would stay a night in John's (the big bloke) caravan. The Clipper was once again used to get down to London on the Tuesday. My musical listening was inspired by The Sun newspaper which told us about Morten Hackett from A-Ha who apparently took young groupies into his room for Bible stories. Young and impressionable as we were, we took none of it with a pinch of salt and imagined what we would do in the same situation (probably panic and make fools of ourselves). After the journey, John and I said goodbye to Burge for a day (who was staying with a relative in London) and we headed to the South Coast.

Rain fell for the rest of the day which made Portsmouth seem a very unattractive place when we stepped off the train at Portsmouth Harbour. It wasn't the sea-side town I had been led to believe from conversations at Roker the previous year, but first impressions are sometimes misleading. We were due to meet big John at a pub near Fratton Park and had an hour to kill while we were waiting. Trying to get something to eat was a chore but eventually we were out of the rain and tucking into the delights of omelette and chips (with bread on the side). This was the first time I had made my own way to a ground before (apart from St James') and found it quite an exciting experience. I had been used to being dropped at the ground and then driven back by a bus or car but now I had complete freedom. There was also something warm about the seediness of the streets around Fratton. I sensed a strange welcoming feeling as we wandered the deserted streets. The ground was silent, there was none of the business of Newcastle, partly because we were a mile or so from the city centre. When the pub opened, we were the first there. I'd been worried because I still looked about fifteen but luckily John could pass for older and so we were welcomed in. Not long later, big John arrived with his mates and I relaxed, safe in the knowledge that we did indeed have a place to stay that night. It was big John's natural warm up before a match, a few pints and a chat with friends before the match and a sign that I was entering the adult world of football. My Shoot and Match magazines weren't a part of this world and neither were walls filled with posters of teams I didn't support or even like. The match was only part of a much larger trip out. Not for them, the hour wait for the game and then straight back for a hot chocolate - this was a man's world. We were treated as equals. My mate John liked to dominate conversations and I enjoyed listening to him trying to impress the others with a sketchy knowledge of Newcastle United. He went occasionally to the matches but pretended he was a fount of all knowledge. I was quietly getting sozzled in a corner of the small but welcoming pub, away from talk of exams, universities and school. I was glad when it was time to go to the match, having started clock watching about half an hour earlier. I wasn't used to getting to matches late and was anxious to get some fresh air to sober me up and to make sure I didn't miss anything. I didn't want to be rude and not trust big John's judgement but it was only ten minutes to kick off, I didn't come all this way just to drink. We were led through endless back alleys, each turn seemed to make the ground further away from us and as fans hurried past us I got more nervous, quickening my pace only to have to slow down again to let the others catch up. I had visions of St James' type queues for the juveniles turnstile at the Gallowgate end and the extra stress that that incurred on a young fan desperate to see his heroes. Finally, we were there. There was only a small queue but the teams were already coming out. A few desperate minutes and we were in, we'd missed nothing. Sighs of relief all round. We stood on the terrace that ran the length of the pitch in one of the most populated part of the ground. I wasn't used to seeing large parts of a ground empty, shrouded in an unwelcome blackness. Portsmouth had been top of Division Two the week before and yet the ground wasn't even half full. It was a shock after being in a twenty-one thousand crowd supporting the bottom club in Division One and thinking it a poor turn out. I had taken a lot for granted at Newcastle and one of these things was the crowd, turning out in all weather, watching all manner of dirge in their droves. Here was a club that had to fight to get its supporters to go regularly but there was again the feeling that there was a hard core of fans who would do anything for it. The ground had the same charm that Roker had and it only made you wonder what both would have looked like when they were first built. The money had dwindled since football's heyday all over the country and it was sad to think of these grounds so rich in history just crumbling away.

The crowd that night was around nine thousand and a dismal night for the Portsmouth fans was made worse when they went 1-0 down. The rain steadily soaked the crowd, and the ground was still, apart from disgruntled shouts from fans who had wished they'd stayed indoors that night. Gradually the rain eased and slowly Portsmouth started to show some life, enough to get the crowd's hopes up. It was to be Mick Quinn's night as he scored a second half hat-trick to waken up the crowd and by the final whistle, what had looked like a dismal experience at one point turned into an exhilarating roller coaster ride. The size of the crowd and the elements also made it feel extra special. The ones that had made the effort were rewarded for their trouble that night, as if the players had done it not for themselves, their bonuses or the club, they had done it for the soaked fans.

We were in high spirits as we headed back to the pub, this time tagging behind a thirsty big John and his mates. Not used to drinking, the rest of the evening swam past eyes. I remembered having a Chinese after leaving the pub we had spent the last few hours extolling Mick Quinn and demanding his inclusion in the New Year's honours list. When big John left us to sleep in the caravan at the end of his garden, my mind was starting to adjust and thanks to the restorative qualities of Chicken Chow Mein and chips the haze was beginning to lift.

The caravan was indeed filled with videos from Portsmouth's television jaunts down the years. Drawer after drawer formed an Aladdin's cave of Pompey memorabilia. I thought about my bedroom, slowly filling up with programmes, shirts, scarves, hats and newspaper articles and had a vision of my own shrine to Newcastle...a house filled with everything black and white. I imagined that big John had been told that his Pompey collection would have to live in the caravan and not in the house and thought about my growing collection. What will have to happen to that? I could see the face of my parents or my future girlfriend /wife, it was a look of despair mixed with anger, telling me that on no account was it staying in the house. Perhaps she would instead scheme different ways to dispose, gradually of the unwanted football debris. I put this image out of my head as we waded our way through 70s TV football programmes on video, complete with the disastrous sets, haircuts and clichés that the era conjured up. In the early hours of the morning, we dragged ourselves out of our beds, cleared up the mess we had made. The forgotten guests, we packed our rucksacks and headed towards the station. It was only when reached the train station that we found out that the town we were in was called Petersfield. We were surprised to discover our location twenty odd miles from Portsmouth but luckily only a short train ride away from London and the rest of our holiday.

Saturday 22na November 1986 - Chelsea (a)

It had only been a month since my holiday in London and I was back again. I was going to stay with some other Portsmouth supporters - Lynne and Duncan. It was going to be my second visit to Chelsea and Newcastle was showing signs of ending their terrible form. Two draws gave me some hope as I arrived in London early on Saturday morning. I had to once again step over the homeless sleeping in the subway at Marble Arch and this symbolised London for me. There was the majestic sight of Marble Arch and Hyde Park but just beneath the surface was the extreme poverty of the homeless. The cans and bottles that littered the subway only served to add to the depression that existed in certain parts of the capital. As an unaffected seventeen-year-old once again escaping from the real world I wasn't going to dwell on this and let it spoil my weekend, there was a team to support. The homeless were London's problem, not mine, I thought as I stepped onto the tube, after all we don't have homeless in Newcastle. How wrong I was there.

Lynne and Duncan took me to Putney for a drink and some food before the game. We sat looking across the river at Fulham on the far bank and watched the hustle and bustle of the streets, the never ending streams of cars, the noise and the grime. I wanted to be a part of all this I once more thought.

We travelled on the Underground to a once proud Fulham Broadway station and for the first time since Sunderland I thought it wise to cover up my shirt and put my scarf out of sight. I had developed a love for the London Underground over the last year. Everything about it was Victorian and despite the dirt and general neglect that had left the stations and trains looking a shadow of their former self, the work that had gone into the system still stood out, from the tiles on each platform to the endless tunnels. Our own Metro system had been built in the early 1980's and showed no imagination, everything was functional, especially the yellow M signs everywhere. But it was clean and tidy, which had its advantages.

There was no sight of any Newcastle supporters as we headed towards Stamford Bridge and I stayed very quiet, listening to the Chelsea fans' conversations. They weren't a happy bunch. They moaned about the manager, John Collins mostly and how bad he was. We had more reason to moan because Newcastle had four points less than Chelsea and were rooted to the bottom of the league, yet I had heard nobody say anything detrimental about manager Willie McFaul. We seemed to be more patient and trusted that he would get us out of the position we were in. As I listened my only communication to Lynne and Duncan was through raised eyebrows and smiles. Chelsea's reputation for trouble preceded them, there was an aggressive air around the fans leaving the station and they were waiting for an excuse to vent their frustrations. Although Chelsea - Newcastle matches were usually exciting, it was the element of rivalry between the two clubs that made them tense affairs. We were the poor relations of the two clubs we had been promoted with - Chelsea and Sheff Wed. Chelsea were the flash wannabe aristocrats while Newcastle were the poor hapless Northerners. Of course we wore our cloth caps with pride and our whippets were faster too!

Stamford Bridge had an immense three-tier stand and the rest was crumbling. We stood on a terrace that was bigger than the Gallowgate and mostly cordoned off, probably because of safety but you couldn't be sure if the bit we'd been put in was any safer than any of the other parts. There was a track running around the outside of the ground which meant you were even further away from the pitch and maybe more significantly the Chelsea fans. We were miles away from anybody else and despite our attempts to liven the home fans up the ground was half full and mostly silent.

The distant figures on the green carpet started chasing the white round blob and from the start the blues were pouring towards us and it looked like our revival of three consecutive draws was to come to an end. Sure, enough Gordon Durie dived in to score with a header and the wind that was whistling around the ground seemed to be accompanied by a bell tolling, like something out of a Western. Where was our John Wayne to rescue us? The Chelsea fans didn't seem that happy at being a goal up and as the half wore on we found out why, as Newcastle started to attack the goal in the distance. Tumbleweed blew across the empty sections of the ground (it seemed) as our hero arrived. It was new boy - gun-slinging Andy Thomas who was that man - taking aim to shoot true just before half time. The buzzards started to land ominously on the roof of the stand to our right. The locals were not happy as we danced our way through half time and then the second half added more venom to their anger as first Thomas and then dancing Beardsley scored a goal each to send a disbelieving group in the middle of a crumbling, empty terrace into raptures. The rest of the ground screamed for the Sheriff's head - "Hollins out," they shouted, along with "We hate Hollins". We were to be given no credit for a remarkable victory so had to praise ourselves as we partied through the rest of the game, oblivious to the anger from the rest of the crowd. The Scoreboard lights behind us seemed to be the only part of the stadium that shone for a Newcastle victory as once again the night air and the cold of a November evening descended upon celebrating Geordies. By the final whistle the ground was virtually empty.

We hopefully made our way to the exit but were stopped in no man's land by the announcement "Would the Newcaarrstle fans please remain behind for a few moments to allow the streets to clear." We waited and waited, hearing shouts from outside the ground but we didn't know where. We watched graffiti-laden District line trains as they rumbled past every few minutes, then we watched the Autumn leaves tumbling from the trees and still we waited. Somebody glanced up at the lights that declared our 3-1 victory and still we waited. Duncan tried to put a brave face on it by talking about the game but after a few minutes even the enthusiasm died down. It was standard practice for away fans to wait behind to allow the home fans to leave first, but it always seemed that all they were doing was giving the home hooligans time to organise themselves to attack further away from the ground. Today, I imagine they just got bored waiting and decided they couldn't be bothered because after what felt like an hour we were released, colours were covered up and fake London accents assumed as our small group disappeared into the wintry gloom of the capital.

Sunday 30th November 1986 - West Ham (h)

I had never seen Newcastle win when they appeared on television. Every time we were on, a draw was scraped or we were beaten - comprehensively or unluckily. It wasn't surprising that I saw television cameras at a ground as a bad omen. Whether it was Brian Moore and his cronies saying how crap the defence had been or John Motson commentating on another shock result in the cup - I hated them all for the bad luck they'd brought to Newcastle. It was like the baddies on Scooby Doo who always said "I would have got away with it if it hadn't been for you pesky kids." Right from the moment this match was announced on TV I knew we were sunk not even lucky underwear could get us out of this one! To make matters worse we were playing West Ham who had completed the double over us the previous season after an 8-1 victory at Upton Park. We had to use three different players in goal (thanks to injury) and the final one had been Peter Beardsley. They were not a lucky team for us. It was an uneasy feeling I had as I queued at the juvenile queue, behind a young lad with a beard and a baby.

The twenty two thousand who were there faced an early West Ham barrage then, like at Chelsea, Newcastle clicked into gear. Inspired by Beardsley we went into a two-goal lead, headers from "Spotty" Neil McDonald and Gunslinger Thomas. At half time everybody confidently predicted a 3-2 West Ham win but it never materialised. They fought all the way for the rest of the match and despite new boy Paul Goddard getting injured, went further ahead through Darren Jackson who people later said looked like me because he was tall, thin and had dark hair.

I was able to enjoy the atmosphere as the usual nerves had flown away. I found my eyes drawn to one particular section of seats. Whenever matches were on TV there were some who were desperate to be seen by their family and friends at home. They usually bought tickets in the benched seating at the base of the East Stand. It was traditionally the most featured part of the ground. It also had no fence to obscure you from the watching millions and the floodlights from the West Stand shone straight at you, illuminating you like no other part of the ground. Whenever the action was at the other end of the pitch, people would stand up at the other end to see better. This started a rippling affect along the side as each group stood up because their neighbour was blocking their view. Whenever the camera panned across there was a group at the front who stood up to wave to the camera, making everybody else stand up too. As I relived the happy memories of the afternoon on video that night I watched the same faces bounding from one section to another, showing off their (supposedly) fashionable dungarees and cloth sun hats, straying miles from their seats, but guaranteeing their place in TV history.

    The atmosphere at St James' mostly came from the Gallowgate at that time. It was the largest bank of terracing and the noisiest. It was split into different sections. The corner of the Gallowgate next to the concrete East Stand built in the late seventies was known as "The Corner". The section next to it was known as "The Scoreboard" for obvious reasons. Most of the time they spent their time trying to out-shout each other. If the team was playing badly then they would taunt each other "Why's the corner full of shit," was a popular one. I stood in the Scoreboard section. When I first went, this was the part of the ground I came to and so I developed an allegiance to it. I worked my way up the ground as my confidence grew, and the crowds diminished. Confident fans would act as conductor - and stand on top of one of the large barriers, it was the same people each week and our leader was a big bloke with blond hair called Darren. Others would try it, but never to the same effect as Darren. Today he was on top of his game, leading his choir in competition with the corner with a resurgence of confidence that seemed to emulate the team's. Every so often one corner of the East Stand next to the Gallowgate would shout "United" or "Newcastle". This would drift from the Corner to the rest of the Gallowgate and then to the West Stand. The sound the whole crowd made when these chants were going around made me shiver. The sound would surround us before drifting into the evening sky. This only happened when the team was performing well but today everyone was playing their full part. To have it all happening on TV made life all the sweeter. I imagined the Chelsea fans who we were going to jump above in the table and all the Sunderland fans at school the next day, unable to match a victory like that. When the fourth goal went in from Thomas I and the fans about me had smiles that would last for days. "The Geordies are back," was coming from every corner of the ground. This was the moment we had been waiting for, and we made sure we enjoyed the moment. I couldn't wait for school the next day; life was going my way and the only way was up!

Wednesday 21st January 1987 - FA Cup 3 -Northampton (h)

Newcastle's season had taken a turn for the worse again. They were once again bottom of Division One and due to play an FA cup game against the leaders of Division Four - Northampton. Thanks to an extremely cold winter the game was postponed twice, along with another against Tottenham. This was just as well really because we had lost the last five league games - the weather wasn't the only thing looking bleak. It was on the Sunday morning before the re-arranged game that me, mum and dad went out for our usual walk along the coast, dressed in sensibly warm duffle-coat, intimidating Newcastle scarf and striped bobble hat. We set off into the frozen Tynemouth wasteland that was a beach. I had heard a rumour that Northampton might be training on Tynemouth Long Sands so I thought we'd suss them out, do our job for Willie and the boys. Sure enough there were some people playing football on the beach, and they looked like professional footballers (my mum could tell by the thighs). As we drew nearer I recognised Neil McDonald (who didn't look that spotty after all), then Peter Beardsley raced into view. I was gobsmacked, here in my village, Newcastle were actually training. The gods I watched each week were here in the flesh. Mum and dad were mildly interested and asked questions such as "Do you recognise any of them?" Did I? Ask a stupid question. As we stood watching the game, I bombarded them with players names, positions, and memorable moments...

    I was so intent on watching the game that I failed to spot Willie McFaul (the guru) standing next to my mum, talking to one of the coaches. It was only when he had shouted an indecipherable range of swear words at one of the players that I noticed him. It was only after he had done it that he noticed my mum standing serenely next to him. Next, to my amazement, he put his arm around her and gave her a cuddle and apologised. I was speechless, beside myself; my mum...Willie McFaul...it was a sign.

    There was the slight problem of my FA Cup record. I had so far seen Newcastle lose both cup ties and with present form as a guide, seemed destined to complete the unwelcome hat-trick. That, however, was before my mum intervened. In the game itself, nerves were eased when Paul Goddard raced onto a through ball and instead of following the time honoured tradition of Newcastle strikers of shooting miles over the bar he actually scored! (I could almost see my mum smiling down on us). Richard Hill equalised for Northampton but immediately after that, 'shooter' Thomas scored the winner. I had seen my first FA Cup victory and I knew who to thank. That cuddle could have revitalised Newcastle's season.

Saturday 31st January - FA Cup 4 - Preston North End (h)

The next round saw us against another Fourth Division team. Thirty thousand fans watched, amazed as first Roeder then Goddard who had rapidly become a hero on Tyneside scored to put us through to the fifth round for the first time in six years. We were drawn against Tottenham next. Could my mum get us to Wembley?

Saturday 21st February 1987 - FA Cup 5 - Tottenham Hotspur (a)

This was it, the round when cup glory would be ours. We had banished the image of Ronnie Radford and his disgraceful seventies hair style (or lack of it) and now we were the minnows to topple the Southern Jessies from their lofty perch. They would replay the moment when Paul Goddard hammered the ball from outside the area and then climbed the fence at the away end, shaking his fist in delight whilst surveying numerous scenes of delirium below him. We were bottom of the league but hadn't a fear or a care. It was David against Goliath...and there was no way we were going to be David. Plucky Newcastle, they would say, turned the league table upside down...I don't think I was the only one who was filled with such dreams. The vast majority of fans probably had nightmares that involved a hat-full of Spurs goals and utter humiliation.... but they were the old gits who never imagined anything good could ever happen to us, writing off great victories as blips in our usual form or the opposition having an off day (realists, really).

In honour of the occasion, the Supporters' Club organised a train to take us to London in style. The cost was £17 for the privilege and for this princely sum, there was a buffet and the chance to arrive in style to the most important (arguably) fixture since promotion. I decided to forgo the chance to see Mark and Jeremy and instead lend my support to the travelling Magpie army.

This fixture saw the introduction of my new match companion. Gary worked in my local paper shop and apart from handing over my copy of 2000AD (a throw-back to my science-fiction days) he would share the ups and downs of Newcastle. I told him I was going to go on the train with Will and said he was welcome to come along. He jumped at the chance of sharing in the glory and so, on his day off we sent him, along with two lots of seventeen pounds to book our tickets. He duly returned with three train tickets (and our own pre-booked seats) and our one (and only) experience of an away day special was set up.

In the weeks between buying the tickets and the morning of the match I had been dreaming of a comfortable trip down on an Inter-City 125, with reclining chairs and a buffet car, complete with a wide selection of hot and cold snacks (nice...or was it?) The reality of it all was a clapped out old diesel with carriages that hadn't been used since the last football special in the nineteen seventies.

It was eight o'clock on a cold February morning and the three of us were standing, shivering on the platform at Newcastle Central Station. We stared at the Neolithic train that had pulled in and I was in heaven. The platform was awash with black and white shirts, scarves, coats, hats...even rosettes seemed to have come back into fashion. We were part of the biggest Geordie invasion of London for many years.

The greatest fear was over the Diesel that was pulling us...the wrenching sound that filled the carriages as it started up silenced the busy corridors. We sat hushed and still as gears squealed and then, one by one each carriage cheered as they felt themselves moving, like a Mexican wave it spread down the train to be replaced by the relieved laughter of an excited crowd. The early enthusiasm swiftly died down and replaced by the blast of personal stereos, card games and the rustle of hundreds of copies of The Journal. One of the advantages of travelling by train was the buffet car, the idea of a handy store of bacon butties, drinks, chocolate, crisps and alcohol for those who could win over the steward serving seemed like heaven. We would get to London quicker than the fans on the buses and we could spend the whole journey filling ourselves with cardboard burgers and teas. There was an enormous queue for the buffet as word spread down the train that it was open, but as the early birds started to filter past us carrying their prized purchases, it became apparent that the dream of a buffet car was just that. There seemed to be nothing but plastic bottles of pop, Mars bars and packets of crisps - and they certainly weren't Tudor! We'd climbed a mountain for this! When I reached the summit of the queue, my fast food dreams were shattered. The buffet car was in fact a dingy guards' van with boxes of assorted chocolate bars, and packs of pop piled up and judging by what was left after an hour or two, not a particularly bountiful stock. To the disgust of the lads onboard, the train had been declared dry, i.e. alcohol was not permitted anywhere. The looming mutiny was quelled by the steady supply of chocolate, but this had a limited existence, London couldn't arrive soon enough for everyone concerned.

    The suburbs of London started to pass by and the limitations of the 'restaurant car' were forgotten as the purpose of the journey was revived in everybody's minds - glory in the cup! We desperately searched the endless rows of streets for landmarks to impress our peers with our knowledge of the capital... Alexandra Palace (it wasn't something anyone dared say they knew much about) ... various train depots (the train-spotters kept quiet..."No... I'm not one, honest!") ...and finally, Highbury. At this point the train erupted into a chorus of "We hate cockneys..." and we knew we had reached our destination.

    The train had pulled into an end platform, away from people, shops and more importantly... alcohol. As we disembarked the sound of police dogs echoed around the Victorian station. This seemed to act as a catalyst to the hordes of fans pouring off the train singing... "Harry Roberts is our friend..." It was the ditty that was always performed when the police treated the fans as potential hooligans and criminals and was about an infamous police killer from the seventies. We were being herded like animals onto waiting buses so we acted accordingly, living up to the image of loud, bawdy Northern football fans. Leaving the group for whatever reason was not permitted and resulted in you being pushed onto any available bus. Trying to stay with friends could be viewed as obstructing the police in the course of their duties and after all, I had learnt from the Daleks on Dr Who - resistance was useless. As if to bait us even more the buses that had been laid on were owned by Tom Cowie -the chairman of Sunderland. The arguments were heated and although most of us happily jumped onboard like lambs to the slaughter, the argumentative ones refused, their justification going along the lines of "I'm not getting on a ******* Mackem bus (insert your own choice of expletive). All the arguments were drawn to a swift conclusion by the intervention of equally irate police dogs and we were soon away.

    White Hart Lane eventually loomed before us, it was over an hour before kick-off. Bill, Gary and I headed straight in, we wanted to guarantee our entry because it wasn't an all ticket match and also to locate a good spot on the terrace. It was only half past one but the terrace was already unusually full. It had only been six months since I last stood here with a few hundred others on a damp September night and the contrast was marked. Although it was an overcast afternoon, it wasn't miserable and the away following was already ten times that of the previous visit... with still well over an hour to go. This was indeed going to be some invasion. I spotted Mr and Mrs Brown, complete with regulation sweets and tea and we remained with them half-way up the terrace, comparing stories and watching the Park Lane stand around us rapidly fill.

    It was about twenty minutes later that we started to feel a bit crammed. There were mini-surges occurring everywhere. Lost footings, drunken barges and over-exuberance added to the increasing feeling that we were gradually losing control of our own movements. Most fans were still enjoying themselves, likening the terrace to a transplanted upper-Gallowgate but by now we were getting closer and closer to the looming seven-foot high fence. Mr Brown was doing his best to hang onto his wife who was looking severely distressed and keep himself upright at the same time, I tried to help him but only ended up becoming a burden myself as I was sucked downwards. Attempts to guide us to the safety of a barrier proved fruitless as we were tossed about, and still fans poured onto the terrace, unaware of the distress that was starting to spread further down. It was clear somebody had made a serious cock-up. We glanced longingly across at the terraces standing virtually empty next to us. Attempts to climb the fences by some people in order to alleviate the swelling crush proved fruitless as they were ordered down but sheer desperation and weight of numbers scaling upwards forced the stewards to give in. Fans at the rear began calling to their compatriots above them in the seats to help them escape the appalling crush. Every available exit from the cells we had become imprisoned in was being sought. Panic filled the air but still the emergency gates onto the pitch and safety remained closed. The Browns had thankfully managed to anchor themselves to a welcoming barrier. Bill, Gary and I kept on passing each other as we desperately fought to stay upright. We frantically called to the stewards to open the gates but our cries seemed to fall on deaf ears. Even more fans were being added to the heaving compress of bodies, and the alarming image of 'sinking' under the surrounding bodies became only too real. Disaster seemed only moments away as each rush of bodies took its toll but the welcoming sight of the emergency gates being opened gave us renewed energy. Desperate fans gratefully poured out onto the running track I had walked around in September under very contrasting circumstances.

What the rest of the crowd made of our toils, was anybody's guess but there was a lot of anger amongst the travelling army. The Newcastle papers had predicted well over ten thousand would make the journey so why had there only been a few sections open that held a fraction of that? When there were obviously too many fans in that section, how come the stewards didn't move late arrivals to a different section? Those who climbed to safety were assumed to be hooligans - the climate of the times - rather than ordinary people trying to escape a looming disaster caused by the very people they assumed were there to protect them.

By the time a form of normality had been achieved the match was already halfway through the first half. The anger that had built up was channelled into supporting the team as the biggest away following for years urged them on. After all we'd been through, we willed the team forward but Tottenham had other ideas. We hadn't beaten a First Division team since December and although there was a lot of effort, it wasn't looking good. Richard Gough (I still spit his name out) fell on top of Peter Jackson and the blind referee, after asking his guide dog what had happened, gave a penalty. This was duly tucked away and all our toils both on and off the pitch were for nothing. We puffed our way through the second half until the closing minutes when Beardsley masterfully dodged past two Spurs players and the ball squirmed across the goal. Hearts missed a beat as Albert Craig dived in at the far post but was far too slow and the ball bobbled off him for the goal kick. Our hearts were broken and our dreams lay in tatters There would be no happy ending and yet again the bad guys got the girl and the loot. Within a few minutes it was all over. The victory was announced by the unnecessarily loud P.A. system blaring out "Glory, glory Tottenham Hotspur." It was the loudest the opposition had been all day. We watched them celebrate and there were the predictable scuffles as frustration boiled over, I felt the same and cynically and hypocritically cheered as the violence carried on outside, safe amid fifteen thousand like-minded fans. We had desperately coveted the slightest hint of victory. .we had a stronger desire but were the ones left wanting.

A subdued bus set off back to Kings Cross. Anger long since replaced by despondency. The walk back onto the train was silent, except for a few lone shouts of abuse at gloating Spurs fans. What did they know about supporting a team? Would they be doing that if they were in Newcastle? Every thought came back to violence. It seemed the only way to get rid of the hurt. We were like bears with sore heads and every sentence started with why?

The train slipped out of London in complete contrast to its arrival, low, disgruntled mutterings the only type of conversation.

There had been no fatalities in the events leading up to the match and although the local papers gave good coverage, the full potential for disaster was never mentioned. The television cameras mentioned that there was some sort of disturbance but never focused on what and so everything was forgotten. Two days later it was as if nothing had happened. There had been more debate about whether Spurs should have had their penalty. Nobody asked any questions and it was put down to an unfortunate incident, we were after all, only over-exuberant football hooligans. No lessons were learnt and the chance that it could happen again ignored with tragic results within a few years.

Tuesday 14th April - Arsenal (a)

After the Spurs game, the result was the only thing that was remembered. There were patronising comments about how Newcastle was too good to go down but no apology to the travelling fans or even a sense of regret at a lack of planning. What else could we, as football hooligans have expected, after all, the toilets hadn't flooded (much).

This was all behind us now. Thoughts were focused on the bottom of the First Division. We'd started to put some results together and despite losing to Wimbledon (which was a tradition anyway) we'd been undefeated. What's more Paul Goddard had scored in his last five games and there was talk of him challenging Len White's post war record of scoring in seven consecutive games. Ever since I had known Newcastle, I'd been constantly informed and enlightened on the subject of their glorious past. League Championships, FA Cups galore but our last major honour won had been one month and seven days before I was born. The teams I worshipped were small fry compared to the real 'greats'. "Jackie Milburn could run rings around that lot..." or "...that wouldn't have been a problem for Bob Moncur." I thought that the signing of Albert Craig was a master-stroke because he shared Albert Stubbins' Christian name, who was certainly a member of the golden oldie club. Shame it didn't take long for my illusions to be shattered on that front, the Albert we had definitely wasn't a Stubbins. Paul Goddard on the other hand had the opportunity to become one of the United greats. As a result I would be able to say I remembered the celebrated Paul Goddard and then bore everyone with a list of his strikes twenty years later.

Will and I forgot about our looming A Level exams and headed off on the coach to London. For the first time we would arrive at a decent time of the day -namely three o'clock in the afternoon. Previously I had made the journey down overnight, arriving at five or six in the morning, looking like a dog's dinner and smelling like one too.

The first difference I noticed was the absence of the homeless from the Underground subways. It had become a

London tradition to navigate my way through the sleeping bodies at Victoria, but they weren't there when we arrived. It was as if they hadn't existed at all, somebody had come along and swept them under the proverbial carpet so they couldn't upset the day-time denizens of the Underground. This group was the far more formidable groups of foreign tourists who streamed out from every destination and whose knowledge of England was restricted to London's famous landmarks. They'd never encountered the unwanted nocturnal Londoners and would have probably found their existence hard to believe. It also might have seemed impossible for them to imagine that anybody lived in any part of England other than the south-east. I imagined they thought the rest of us lived in little isolated farms and quaint villages, occasionally coming to London to sell our livestock and produce. The only other big city in the UK for them was Edinburgh (where all the Scots lived).

    The day-time London atmosphere, a mixture of annoyingly loud American and European voices, instantly brought on my practised Newcastle match accent. This was the voice I used to avoid being called posh. The trouble with being from a middle-class family from Tynemouth was that I'd no noticeable regional accent. My accent was the source of a running battle with the rest of my family because they hated my attempts at a Geordie accent and didn't want to "Hear it in this house..." There had been no problems until I started going to Newcastle matches, but standing on the Gallowgate my voice stood out like a sore thumb. My Grandma always said that we had Northumbrian accents... but sod that as well. There was only one accent I wanted and that was Geordie. I was intensely embarrassed of my upbringing whenever anybody talked to me and so that I could feel a part of the terrace group, developed and cultured my match accent. The first year was spent listening to the conversations around me and mumbling answers to questions asked. By my second year I'd developed the accent sufficiently to answer most questions without any trace of 'poshness'. Three years on I was able to hold relaxed conversations with most of the Gallowgate regulars. (I was still only seventeen, however, and as such not considered worth talking to anyway - accent or no accent). I didn't realise that I wasn't alone in disguising my upbringing. It wasn't something that people admitted to freely. An assortment of young lads had to lead a similar double life but with a variety of success. The popular technique was to use the words "Man" (with a short, sharp 'a'), "Gannin" instead of "Going", end every sentence with the word "aye", "How" (instead of 'hey' and said very quickly to avoid confusing it with "How are you doing". For instance, you could say "How man where're ya gannin...). Everybody was either a lad or a lass; or your mam and dad. Everybody became a "knacka" if they did something stupid and if you ever found anything you happened to like it could be described as "sound" or "tops". Armed with this survival kit, you avoided being singled out and were treated the same as and ignored by the rest of the lads. Will had no such fears of detection and didn't feel any need to be anything other than the person he was. This was admirable but because I was always so conscious and embarrassed about myself, I shamelessly disowned him whenever he revealed any hint of being educated anywhere else but the School of Life and the University of Hard Knocks. On the whole, Will followed the same rules as me and we both spent a good deal of time trying to avoid being exposed. Some lads got carried away at times, inventing words that belonged to no known accent and left themselves open to be labelled as an impostor. The lad who commented how tired his "leegs" were, was ridiculed and forbidden from joining in with the Blaydon Races because it "wasn't his song". The way to succeed was not to draw attention to yourself and only say things you were confident saying. Away from Newcastle it was a different matter - nobody had a clue what you were supposed to sound like so you could say whatever you liked, as long as you sounded Northern.

I felt it my mission (as most Newcastle regulars did) to let people know that Newcastle existed. I had quickly learnt that although Londoners knew that towns existed outside of the South East, they were completely uninterested in their existence, along with their character-less and miserable inhabitants. After all, not everybody could live in London. It was this arrogance that set my adrenaline going and made matches against Arsenal, Tottenham and Chelsea more important - we were playing for North East pride. My main aim was to act as cheerful and annoyingly polite as possible - smiling at the miserable faces that passed me, while attempting to engage anybody in conversation around me. I failed miserably on the last count (finding out later in life that being drunk was a great advantage). I enjoyed smiling and found great amusement at the sight of the stressed and fed up faces about me. I was determined to show how Geordies enjoyed life to the full and there was a better life outside of London.

For the next few hours we did the football tourist bit. We visited a morgue-like Wembley and joked about how we'd be back next season, then headed off to Arsenal. Nine days earlier, Arsenal had beaten Liverpool to win the Littlewoods Cup so we weren't confident, despite the face of optimistic bravado we put up. When we reached the away end, there were a few hundred Newcastle fans and a half-empty stadium. Obviously, after seeing their team win at Wembley most of the fans had decided to take an early Summer holiday - loyal fans, I thought. We were desperate for the points and they'd no need for them, my mainly pessimistic mind dragged me down to earth. We hadn't won at Highbury since 1973, what chance did we have against the Wembley winners? All the faces I had tormented on the tube with my happy, smiling facing were coming back to haunt me - "You're going to lose, and then you'll be as miserable as us...", "It'll serve you right..."

The team lifted me. Gascoigne was having a stormer. A Beardsley cross was cleared by Lee Dixon. A couple of shots by Steve Williams and Tony Adams had Thomas performing acrobatics and suddenly the twisted faces were there staring at me - "Nobody smiles here - not on our Manor!" But at that moment, a Gascoigne dribble broke down... (faces sneered at me, laughing at my pathetic desire for a goal), but Goddard picked the ball up and darted past four Arsenal defenders before, from the corner of the penalty box, lofting a shot goal-ward. The faces and I watched as it sailed through the air. John Lukic in the Arsenal goal pushed a despairing hand towards it but the ball carried on into the net. There was the momentary calm, as the faces disconsolately disappeared one by one, cursing my good fortune, then my small band proceeded to leap around the empty spaces surrounding us, using barriers to vault higher in a manner very unlike ballet dancers. Goddard shared our delight along with the rest of the team. Once the dust had settled, talk immediately sprung up of Len White's record...Goddard was one goal away from *a* place in the history books (the ones I read anyway) and I would be able to say... "I was there..." The record suddenly became so important to me. It was as if I could claim some part in it, a boost to me self-esteem. It would be the boost I needed to see me through my exams. It had to happen!

I wished the rest of the game away, wincing each time Arsenal came close. But we were not to be denied, it was a warm April evening in muggy North London and those cheerful chaps from the North East had been rewarded for their chirpiness. Will and I celebrated with a pint each, raising our glasses and toasting the great Paul Goddard, our hero and friend before setting off to Victoria and the night bus back to civilisation. We were now the Glory Boys, heading home to a rapturous reception.

Unfortunately, when we arrived into Gallowgate bus station at 5:30am, there wasn't a soul about. No welcoming committee and no flags flying. There weren't even any Metros running until 6:30. Will tried to ring his dad to give us a lift home but the phone just rang and rang without answer. Maybe everyone had been celebrating the victory and was sleeping off the excesses. Whatever it was, we ended up sitting and half sleeping on a couple of benches outside the George and Dragon pub, while hot air from a ventilation hatch kept us warm-ish. It was a familiar story, you had to be there I supposed as I stepped onto an empty but clean Metro. I remembered the empty and run down Underground carriages we had travelled on only fourteen hours earlier and compared the two trains. One was ugly and familiar, the other exciting and in a place where I'd had the last laugh. I'd been somebody, now it was back to exams and school.

The tube was three hundred miles away and would by now be filling up with the same morbid faces I had laughed at yesterday, it all seemed such a long way away and it was now no more than a memory, but a happy one at that.

Saturday 18th April 1987 - Manchester United (h)

Today was make or break. If Goddard scored, he equalled Len White's achievement, if he didn't, it would all have been for nothing. The omens looked good, we hadn't beaten Manchester United since 1973 but ironically, it was the same year we beat Arsenal at Highbury. The gods were looking down on us, today. I was sure of it. There were six thousand fans locked outside and the atmosphere was throbbing. Everywhere, the talk was once again of Paul Goddard. The match started with a fight between the large and looming Peter Jackson and the annoying gnome Terry Gibson who played for Manchester. Then just as things were quietening down, Glenn Roeder scored with a glancing header to ignite the animated crowd once more. The league title could have been at stake for all the emotion in the ground, but when Beardsley limped off injured and Gordon Strachan scored the equaliser, an awkward and eerie stillness descended. Worse was to follow as John Anderson limped off injured, Len White wasn't going to be equalled. The match ticked on into the last quarter of an hour, shots were flying in at both ends, but Manchester looked the more likely winner.

The team seemed desperate to help Goddard, but it just seemed to be beyond us, I started to think that a draw would do. I would have to just accept the fact that history was not going to be made. Just as this seemed inevitable, there occurred a Roy of the Rovers moment that make football the game it is. The ten men were playing their heart out but to no avail...until, Gascoigne crossed and Jackson (large and looming) helped the ball to Goddard who scrambled the ball into the net. The foundations shook with the emotion that frothed in every corner (bar one unhappy one, I was pleased to note). The wooden West stand rang out as thousands of wooden seats were pushed back in delight, the terraces were a sea of hands greeting their hero - against all the odds, the record had been matched, and what's more we had beaten Manchester United in the process. Safety from relegation was within our grasp, the town would be buzzing tonight without a doubt. As for me... I would be able to say, I was there, after all. I'd seen five of the seven goals scored and I felt a great sense of pride. True, I hadn't kicked a ball myself, but if it hadn't been for me and the other few hundred at Arsenal and the thousands here today, it wouldn't have been special at all. *We'd* made today, and the atmosphere had been so thick you could have tasted it...it tasted very sweet indeed, a cure for all the problems I and thousands of like-minded souls had. At least for the next few days anyway.

The end of an era.

Two wins at home, against Chelsea and Charlton ensured First Division survival. Paul Goddard didn't manage to set a new record for scoring in consecutive games, which was probably just as well. Instead we were trounced 3-0 at Everton, which was only to be expected. The final game of the season turned into a party. We were safe whatever happened and despite losing 2-1, it didn't seem to matter. On Nottingham's Bridgford Road terrace, the interest was firmly fixed on Sunderland. They had to go through the anguish of the Playoffs to avoid being relegated to Division Three. "Ha ha ha, Hee, hee, hee, Sunderland are in Division Three" we chanted as we conga-ed around the spacious terracing. Indeed, a few thousand Newcastle fans made the trip to Roker Park to witness the happy (from our point of view) event, as Gillingham beat them on away goals in one of the most exciting games I've ever seen. Tony Cascarino scoring three as they won 4-3.

Everything seemed rosy in our garden as the season finished. We were still in the First and Sunderland was in the Third, which was nice. After the buzz had died down, there was the drudgery of my A Levels. All I needed was a D and an E, but like United I was going to make hard work of it. I eventually got a D and two E's and so I had passed with flying colours. I wouldn't have to suffer any more at school and was off to college in London, scene of those magnificent triumphs against Chelsea and Arsenal.

As I was leaving Newcastle, so was my hero. Peter Beardsley had decided he wanted to win trophies and that he wouldn't do it at Newcastle. He was off to Liverpool and in so doing, broke my heart. Despite offers of an improved contract at Newcastle he chose the glory of Liverpool. The rumours had been going around Newcastle for ages and everybody knew he was off. It was only a question of when. The brush with relegation had been too much for him. I hadn't cared about Waddle leaving, but Peter's departure hurt. For the three seasons I had been supporting the lads, Pete (as I always called him) had been the star. He'd brightened up dismal days at Spurs, Villa among others. He was the other half of my love for Newcastle and it was like being mercilessly dumped by your girlfriend after a fantastic relationship. Sure, we'd been through a sticky patch, but didn't everybody? We'd come through it, we had survived and our love was intact. He wanted more than love, he wanted Cups. He wasn't happy with an old Ford Escort, he wanted a shiny BMW with leather upholstery and a sunroof. That was something he wasn't going to get if he stayed in this alliance. He wanted more than we could give him. You couldn't blame him, but it didn't stop you feeling depressed, after all we'd put everything into this affair and been left with ...Albert Craig. Would we ever be able to love again?

    Course we would... Peter who?
***

My last few weeks in Newcastle were great. The arrival of my eighteenth birthday meant that I could be entered into the adult world of the public house, without having to hide behind my tall mate. I could go to any pub I wanted and be served, instead of the few pubs that I was confident would serve me in Tynemouth. The world of the night-club opened up to me as well. Although I looked thirteen still and therefore had no hope with any girls, I could (get a friend to) buy a pint and, armed with three straws happily share it with my mates. The Tuxedo Princess, a floating club, gave free flyers out to students so we would go along every Thursday during the summer, making a pint last all night, due to the limitations of our personal finances at the time.

    On the football front, Peter Beardsley was but a distant memory. We had a new hero to worship. Mirandinha, the first Brazilian to play in the First Division had replaced him for the princely sum of £650,000. Dusty and flea-bitten Sombrero's had been dragged out of forgotten cupboards along with sets of steel drums and maracas to make him feel welcome on Tyneside while everybody started dancing to "La Bamba". The club started making sensibly warm bobble hats with Newcastle on one side and Brazil on the other. They also stocked up on Brazil scarves, hats and flags. The Supporters Club sprang into action and even produced a T-shirt themselves - a disgustingly tasteless yellow affair with a badly drawn cartoon figure in a Newcastle strip, containing the side-splitting caption, "Mirandinha, now he plays for the Toon!" This sort of marketing was unheard of prior to his arrival and seems quaint by today's standards but, a few days before leaving to go to college, I purchased one of the aforementioned tasteless shirts and wore it for weeks on end with pride and very few friends.

The little fella in question took time to settle in. A screaming shot from nearly forty yards on his debut and a few nice touches had been the sum total before, on my last weekend on Tyneside, he set me screaming in the middle of the ladies' shoe department in Marks and Spencer, Newcastle. Mum was taking me shopping to fit out my wardrobe, and my radio informed me that Mira had scored twice at Manchester United, I shook with delight. The men nearby were instantly drawn to me for more news and in the end a draw was the result. It was the first time we had gone to Old Trafford and not been soundly trounced. Could we be on our way at last?

Sunday 20th September 1987 - Liverpool (h)

Going to college is the most exciting part of a young person's life but I didn't want to go today. Tomorrow maybe, but not today. How had it worked out this way? Here I was packing for my life in London and the lads were playing Liverpool. Not only that, but we were live on television. To add to my sense of grief, we had drawn at Man United the previous week, with Mira in sparkling form. I was going to miss out on the performance of the year, all in aid of a crusade to bring the Geordie word to the Southern heathens. Mum and Sue were going to drive me down, and much to my downright annoyance, we would be in the car while the match was playing. At least dad wasn't going to be there to tell me to stop cheering excessively after every goal scored. The obvious suggestion that we set off early to miss the traffic, perhaps seven in the morning would be a good time. By allowing five hours to get to London, at an average of sixty miles an hour (allowing for traffic jams and other unforeseen obstacles) would get us in at twelve, leaving three hours to unpack, get rid of family and socialise before the match began. Startlingly this wasn't anybody else's agenda. Hurrying down to London, just so that I could watch football was disregarded. My family just called me selfish, saying if that was how I felt, I could bloody well walk there. I know they couldn't see how important the match was. It would have given me the perfect opportunity to start my missionary work on any fellow football fans. I would be able to bamboozle them with obscure facts and tales of my travels ("...when Beardsley lobbed the keeper I..."). As the lads ran circles around Liverpool I would reflect in the glow of both the performance and my bright yellow performance, instantly becoming the popular Geordie at college...renowned for my knowledge on all matters football and a 'sound' bloke. Of course now if anybody asked me if I saw the match I would have to lie about the fact that my mum and sister were driving me down to college while I sat quietly in the back of the car, listening on the radio. Not exactly a cred-worthy thing to say.

As it was we didn't set off until well after ten and also stopped to have something to eat, wasting more time in the process. By three o'clock we were approaching London. The atmosphere in the car was dire. I'd moaned incessantly... why did we have to stop for lunch, what was wrong with a bite on the way and would they please not embarrass me when we got there? The match had kicked off and since my name was mud, I sat silently in the back. How lucky I was, mum kept telling me to have a family who would drive a six-hundred mile round trip, just to take me to college. I didn't feel privileged at the time. Worse was to follow as Liverpool was running the rings and as goal after goal followed my mood worsened. As we pulled into the picturesque grounds of my college, a Newcastle penalty made the score 1-3, and the possibility of a fight-back on the cards. We pulled up in front of my hall of residence and the engine turned off, the radio with it. I complained vociferously, but was ordered to carry my own stuff up to my new room, without the car radio to keep me informed of the lads' progress. I furiously rushed to empty the car, harassing the others to go faster so that I could hear or see at least the end of the match. I passed open doors with the sound of televisions blaring out, straining every part of me to hear the score but no-one was watching the match. More frantic unloading followed by more histrionics from an (understandably?) irate young man. As the last box had been deposited in the room, my new next door neighbour, walked past my room. He noticed my fetching T-shirt and informed that Newcastle had been beaten 4-1. My mum smiled politely at him as I cursed silently and thanked him for the news. My sister looked daggers at me, as if to say, "I hope you're happy with yourself!" Of course, how could I be happy, we'd been thrashed to punish me for leaving the lads, and for selfish disregard for everyone's efforts to get me here.

Mum wanted to look around the expansive grounds, perhaps stay for some welcome food, before the long journey back. This idea horrified me. So I packed them off and then set about mixing with the fellow students, armed only with a bright yellow T-shirt that said everything about me at the time. In spite of everything - I was Newcastle and proud of it.

As I look back now, I can't help feeling a sense of regret at the terrible way I treated my mum and sister, especially as they had to drive back to Newcastle and then stagger into work the next day. But... if I had the time again, I would shamelessly do the same again. It's the sorry side of being an eighteen-year-old... you just don't admit to having any family, especially when they failed to understand your passions and need for street-credibility.

London life

When people think of student life, what are the first things to spring to mind? Nonstop social lives, weird appearances and an endless daily diet of Aussie soaps and quiz shows. All this at the tax-payers' expense.

The Young Ones seemed to personify everything about students that everyone who wasn't a student hated - their enjoyment of living in squalor and the desire to look and act different.

I had no desire to look like Neil the Hippy or Vivien the Punk but an improved social life appealed.

After a first week that included a drunken riverboat disco on the Thames, the college's social life turned out to be worse than that of a church hall.

The only event of note was the Friday Frolic which seemed to be run for the soul purpose of providing the football team and the Students' Union members with a drunken love-life.

It was thanks to these nights that I discovered the advantages of drinking lager, cider and black-currant together (nicknamed a snakebite and black), after being told it was 'cheap and effective'. I expect the same could have been said about meths.

From time to time, the lads from a nearby estate would arrive. They were usually seen off by the doorman, a dour-faced Irishman (who we nick-named Disco Dave) and his two mates. Their psychotic activities provided a rare source of entertainment that was sadly lacking.

However, by Saturday morning the college was always deserted bar a select few. These were the ones who lived too far away from college to 'pop' home every weekend.

For those left behind, the college was set in beautifully wooded grounds, with an extensive lake populated by some exceedingly vicious geese. On top of this was an ornate mansion that had once been owned by Winston Churchill. Culture surrounded me.

Inspirational? Sadly not! I needed to find some fellow football fanatics to share my obsession with. There existed an extraordinarily large number of Leeds United fans but they turned out to be of the often spotted armchair variety.

Despite the frequency of Leeds United's visits to London they hadn't ever made the effort to see their 'heroes' in the flesh. Sure they knew the score each week, but ask them to select their favourite terrace ditty they would have been hard pressed to recite anything more than "Leeds, Leeds...etc." I would instead be entertained by the timeless classic "We hate Geordies..." Maybe they chose Leeds in the same way lost souls from around the country supported Liverpool. Leeds however was a mediocre Second Division team at the time and as none of these "supporters" actually came from Leeds the reasons for their chosen allegiance remained a mystery. I managed to sniff out the only other person at college who was as mad about football as I was.

Paul, however was an Arsenal fan and actually attended all of Arsenal's home games. It was evident that he was a fellow 'sufferer'. He had turned out in the worst conditions to watch dire 0-0 draws. He was able to talk at great length about football catering facilities, collars on replica shirts and the experience that was the terrace toilet. We were kindred spirits, in love with the football ritual, from the choosing of the match underwear to the match programme and its undeniable dullness.

The best thing about meeting him was relating my memorable trip to Arsenal the previous April and Paul Goddard's winning goal. I was immediately at an advantage - a rare position for me to be in. Of course he denied any interest in the result, due to their appearance at Wembley weeks earlier, which somewhat blunted my sword but I looked forward to the day when our two teams met and the potential for unchallenged gloating.

As part of my missionary work, I wore my black and white uniform continuously and spent my time preaching to the predominantly armchair supporters that I met. My favourite victim was, unusually for London, a Manchester United fan. She was the girl who served us our chips at the local chippie and had turned the phrase "open or wrapped" into an art form. We affectionately nicknamed her Grimelda, mainly because of her tattoos (that looked like she had put on and tried to remove herself) and her pleasant attitude to 'Norveners'. I would adopt my match accent whenever I visited, daring her to understand me. She in turn would persistently ask me "Ooo are Nucarsel?"

Most ignored my devotion and on the streets of London I was just another nobody in a sprawling metropolis... there was time for this to change. The absence of Newcastle matches was proving the biggest disadvantage of London life.

Tuesday 29th September - Fulham v Sunderland

The mark of a true football fan was the desire to attend a game, any game. It didn't matter whether it was Liverpool or Whitley Bay, if there was a game on nearby then you felt the sights and smells of the ground calling to you. It was like the Sirens in Greek mythology luring unwary sailors to their death with their beautiful singing. So it was that Paul and I were lured to the nearest league ground - Fulham.

Lured by the smell of burnt burgers, cold chips, Bovril, and the chance to swear our way through a couple of hours in the like-minded company of some of the least popular members of London society. There was the added draw that Sunderland was the opposition and the chance to hurl abuse at the old enemy was too great. We set off in his battered Vauxhall Cadette, littered with piles of accumulated cassettes featuring bands I had either never heard of or couldn't stand. Names like The Cure, The

Smiths and The Cult would grip me later, but for now I held them in complete contempt and I was perfectly happy in my ignorance.

It took us ten minutes to reach the ground and then half an hour to find a parking space as I learnt my first lesson about London - there are hundreds of thousands of cars, but nowhere to put them. In order to be a successful driver you had to be able to park in a space half the size of your car. With the aid of a shoehorn Paul managed to squeeze into such a space and we then raced to the ground.

The ground was set amongst endless rows of the expensive style of Victorian terraced houses, with patterned black and white tiles adorning the short paths to each house, we could only see the glare of the floodlights that lit up the night sky. It was enough to give that rush of adrenaline that we both thrived on. The approaching streets were devoid of life as we instinctively quickened our paces. The welcome signpost of a programme seller convinced us we were heading in the right direction and eighty pence later, the smiling and chin-dominated face of the Fulham Chairman, Jimmy Hill, shone from our sweaty hands.

It was two minutes to kick off and there was barely a murmur from within the ground and the streets weren't too lively either. Poorer by £3, we pushed our way through the hefty turnstile and onto the huge expanse of home terrace.

The covered home end was sparsely populated and spread behind each black and white metal barrier was clustered a group of two to four middle aged and elderly men. There was the occasional young boy, dragged by an enthusiastic father or grandfather to the game, even the odd wife or girlfriend but they were the exception to the rule.

At the far end a small group of dedicated Sunderland fans cheered as their heroes emerged for this Third Division game and it was with no sense of remorse that I remembered cheering Gillingham on as Sunderland were relegated only five months earlier.

A Newcastle bar scarf was worn in honour of the occasion and blended in nicely with the black and white patches that were scattered around Craven Cottage. As the game started there was a stirring, but after a few minutes this was replaced by the hubbub of conversation as the game became no more than a distraction.

Occasionally play would drift towards one of the goals and the talk stopped as the fans vented their frustration at one of their players before returning to complain to their neighbour and resuming the chat. It was a relaxed, somewhat resigned atmosphere round about us. Nobody expected much from Fulham and when Marco Gabbiadini scored for the visitors it gave them the opportunity to reminisce of old heroes and lament their passing - "Do you remember..." or "What about so and so, he'd have sorted this lot out."

They seemed to accept that nothing would come of Fulham and any small achievement was a bonus. At times the crowd was hushed, perhaps absorbed in sentimental nostalgia. The smell from the burger van parked in one corner of the ground drew us away from the action and as we ate, we could just hear the River Thames as it flowed behind the stand to our right.

Everything about Fulham reflected a by-gone era, from the stands to the supporters, what would happen to Fulham when these supporters were no more?

The experience lacked the passion of a North East match with a partisan crowd but in its place was a unique charm which drew us back time and again over the next few years.

Fulham could have gone top of the Third Division if they'd won that night but you wouldn't have guessed it from the crowd. A second Gabbiadini strike put the game beyond them and pushed Sunderland further up the table.

When we told people where we'd been, we got the usual comedy stares and smart comments, but we had experienced a piece of London that time seemed to have forgotten and Fulham was a better and more remarkable place for it.

Saturday 3rd October 1987 - Chelsea (a)

It was back to the serious business of Newcastle, and a return to the scene of one of the comebacks of last season. I couldn't wait to return and once more rely on either binoculars or guesswork to follow the match.

Today I was starting from behind enemy lines. Chelsea was only a few stops on the tube and apart from Grimelda, the local population outside of college supported Chelsea. I hadn't inspired anybody to come along, despite a great deal of effort, so I travelled alone. It would be better this way, travel light...no ties, the lone gunman on a solo mission.

I didn't even hide my shirt at Putney tube station, not that anyone noticed or even showed the slightest bit of interest.

The journey to the away end was equally uneventful and by the time I passed through the turnstile it was turning into the biggest non-event since drinking became legal for me.
Still, at least being among my kin would inspire me. This proved not to be. Newcastle were 2-0 down before any hopes could be raised and the mood was extremely gloomy. There was no noise, just a few hundred fans reflecting on the warm beds they had left, three hundred miles away, in the wee hours of the morning.

Tube trains rattled past the back of the away end like dust sweeping past a ghost town. There was just no atmosphere at all. The home fans seemed so far away that any utterance we might have heard disappeared into the still Autumn afternoon, twenty-two thousand people were unbelievably still.

From out of nowhere, a lob from stocky Irish battler John Anderson strayed to Mirandinha who picked out Goddard to score. The mood brightened considerably and it seemed the atmosphere I had been missing had only been put on hold, but as quickly as it had sprung alive, the terrace died.

A penalty five minutes from half time could have kick-started the party but Neil McDonald missed. Suddenly 'Spotty' was public enemy number one.

As the second half dragged on, Chelsea looked like burying Newcastle though they never quite managed it and Kenny Wharton knocked in the equaliser to prompt another brief fiesta.

The lads poured forward for the winner but it was not to be and as we waited the usual hour to be let out, I was disappointed that in the few weeks since my departure from Newcastle, an air of despondency had crept in.

It seemed contagious and I returned to a nearly deserted college with a depressed cloud about me. What had happened to the happy fans I knew? Were they suffering from collective hangovers, or was there something more serious afoot?

I was so incensed that I wrote to Newcastle's football Pink describing my disappointment with the support that day. The comment underneath my letter when it was published informed me that the fans' frustration with the team's lack of success was to blame and the time for goodwill was over.

The honeymoon since promotion had ended and though the Newcastle board had bought Mirandinha, it had been at a fraction of the cost of Beardsley. The team would have to work for the fans' support and if they didn't they would certainly know about it.

I tried to look on the bright side that night as Grim (elda) served me my chips - open and not wrapped! Even the thought of her specially battered jumbo sausage and chips couldn't rid me of the frustration at being miles from home and starved of information on the lads.

Like so many exiles the only way to keep in touch was for Dad to become my eyes, ears and personal newsagent.

Saturday 31st October 1987 - Arsenal (h)

Paul was the sort of person you'd hate to have as a mate. He was much more successful with the opposite sex (or convinced you he was), he was never stuck for words and awkward silences never seemed to happen to him, he always seemed to have loads of mates and worst of all - he supported a more successful football team.

The fact that last year we had won at Highbury didn't matter one bit because they'd finished much higher in the league and won the Littlewoods Cup, consequently they didn't care who beat them that day. He constantly patronised me about my love for a team that, in his words, was "hopeless".

We had lost Beardsley and despite buying Mirandinha, we were still in the bottom half of the table. He was amazed that I got so excited when we beat Third Division Blackpool in the Littlewoods Cup. Arsenal made no mistakes against smaller clubs, winning by three or four goals each time, whereas Newcastle always struggled to win by one. I never entered into football arguments with him because I knew that in Newcastle I would always have the weaker card.

In Top Trumps terms - Newcastle was a Boeing 707 airliner - quite good in its time but very ordinary now, while Arsenal was a Boeing 747 - one of the biggest planes that knocked spots off most opposition. There were better teams than Arsenal, but Newcastle wasn't one of them.

When the time came for the two to meet at St James', we braved the night bus to Whitley Bay and I took my chance to educate him. He had never been to the North East and believed all the stereotypes that existed.

He was amazed to find himself in a quiet, sleepy seaside village, with no outside toilets to be seen. He was also not expecting the Metro system and I took the opportunity to remind him of London's ancient and run down Underground (despite my fondness for it, very much a Boeing 707).

I desperately wanted Newcastle to put Paul and Arsenal in their places, to wipe away the amused, smug look of pity that appeared on his face whenever we lost to some 'lowly' team.

There had to be some justice in the world, he couldn't have the charm and the successful team. Today was hopefully the day I extracted some revenge. Paul, however, imagined my further humiliation - a late winner by Alan Smith or a four or five nil drubbing.

Paul was impressed with Newcastle. In fact the only thing he found to moan about was the weather which was, in his words - "parky".

We travelled by Metro to the ground and the instant Paul saw the first black and white scarf, he fell unusually quiet. He communicated with eye contact and from time to time would nod and mockingly utter "aye". He was carefully studying the rest of the carriage while trying to make himself as small and insignificant as possible.

He came with me into the terraced paddock in front of the West Stand constructions, relying on my charitable spirit not to reveal his identity. I was reminded of the atmosphere that I'd been deprived of. The cold wind that blew in off the Tyne, the sight of the Gallowgate, busy and bustling. For the first time I noticed the absence of the battleship bridge that had been the old wooden stand. I took a moment to think about what had been lost. The ancient eighty-one-year-old grandfather who had passed away to be replaced by more concrete. It would look impressive when finished but would it have the character? The image of Keegan waving to his family sitting underneath the 'ship's bridge' before being whisked into the April night sky was all now just a fading memory.

I started to notice things I had never noticed before, across the city that stretched away beyond the ground, the Newcastle Breweries building and gothic Saint Andrew's buildings which I'd previously ignored but now represented a missing part of my life. I glanced into the steadily darkening sky and watched the starlings. Their massed groups made ever-changing patterns above the city as they swooped and banked in near unison. Their never-ending dances grew quicker and more elaborate the louder the crowd became. They became one of the first things I looked for when I approached St James', and a sign that I was home.

Once we entered the ground Paul relaxed a bit, glad to be under the watchful eyes of a nearby policeman, but I was glad to see he was still squirming. The game kicked off and from our vantage-point near to the half way line, we watched Newcastle tear Arsenal apart. He joined in with his own frustrated shouts each time a chance went begging, however each comment was accompanied by a wry smile and satisfied grin which was solely for my benefit. He pretended to be pleased when we were awarded a penalty but disguised his amusement when it was squandered. There was no way we were going to score and he knew it. I desperately hoped for a change in luck and there was, but it was a change from bad to worse.

Arsenal had hardly threatened and in the 89th minute, won a corner. My only thought was to get the ball to the other end of the pitch as soon as possible to end the torment. Instead, the corner went straight to Alan Smith, with his back to goal and he flicked the ball over his shoulder and into the net. The ground was stunned. The small band of away fans, overcame their initial surprise and danced away in their little corner. Paul's face had now acquired a broad smile and while the supporters around us tried to voice their disbelief, there was a barely audible "Yes", then a return to the role of depressed United fan. The final whistle brought reality of it all crashing down on me. This one moment had brought the weekend to an abrupt halt.

I never felt like hitting Paul or revealing his true identity to the supporters nearby, there was just a bitter sense of humiliation. I had been so desperate to see Arsenal, Paul and his cockiness beaten, the team had responded and Arsenal didn't look at all bothered or interested and won without putting in anywhere near the effort.

It was like getting the girl of your dreams to go out with you and then after you had worked so hard to win her over, your mate comes along and taking a passing interest in her, whisks her from under your nose only to dump her the next day. The win didn't
matter anywhere near as much to Paul as it did to me.

Here had been a chance to put London's arrogance in its place, and give me some pride to carry back to London with me, but I was now in a worse position than before.

He had the top three team, success in the cup and the one with the girlfriend, while I had the bottom half team and the shattered dreams. We sat stoically silent on the way back to Tynemouth. He was afraid of being uncovered and I couldn't bring myself to lift myself out of a self-pitying state.

This lasted until we reached the safety of Tynemouth station and then he couldn't contain himself any longer. Realising he had reached relative safety, he bravely sprinted out of the station and up the empty street screaming and punching the air, frightening the pigeons settled on the nearby school roof. He laughed all the way home, until we arrived within earshot of my house and then turned on the sympathetic charm which would make me out to look the bad tempered loser that I and twenty three thousand others had become that afternoon.

There were the usual comments "...it's only a game..." or "don't let it spoil your weekend" from mum and dad but how could they have understood?

At least Gary came out that night for a drink in Tynemouth. We took every opportunity to remind Paul what might happen if we happened to mention which part of the country he was from or where his allegiances lay. Paul heeded the warning and the match wasn't mentioned that night. Needless to say, the journey back to London was a very muted affair.

Saturday 20th February 1988 - Wimbledon (h) FA Cup-5

It was time for the FA Cup. Newcastle was once again into the fifth round. Gascoigne had launched a screamer from thirty yards out that got stuck between the netting and the post to dispatch Crystal Palace.

We then trounced Swindon 5-0, only to find out that Lou Macari, the Swindon manager, and his mates had had a bit of a flutter on the result and coincidentally picked the winner and the score. How bizarre!

Into the fifth round and a home draw against Wimbledon. The warning signs should have started sounding when the draw was made but I wanted that elusive Wembley final so much that my knowledge of Newcastle and their ability to build your hopes up only to throw them cruelly from the top of the Tyne Bridge was foolishly ignored.

They had already knocked us out of the Littlewoods Cup in the last minute, beaten us on Mirandinha's home debut and just two weeks earlier, at Plough Lane, an unknown Vincent Jones had kicked Gascoigne all over the pitch. To add insult to injury he grabbed hold of Gazza's pride and joy for the benefit of delighted reporters.

Since that game, we had been beaten at St James' by a struggling Norwich team 3-1 and Mira had been anonymous and was booed off. The vultures had started circling and I never even noticed.

London was going well, I had a few mates and, more importantly, a girlfriend called Rachel. There was none of the nervousness of my first romantic involvement, the Coke stayed in the cups and I decided that it would be a good opportunity to take my new girlfriend home to meet the parents.

She was from Bournemouth and four years older than me, needless to say she had never been to Newcarstle before and needed educating.

It was only £10 to travel home on the train so we did just that. I took her on the sightseeing bit around town and then in true North East tradition, I went off to the match while, instead of doing some shopping, she diligently tackled her latest essay (after all, students have to work sometimes).

Cup fever had hit Gallowgate. The ground was packed and every corner in full voice, willing United to success. The new West stand was starting to show signs of emerging from behind the wooden boards and the stage was set for us to go one better than last year. In the first five minutes Wimbledon were rocked as Goddard and then Peter Jackson missed good chances, the expectant crowd roared the lads on, as a jittery Wimbledon struggled to cope.

In time-honoured tradition, Wimbledon spoilt it all. Dennis Wise crossed and Terry Gibson headed in. The smallest players on the pitch had burst the bubble. Silence instantly fell upon us, as twenty-nine thousand dreams evaporated into space. This wasn't supposed to happen.

They'd gate-crashed our party. We'd seen it all before and knew that no matter how much we abused them, they wouldn't leave and in fact thrived on these situations. At half time the Bros song "When will I be famous" seemed apt, because it sure wasn't going to be us that was destined for glory.

Second half brought more misery as they doubled their lead then a brief glimmer of hope with a Neil McDonald goal. A ludicrous lob from John Fashanu sealed our fate. Tempers boiled over at the final whistle when Mira once again having flattered to deceive, showed the wrong sort of fighting spirit by attempting to kick Wimbledon goal-keeper Dave Beasant. He only succeeded in embarrassing himself, due to the relative sizes of the two - a bit like watching a Terrier sizing up to a German Shepherd dog. For that he received a police warning.

I just wanted to rewind the previous two hours but I couldn't. In true FA Cup tradition, the TV cameras were there to remind the country of our exit. Arsenal had beaten Manchester United so Paul would be full of patronising pity.

At home, Rachel was standing there, smiling expectantly. How was the match, she asked naively? How could she ask such a question, didn't she know what I'd been through that afternoon? All the built up frustration spilled out. I launched my programme through the thickening atmosphere that was developing, it lodged itself nicely in the crack between door and frame.

I tried to explain calmly about the Cup, my dream for this season, Gascoigne's performance and life would never be the same again. All I succeeded in doing was ranting for ten minutes, blaming Newcastle for building my hopes up and Wise, Fashanu and the rest of Wimbledon for destroying them.

I then proceeded to make a sacrificial offering to anybody who was prepared to have it by burning my Brazil/Newcastle hat in the back garden. The rant had finished us both off. She stormed off muttering something unpronounceable while I steamed in a chair looking at the football scores on Ceefax, hoping that a mistake might have been made and we had in fact won (a draw would have done).

Alas, no. We were out. Unbeknown to me, my first football argument with a girlfriend had taken place. It hadn't even been her fault. Her only crime had been that of trying to be supportive but in my deranged state, it had been the worst thing she could have done.

Eventually the reality of the situation dawned on me and the appeal of the same repeated Ceefax page diminished so I sheepishly slunk upstairs to make my peace with her, still wondering what would have happened if Jones hadn't grabbed Gascoigne's valuables.

Saturday 30th April 1988 - Coventry v Portsmouth

Moving to London had brought me close to Portsmouth so I went down to see them whenever I could, making a lot of good friends along the way. I'd been lucky enough to sample two emotional South coast derby matches against Southampton, (a draw and an unheard of 2-0 win). Just like Newcastle, there were like-minded passionate fans that followed them everywhere, such as Big John but there was always a friendly welcome for infrequent visitors. Today was the day Portsmouth desperately needed to win to avoid relegation. They'd slipped down the table, usually losing by the odd goal and were now in deep trouble. A large group of fans travelled cheaply from London and I tagged along with them.

We taxied to a pub near the ground and I was able to witness a modern day gathering of the clan. Just like the Scottish kinsmen gathering nearly a thousand years before when one of their number was threatened, this was the Southern modern-day equivalent.

There were Pompey fans from as far apart as Plymouth, Darlington and Glasgow. Most either had lived there and moved away or followed in parents' footsteps, the love passed down, along with tales of days gone by. The team was in need and they answered the call for support.

The game itself was filled with tension, Coventry was comfortably off in ninth place and in no real need for the points but Portsmouth were desperate. There were precious few chances and Pompey's nervousness proved their undoing when Brian Kilcline, looking like an ancient warrior with his long moustache and curly hair scored.

The atmosphere of expectancy disappeared from the Portsmouth contingent on our terrace. Heads dropped and there was a stunned silence. Unfortunately, the fans in the seats decided that they would exact their own revenge on the home supporters. Portsmouth's notorious hooligan element, known as the '657 crew' (named after a London-bound train time) launched themselves at a fragile fence that divided the different fans, using themselves as battering rams. I had a clear view as they wildly attacked it. Once through this brittle barrier, they ran into a group of Coventry fans, who proved no opposition.

In full view of a stunned ground, they kicked and punched anything in sight. I had never seen anything so vicious. All anybody could do was watch as one thug repeatedly kicked a Coventry fan when he was on the ground. I was sickened as I watched the victim's head jerk with each blow.

Satisfied with their 'work', the thugs returned to the protection of their own fans. Too late, stewards and police arrived on the scene, but the damage had been done. Boos and threats rang around the ground and their anger was directed, not only at the seated fans, from whom the louts had emerged, but also our group of fans whose only interest was the football, which had carried on, oblivious to the sickening scenes that had just taken place. That fact was immaterial to those on the receiving end of the violence, our 'shared' allegiance had put us all in the same pot.

After the game, needless to say, we were kept in for half an hour then released to run the blockades of vigilantes that paced out of view of the police.

This situation always seemed to me the human equivalent of a fox hunt, only this time, instead of releasing the foxes first, they held them back so that the hunters could set traps to catch them in before ripping them to shreds. Once again, a sense of survival was called upon.

Keeping to the back of the group, a few of us vainly searched for a taxi to return us to the station, but there was no sign of life anywhere. Highfield Road and the surrounding streets had become a ghost town.

Perhaps all the residents had teamed up with the home fans to give us a send-off to remember.

Whatever the reason, the situation looked decidedly dodgy. The Portsmouth fans had quickly dispersed, most on to waiting coaches leaving myself and two other fans standing, disorientated and desperate to find the station and escape.

The effect of lunch-time drinking had unfortunately dimmed my knowledge of the outward journey. Clue-less about which direction to go we took pot-luck and headed along one of the main roads, in a generally guessed direction.

The streets were still deserted and from time to time, our tensed state was heightened by shouts along adjacent side streets. We didn't utter a sound in case our foreign accents were picked up, not that there was anyone anywhere near us to hear.

We reached numerous cross-roads, and had to rely on an extremely patchy knowledge of Coventry gleaned from the inside of a speeding taxi. More by luck than judgement, we eventually reached the town centre and what seemed a labyrinth of concrete passages.

Each one seemed to remind us of a previous walkway, which might have been by design, but more likely down to our completely hopeless navigation. Walking through each underpass became a trauma in itself. Like a scene from the film Poseidon Adventure, which was always repeated each Christmas and Easter it seemed, we picked up similarly lost groups of fans and shuffled warily through the concrete jungle that was Coventry city centre.

Groups that joined us elaborated their own tale to spark our already over active imagination, until finally - there it was, towering above us, our journey's end, and salvation - Coventry British Rail station. We hadn't met any hunt members (perhaps it was all in our imaginations) but the motto "It's better to be safe than sorry" seemed apt. At least we didn't have the embarrassment of locking ourselves inside an empty ground at the slightest hint of trouble. We'd live to bore children and grandchildren by what was a non-event in all but our minds.

The violence that afternoon had been the final nail in the season's coffin. Portsmouth's imminent relegation contributed to the gloom that surrounded the fans who made their way back to London. I doubt whether the thugs were caught, perhaps they were travelling back with us on the train, happy with their afternoon's work.

They certainly weren't one of the groups of scarf, cap or bobble-hatted fans who were devoted to watching the on-field exploits of Portsmouth craving nothing more than a successful team to follow.

The hooligans only jumped on the back of the team for their own purposes: to find different fans to attack and different places to cover themselves with their own idea of glory. Never mind the effect that it had on fellow supporters or the team that gave them the vehicle to hitch aboard.

How many innocent Portsmouth fans had been attacked because of others' selfishness?

My mind was cast back to Woodall services and the stabbed Newcastle fan, as the night sprinted by the carriage window. His love for Newcastle had seen him resume his travels, just as the Coventry and Portsmouth fans attacked that day would probably do so in the future, today would eventually become just a painful memory.

Monday 2nd May 1988 - Portsmouth (a)

This was supposed to be a great get together of all my Pompey mates, but Saturday's result had put an end to that. I'd been cheering Portsmouth on, but now I was on the other side of the fence. I was the Judas that had been accepted into the enemy's fold. Today, I'd be a target so decided covering up colours was the safest option.

The mood around Fratton Park was sombre and so I just drifted into the ground. There wasn't a particularly good showing from the Newcastle fans day and amongst those that did turn up, the only topic of conversation, was John Hall.

The man who'd made millions from the Metrocentre wanted the board to allow the fans to buy shares in the club and have a say in its running. The board, under the chairmanship of Stan Seymour, or Fat Stan as he was affectionately known, thought this wasn't such a good idea.

There was a defiant mood on the uncovered terrace we had been placed on. "Sack the board" could be heard at times from sections of the travelling crowd. Newcastle was heading for a comfortable mid-table position but there were worries that once again a star player was going to be allowed to leave.

This time it was Paul Gascoigne, who had provided Newcastle's major spark that year. All the top clubs wanted to sign him and, if previous form was anything to go by, rather than build a talented team around him, it would be easier (and surprisingly cheaper) to sell him.

The board could sell him for a couple of million pounds and then buy a cheap replacement who could never quite live up to his predecessor.

John Hall had become the fans' champion and he'd enough financial clout to make the club sit up and take notice. The Evening Chronicle got in on the act with a campaign for a share issue, supported by Newcastle Breweries by producing a sticker with the title "Why are we waiting?" It featured a bad tempered cartoon magpie, complete with black and white waistcoat and impatient stance.

On the field, activity became of secondary interest. As the Newcastle players ran out there was only polite applause from the fans who had travelled over four hundred miles to see them. There was no Mirandinha, who had been injured in March and never fully recovered. He had failed to set Tyneside alight after all the hype had died down, and his meagre total of twelve league goals was in danger of being surpassed by young Irish beanpole of a star, Michael O'Neill.

This had angered the fans because money hadn't been made available to sign anybody more than an eighteen year old A level student. A 2-1 victory seemed irrelevant as Pompey left the First Division without a fight and in depressing fashion, while the

Newcastle fans spent most of the time shouting abuse at the board.

The goals from Kevin Scott and Anth Lormer seemed to annoy them, because it meant they had less to complain about. That didn't deter them and it seemed insulting for the home fans who had turned up to see the fans of a team destined to finish a respectable eighth calling for the board to resign while they were to suffer the ignominy of relegation.

It also signalled a parting of the ways. I realised that supporting two teams was beyond me. The feelings I had for Newcastle couldn't be transferred. There were hard times ahead for United and, although I'd still watch Pompey when I could, the old adage "Home is where the heart lay," held true.

Saturday 28th May 1988 - Chelsea v Middlesbrough

After Newcastle's mixed season and Pompey's terrible season, it was time to cheer myself up with a party.

Middlesbrough were a game away from promotion to the First Division. It was the playoffs final, second leg and the Boro were 2-0 up from the first leg and looking good for promotion. The pessimist in me was put in a locked box which was then covered in concrete and dispatched to the bottom of the Thames. Chelsea was only a couple of miles away, the weather was glorious and it was just the sort of day British open terraces had been designed for. What could go wrong?

The first leg of the contest, at Ayresome Park had been beamed live to the Hammersmith Odeon cinema. I asked Paul if he fancied going to watch it, but thankfully he declined my kind invitation, perhaps because going might be a bit like putting your head in a ravenous lion's mouth and expecting it not to have a nibble. Thinking back, the urge to cheer when Middlesbrough scored would have been too much, bearing in mind my delight whenever Chelsea were beaten. Reading the papers the day after, it turned out that some fans had done just that and had had their celebrations cut short by the less desirable members of the Chelsea following. The subsequent Northeast visitors to the local casualty department were a direct result of the Bora's success.

Putting that to the back of my mind, I set off for Fulham Broadway for a relaxed afternoon in the sun.

The away end filled up as kick off approached. The atmosphere was charged with the traditional humorous trading of abuse. For the first and only time, I saw Stamford Bridge and its huge expanses of terracing full. "We hate Geordies..." drifted from the far off home end, which was joined by the Boro fans singing "So do we..." (To call someone from Middlesbrough a Geordie is one of the worst insults imaginable, comparable to calling a Scot an Englishman).

Even the light-hearted ditty "You're going to get your f...ing heads kicked in" seemed jovial as the sun beamed down upon a crowd clad in shorts and T-shirts. This was the way football should be, I thought to myself as the away fans bobbed up and down singing "E, I, O, E, I, O", a bizarre Boro tradition.

The teams entered and the volume shot up as the whole crowd committed themselves to their team. Torn up newspaper confetti drifted down onto us, along with red, blue and white balloons that had been lofted as a ceremonial welcome.

It was just how I imagined a cup final to be, the only drawback being Newcastle's absence. Since Boro were from the Northeast, and the nearest you could get to Newcastle without being Sunderland, I gladly transferred my allegiances for the day.

The first sign that this wasn't going to be a 'quiet afternoon at the Bridge' was in the second minute of the game. The home club had, in their wisdom, thought it a good idea to sit fifteen hundred Boro family enclosure members at the farthest corner of the covered West Stand to our right. Unfortunately this was where most of the Chelsea 'lads' sat. They were soon in the firing line. There then followed a mass evacuation as fighting continued throughout the stand. The true horror wasn't obvious initially but the fans around me were talking about friends who were sitting with their families there.

Once again, the players on the pitch ignored, or were oblivious to the clashes that littered the home end. Middlesbrough were too busy trying to fend off constant Chelsea attacks, with a young pairing of Gary Pallister and Colin Cooper keeping them at bay. They managed this until the nineteenth minute when a Nevin cross was turned in by Gordon Durie. There was a lull in the fighting as three quarters of the crowd assumed that victory wasn't far off but as the game wore on they became increasingly restless and even more aggressive.

By half time most of the obvious Middlesbrough fans in the home sections had escaped to our open terrace with police assistance. The fans who remained either had convincing London accents or had been extremely lucky.

The ground suddenly seemed claustrophobic. There was only one way out and the fences that separated us from any pitch invasion seemed incredibly flimsy indeed. The evacuated fans were filling our enclosure with stories of unprovoked attacks.

I started subconsciously scanning the ground, looking for signs of a possible strike. My mind was going into overdrive, the match hadn't been all ticket so what if Chelsea fans had infiltrated our end? I scrutinised and assessed the faces around but relaxed when I saw the immense stomachs that had been crafted over great periods of time spent in Middlesbrough drinking establishments, and the way they had been delicately crammed and stuffed into a variety of Boro T-shirts.

Casting my mind back, memories flooded in of the Milk Cup Semi Final that Sunderland had played in 1984, when Chelsea fans had raced across the pitch towards the away end, carrying metal chairs, bricks and anything that they could prise off the terraces.

I cast my mind back to pitch battles fought by the Central station in Newcastle when Chelsea had been visiting and at Kings Cross for the return matches. Basically, Chelsea didn't like anyone from the North East, or anybody, anywhere who wasn't a Chelsea fan, I concluded.

My mind was proving to be my worst enemy, recalling every single piece of hooliganism carried out by the Chelsea hooligan element who wittily called themselves the 'Head-hunters'. There was also a chance that the Boro fans might take exception to my faint traces of a Newcastle accent. I was desperate for the match to restart, to take my mind off any fate that awaited us, if Chelsea failed to score another two. Despite the possibility of becoming a victim of the home fans wrath, I desperately wanted Boro to win.

Boro fought back in the second half and turned the cards on the Chelsea team that had swarmed around them. The home team tired and for their fans, it became too much to bear. I watched the West Stand as more and more fans started gathering along the perimeter fences.

At first, stewards and police managed to return them to their seats but gradually the trickle turned into a sea of 'fans congregating by the flimsy barriers.

The final whistle was still over ten minutes away when one group started tugging at a gate onto the pitch. There was no-one to stop them, the hapless stewards having either gone for reinforcements or been overrun. The tugging became more violent. Each drag on the door saw it bend and sway with the fans' fury. Along the length of the stand Chelsea fans converged on each gate until at last the first gate gave up its fight and crashed open. Fans poured out of the small opening but were easily pushed back as more stewards arrived, but this seemed to goad the rest of the gathering and the entire length of fencing rattled and shook. The score was still 1-0 and Boro were looking good. It was injury time and Stuart Ripley found himself on the end of a cleared corner. He sprinted towards the Chelsea end as the ground seemed to pause... .and shot weakly from the edge of the penalty area. There were mixed emotions from either end of the ground but the final whistle blew and Boro were up and Chelsea down.

A few brave fans ran onto the pitch from the Middlesbrough end, to congratulate their heroes but, before long, most of them had long since sprinted from the field, aware of the riot that was brewing. As we watched, every available piece of fencing below the towering West Stand and the sulking Shed was filled with waves of bodies with one thing in mind... revenge. The North East fans, suddenly aware of the danger they faced, raced back to the away end and safety. Some were lucky and managed to scramble back but the rest were cut off by fans charging from the nearest section of the West Stand.

It was even more sickening than the scenes I'd witnessed at Coventry. Even the stewards joined in, as I watched one fan being held as karate kicks were aimed at him. As more Chelsea fans arrived without any visible hindrance, the Boro fans left on the field knew they were fighting for their lives and fought even harder to escape and after a few tense and sickening moments most if not all managed it.

Stewards managed to push the invaders back and delay their assault on our enclosure. Those who didn't fancy their chances, not surprisingly myself included, tried to ease themselves further back without making it look like they were afraid. Others shoved fellow fans out of the way in their desire to defend their territory from possible invaders.

Fury raged at the scenes that we'd just witnessed. Masonry rained down as the Chelsea hordes became frustrated at their lack of progress. This was returned as quickly as it had arrived, until from out of nowhere, police horses appeared and split the Chelsea supporters up, before sending them packing.

At this point, the small group who had been celebrating promotion at the back of the terrace was joined by waves of jumping and leaping fans across the terrace, not only because of the footballing success, but also the routing of the foe.

The sounds of battle continued in the streets around the ground but thoughts turned to The Boro. They screamed for the team to return and they duly obliged, sprinting across the pitch spraying each other with champagne and generally sending the sense of delirium one notch higher.

I joined in, but couldn't share their mood of relief and delight so keenly. I was an outsider looking from a corner at a party I hadn't been invited to but was welcome at anyway. Just two years earlier their club looked doomed, I'd seen it on the news but couldn't possibly have known how it felt. To see your club go from that to promotion today must have been an amazing feeling and although I hoped I'd never have to experience it with Newcastle, I loved the buzz that the peaceful fans generated.

Saturday 27th August 1988 - Everton (a)

For the first time in most peoples' lives, the Newcastle board seemed to be going all out to prove that they were ambitious. John Robertson was signed from Hearts, John Hendrie from Bradford City, Andy Thorn from FA Cup winners Wimbledon along with curly-haired goalkeeper Dave Beasant. The four had cost a cool £3,000,000. This had been offset by Gascoigne going to Spurs for just over £2,000,000. But hey, it was his loss. Newcastle was going places!

The reason for this sudden need to invest was the threat from John Hall. Hall had the financial clout to challenge the board and had become the fans' champion with talk of giving the club to the people and sharing our disillusionment at the lack of success.

Hopes were high for the first game of the season at Everton and the away end was packed on a warm August afternoon.

Everton, however had also had their wallets out and bought Tony Cottee (West Ham), Stuart McCall (Bradford), Pat Nevin (Chelsea) and Neil 'Spotty' McDonald from Newcastle. In all they had spent over five million pounds, which put our 'modest' three into perspective. However, considering that before Paul Goddard arrived for £750,000, John Trewick had been our record signing at £250,000, historically we were not exactly big spenders.

Dreams of glory lasted exactly 34 seconds. For the hour before kick-off we had stood, marvelling at our new acquisitions warming up, studying their lazy passing and clever flicks. Confidence grew as we predicted a two or three goal victory, Robertson hat-trick, Hendrie screamer, sensible predictions went out the window. But, it all boiled down to a big boot from Spotty, a shot from Sharp and a nice rebound for Cottee to stick away. We were torn apart and lucky to escape with only 4-0.

The doom merchants all ranted that they could have predicted the score, while the optimists said that this was only a settling in period. Most were too stunned to comment. So much hope and belief, gone up in smoke. Dave Beasant's comment after the match summed it all up: "It can only get better- can't it?" Even the number one song in the charts seemed to agree with him - Yazz and the Plastic Population singing "The only way is up". It was an unhappy coincidence.

Saturday 1st October 1988 - Liverpool (a)

It was early days to start panicking but since the disaster at Everton, we were second bottom with a meagre two points to our name. Hardly the time to visit Anfield to play Champions Liverpool.

The Magpie Group was still slugging it out with the board and gaining more support thanks to the worsening situation. A 3-0 Littlewoods Cup defeat at Second Division Sheffield United hadn't helped confidence.

The start to my second year in London had been as successful as Newcastle's season. A Summer spent revising for resit exams, along with a broken relationship after eight months (a definite record) ended when I moved into a house that was miles away from friends and college social life (such that it was), populated by four mad children and their strange parents. The idea of travelling to Liverpool to see us totally humiliated seemed an attractive prospect. I travelled with the Newcastle London Supporters Club which made the trip that little bit cheaper.

On reaching Merseyside, everybody seemed to disappear before I could ask for directions. This left me and another lad stranded on the platform without a clue where to go. He looked younger than me and spoke with a London accent but he was wearing a Newcastle shirt and appeared as clue-less as I was. We asked for directions from every Scouser we could see and was given a different set of incomprehensible instructions each time. Forgetting our previous efforts, we took pot luck hoping we'd reach the ground in one piece.

It turned out that my companion's dad was a Newcastle supporter but most of his friends supported West Ham and Millwall, two clubs whose fans hardly had a great affinity with us. We chatted about previous matches but his knowledge of the last few years was sketchy. He said he'd been away for a while at Her Majesty's pleasure.

I'd led a sheltered life and was taken aback by this. Okay, I told myself, it was probably nothing serious (anyone could make a mistake) and I relaxed. When asked why, he said that he'd knifed a Millwall fan who'd laughed at Newcastle. He happily added that this was his first game since being locked away.

I was glad that he was wearing the same colours as me but started thinking about what might happen if, after being humiliated 5-0, a Scouser had a little joke at our expense, would my time bomb of a friend start his own one-man war? I made a mental note to use my legs at the first whiff of trouble.

By pure fluke, we stumbled across Anfield. Once inside we took our front row seats and waited for Newcastle's systematic destruction. Sure enough, on three minutes Gary Gillespie headed Liverpool in front. Of course, we reminded them that they only sang when they were winning. This was down to the simple fact there weren't that many times when they weren't on top. Liverpool dominated as usual but occasionally, Mirandinha shocked them by having the cheek to shoot... at least we were going down fighting, we thought. But no, Michael O'Neill, last season's wonder boy laid a ball down the wing for John Hendrie to chase. John's little legs reached it, cut into the penalty area and blasted a shot past Hooper in goal. We had gone through the motions of thinking he could score, but when he actually did, it was a shock to the system. You could never plan these moments because when they come along, all thought is lost and you end up throwing yourself onto the nearest person, screaming deliriously into their ear. Today was no exception. You had to take a few moments to draw breath and even then, were still gasping for air.

Liverpool attacks blurred by as we prayed for first half time and then the final whistle. There were brief moments of respite when Newcastle attacked but they were rare and short-lived.

With seven minutes left, John Hendrie chased a long ball from Beasant and was chopped down. To our amazement the referee awarded a penalty. Surely, this wasn't our Newcastle. This sort of thing didn't happen to us. You just didn't get penalties at Anfield, unless you were wearing red.

All expectation evaporated when we saw Mirandinha pick the ball up. He hadn't scored all season or looked like it, so why did he think he could score now? I pictured the headlines in tomorrow's papers, "Basement boys blow it." I could see myself on the trip back to London reflecting "If only he hadn't..." But he did, and instead of the anticipated despair there was unrestrained delight, Mike Hooper in goal dived one way, the ball shot the other.

The remaining seven minutes were spent in a dazed state. "The Football League is upside down," we sang and when the final whistle blew it signalled the type of celebrations you'd expect from a championship-winning team.

The chances of a Newcastle team ever being in that position were extremely thin so we had to make the most of this golden opportunity. After all, we had beaten the champions.

The merriment spilled onto the street, the Scousers walking by seemed happy for us. They gave us patronising comments on how well we'd played, as fans besieged the surrounding pubs and off licences. My new-found friend and I took similar action, determined to enjoy our journey home. After merrily waving to the departing Liverpool supporters' buses we scurried off to Lime Street Station after they failed to see the irony in our win.

The train was alive with jubilant Geordies. This was the greatest result of my supporting career and as we pulled into Euston, the party showed no signs of ending.

I staggered back to college in a drunken stupor. The rest of the night became a blur. I eventually collapsed on Arsenal Paul's floor still singing. The room was packed with my mates, ready for the college dance. They were dressed to the nines, I was still in my Newcastle shirt and we seemed worlds apart.

Saturday 19™ November 1988 - Millwall (a)

For the great result at Anfield and the excesses that accompanied it we were to be made to suffer. Apart from a Mirandinha inspired 3-0 victory against Middlesbrough, we failed to score in the league for a run of five games. Willie McFaul was made the scapegoat. His deputy, Colin Suggitt took over.

John Hall must have been delighted at the mess Newcastle were in as it gave him plenty of ammunition to aim at the directors.

Millwall were fourth in the league and had only been beaten once. The chances of anything but defeat for Newcastle looked remote.

Their fans' reputation for being inhospitable convinced us that colours were best concealed. It was a gloomy afternoon as we passed through the metal detectors set up outside the terraces to deter fans from bringing cutlery to the game.

There was great amusement as the announcer spelt out the teams for the mentally challenged members of the crowd "...Steve Wood, that's W...o...o...d."

The amusement this caused was cut short as we stood at the top of the corner of terrace we had been allocated, staring gloomily at the seven-foot fences that hemmed us in on all sides. The pitch was given the extra protection of a series of metal spikes designed to rotate and ensnare any would-be invaders. We were kept away from the home fans by giant steel curtains that challenged any view of the nearest goal.

An eerie and sinister atmosphere seemed to surround The Den, which despite the flashes of yellow and blue everywhere seemed as welcoming as the North Sea. The terracing on three sides helped generate the hostile environment that it was renowned for.

Newcastle welcomed new signing Rob McDonald, signed from PSV Eindhoven for about £100,000. It was rumoured he was their top scorer but this was greeted with scepticism since good strikers were rarely available that cheaply.

For twenty minutes, Newcastle actually matched Millwall but three unanswered goals showed how bad we had become. The only highlight was when big Rob McDonald stooped to head in a John Hendrie cross only to be ruled off-side. Our corner celebrated by singing "We nearly scored a goal."

Our depression was made even worse when the Millwall fans started up their haunting chant of "Millwall" which they managed to stretch into a full ten minute 12" version. It made your spine shiver as it reverberated around the old ground and into the rapidly darkening sky.

A fourth goal completed the rout and the chants of "Sack the Board" hit the roof above us. Millwall fans laughed and then joined in to confirm their superiority on and off the field.

The fans' mood was dark. How could we have sunk to these depths? Being made to look so poor.

We were made to stew for forty minutes as we waited to be released from our pen eventually being herded along the side of the ground that contained the executive suite but looked amazingly like run-down Portakabins. Fans, frustrated with our treatment by the police, the team's performance and our own board, vented their anger by smashing any available windows. We were pushed onto express trains at New Cross Gate that took us straight to Kings Cross. The atmosphere was subdued by now. I stood watching the majority of fans heading for North-bound trains and wished I was going with them.

My first visit to Millwall had been the loneliest feeling I had experienced since moving down to London. My love for my new home was waning. I was becoming as despondent as the poor souls I used to laugh at only a few years ago. The miserable faces around me made my problems seem ten times worse. Faces were fixed firmly on the floor or staring at the adverts that had been read thousands of time. Eye contact was to be avoided, laughing was only attempted by the brave or drunk. I now ached for a night out in Tynemouth with the lads but that was a world away.

Wednesday 18th January 1989 - FA Cup 3 (3rd replay) - Watford (a)

After a month of hearing about all the managers that didn't want to come to Newcastle, Jim Smith eventually said he'd be our saviour.

His first game saw John Hendrie score our first goal in 588 minutes against Wimbledon in a 2-1 win. This combined with a 2-1 fluke at Sheffield Wednesday thanks to Michael O'Neill's knee who also starred in a 3-3 draw with Southampton, when the lads trailed 3-1 in the second half.

Optimism was starting to creep back in. Were we picking up form in time for the FA Cup?

The third round draw had seen us paired with second division Watford. After a 0-0 draw at St James', Paul decided to join me for the replay, a tube ride away at Vicarage Road. An exciting game finished 2-2, the return at St James' finished 0-0 and so it was back to Watford on a mild Wednesday night.

Two girls from college came along with us who supported Watford. One had a long-term boyfriend. I fancied her friend but typically lacked the courage to do anything about it. The hope was an emotional Newcastle win might conspire to give me the confidence to sweep her off her feet. This was reliant upon her also being filled with the same emotion, amount of alcohol and therefore susceptible to my Geordie charms.

What could be better? A step closer to Wembley and a long-awaited romance?

They headed for the home end without any alcohol consumed, which spoilt my plan somewhat, so Paul and I headed for the away end.

All thoughts of the girls stopped as the action got underway. For ninety minutes, Tony Coton denied Newcastle but extra time was a turning point.

Watford pounded Dave Beasant's goal and with another replay looming, Rick Holden lashed at the ball. His shot was going nowhere near the goal until Glenn Roeder helped out. He stuck out a foot and the ball trickled into the net.

My world and that of thousands of other Newcastle fans caved in. The reality of being bottom of the league was brought home. We were the worst team in the first division and now, Glenn had killed off our chances of restoring any pride.

I sat on the cold steps that lead away from the stadium, wallowing in self-pity. I thought about Roeder's abomination and my non-existent love life. I'd made a fool of myself desperately chasing girls who didn't want to know, scoring own goals ever since girls had become more appealing than outer space.

In footballing terms, the easiest thing would have been to let the ball sail out for a throw in and not risk losing face with a desperate lunge which usually ended in an own-goal. I hated the thought of being on my own but would have to make the most of it, I decided. I was no longer prepared to chance the humiliation that followed rejection.

In this case, there was no way the object of my affection would return the compliment, I thought, so I wouldn't bother. Life would have to stay as it was. We were out of the Cup, doomed to relegation but at least I wasn't going to knock in another howler by embarrassing another female friend.

Paul joined me on his way out, I hardly said a word. Neither did I say much to the two girls, who felt sorry for me. I started on the "You just don't understand..." routine, but in the end, silence (or sulking) was the most credible alternative. In my forlorn state, the funeral parlour opposite the ground seemed the best place to stay that night. The fact that I would have looked stupid and didn't fancy a night in Watford's streets convinced me otherwise.

Saturday April 1st 1989 - Southampton (a)

The naive eighteen-year-old that had arrived at college had been transformed. I'd dyed my hair black and shaved the sides to make some attempt at appearing weird. The image was spoilt somewhat by the natural Kylie Minoque curls that crept towards my back.

My red ski jacket and 'nice sweaters' had been replaced by black T-shirts, black shirts, black jeans and black bikers' jacket. A pair of black suede pointy boots completed this, my Spring / Summer collection going into Autumn and Winter. I was, unfortunately, proud of my new look and pleased by the admiring glances of passers-by. The calls of "Bloody student," didn't put me off. I had become what was known as a "Goth".

As a young Tyneside lad, anybody who had long hair was either a poof or a lass and to be given a wide berth. I had transformed myself into just the image that provided me with so much amusement a few years earlier. I could now comfortably stand with the like-minded individuals in old Eldon Square being avoided and tutted at by the elderly and sneered at by the young. The fact that I never felt any inclination to stand there drinking cider and still try to appear cool, meant my image didn't affect my mentality.

My musical tastes changed considerably. Out went teeny-boppers Debbie Gibson, A-ha and T'Pau, while a Level 42 tape was deservedly diced. In came The Cure, The Cult and Sisters of Mercy, bands who seemed to thrive on the miseries they imagined life presented. There was an abundance of concerts to go to in London and back in Newcastle the Mayfair's rock night provided me with a weekly holiday dose of alternative music. I even met up with Jon, the Manchester United fan from school, who'd followed a similar path, latching onto him and his mates. A new circle of friends opened up to me.

It was the Easter holidays and exams were looming over the horizon. There was a good possibility that I could be spending another Summer revising for re-sit exams. This was mainly down to choosing to study maths instead of PE or history. Everybody else seemed to be breezing through their courses while I was sinking deeper into a world of mixed-up numbers and ideas. I didn't care who invented numbers or how to prove that one was an odd number, despite the obvious enthusiasm the lecturers had for such matters.

The only numbers I cared about didn't make good reading. Newcastle was second bottom, seven points above West Ham who were bottom. However, the Hammers had three games in hand. Today's opponents had the same number of points as us but a game in hand. A win today could see us climb four places, defeat didn't bear thinking about.

In my right mind, I would never have gone. But, the thought of spending my day locked away with maths text books convinced me that a trip to the other end of the country was a good idea.

Only a few years ago a trip to Arsenal had seen me through my A-Levels and helped Newcastle in their fight against relegation. The same could happen again. It was a return to the much-loved overnight non-stop Clipper, leaving a Gallowgate that thankfully was still as smoky and rundown as I imagined. I thought I was the only fan making the trip which made me feel, once again like the devoted missionary.

After unfolding myself from the twisted shape I'd been moulded into, I stepped off the coach and headed for Waterloo... glad to be breathing in London fumes again. I'd had too much sea-side air lately. The mustiness of the tube seemed to welcome me back as well.

What made the experience so enjoyable was the fact that I was "just visiting". All this to enjoy and only six in the morning.

The morning was spent in Bournemouth trying to convince my ex-girlfriend I wasn't going to mess her around anymore and perhaps we might go well together after all. I failed to mention how lonely I was finding college. Did she really need to know this?

My selfish needs met, it was off to a sunny Southampton.

No matter when we played at The Dell it was always sunny, a South coast ruse to lull us into a false sense of security. As a consequence we became welcome visitors with gifts galore for our hosts. The role of generous Geordies had been played too well judging by our lack of victories here, the last being in 1972 (thanks to Supermac and Stuart Barrowclough - the type of players sorely lacking from the present team). Today was to prove no exception!

Southampton was here for the taking. They hadn't won since November, were the only team in the league not to have won in 1988 and were two games away from equalling a club record of 22 games without success. We, on the other hand, had beaten second placed Norwich the week before. How could we fail? Easily.

The team seemed to have settled for a point early on and offered few shots on the home goal. Southampton laid siege to our penalty area but didn't look like they could breach our massed defences.

Watching from the away "pen", our only consolation was that we'd secured a point. The day was about to be completely ruined in the last minute. Southampton's Rod Wallace chased a long punt. We watched, in disbelief, as Newcastle keeper Gary Kelly sent him flying through the air. Before he had landed, the referee awarded a penalty. Neil Ruddock scored to deprive us of any hope that we'd stay up.

Our silent group didn't linger. After the final whistle, we filed out. Thoughts turned to Swindon in the spring and Watford in the winter and the relevant merits of each.

The worst thing about away travel was the journey back. A week spent thinking about the match, an early start and lengthy journey made you more agitated as the adrenaline started pumping. Nearing the ground all was forgotten as thoughts turned towards the impending match.

The match over with, there was the return journey to dwell on mistakes and misses. Today, a twelve-hour journey beckoned. It was at times like these that I wondered why I was here (wherever "here" was). Cold and wet on a remote platform in Oldham or lost in Coventry's strangely empty town centre, the start of a return journey always made me question the wisdom of these journeys.

When darkness set in I was in an enclosed world, the buffet car my only entertainment. I'd listened to the tapes until my ears buzzed louder than the headphones. The match programme held my interest for five short minutes. Meanwhile, the outside world whizzed by unseen.

Thoughts soon wandered to mates who hadn't come, their lie-in that morning, what were they doing now? Sitting in the warmth watching TV or out on the town?

I sat on the train back to London turning these thoughts in my head and started to make myself miserable, feeling sorry for myself big-time! Here I was in the prime of my life, sitting on my own watching a bunch of pissed middle-aged blokes playing cards. The only memory I had to reflect on for the time and money spent was a last-minute soul-destroying penalty.

I, along with so many other like-minded fans, spent so much time and money watching football because it was an escape from life. Personal problems could be replaced with footballing ones. Thinking about team selections and match results was preferable to thoughts of money and work.

By ignoring the real life difficulties, they were never resolved. They tended to creep up on you when you were sitting alone on an evening or sitting on a bus or train, returning from an equally depressing match.

As if you hadn't been through enough that day, the real world would come back with a vengeance.

It was during such trips that I realised why a lot of fans either drank themselves stupid, the eventual return of reality temporarily postponed.

I was in a college filled with women and was still single. Football filled lonely weekends but in the process my chances of meeting anybody were poor.

During the week, I enjoyed comparing notes with Paul because he shared my love for the game. Potential friends were put off by my initial question of "Who do you support?" and the subsequent interrogation on football I subjected them to.

"What was the last match you went to?"

"What do you think of Sunderland."

I had difficulty talking about anything but football or music. Both were past-times Paul and I followed religiously. I came to the conclusion that I was skint and on my own because of football, but there was nothing I wanted to do to cure my addiction. After all, one day it would all be worth it, wouldn't it?

It was that thought that kept the likes of me going and in the meantime, it gave purpose to lives that lacked one.

Saturday April 15th 1989 - Arsenal (a)

With Newcastle's interest in the FA Cup so cruelly ended by Watford and Arsenal's by West Ham, we had no interest in the semi-finals being played that day.

Arsenal was joint top with Liverpool and Newcastle was second bottom and sinking. I got a lift with Paul and his dad and tried desperately to pretend we had a chance.

By half time, the expected deluge hadn't taken place and the score was 0-0. Rumours had started circulating that there had been some crowd trouble at Hillsborough and that the game had been stopped.

This news was greeted with only passing interest, with a good number of assumptions made about Liverpool supporters based on the unfortunate Heysel disaster.

During the second half, more information was passed out from those fans with radios. There had been people hurt. The match carried on, with both sides oblivious to the horrors taking place in Sheffield. Brian Marwood scored when he looked off-side and Kenny Sansom scored for us but was ruled off-side.

Only after the game did people turn their attentions to Hillsborough as car and coach radios stunned fans with the full extent of the disaster. The fact that the match had been abandoned gave us an indication that things had gone seriously wrong. Matches were only ever abandoned if the pitch was unfit. Even Heysel's European Cup final had carried on, despite the fatalities.

The walk back to the car was still dominated by Kenny Sansom's off-side goal but all that was forgotten when we sat in the car.

The number of deaths rose as we listened. It was impossible to believe... as the figure crept up towards a hundred. The radio was turned off after a while - it was all too close to home.

The television pictures that night couldn't tell the full horror. We were a nation of shocked spectators unable to escape the scenes of carnage and suffering. As football fans there was a frightening sense of deja-vu. It could have happened at any ground in the country.

I thought back to Newcastle's FA Cup visit to Tottenham two seasons ago. The difference had been that the crush had gradually built up. Bill, Gary and I had been standing towards the front of the terracing, just like most of today's victims. We had been lucky but it could have been very different.

There was my first visit to Norwich on the day of the Bradford fire. Their stand had burnt down not long before. Why hadn't anybody thought about the chance it might happen again? There had been so many warnings left unheeded.

Things only usually change after tragedy has struck. Football clubs didn't need to do anything to improve safety because fans were still paying for games and nobody was kicking up a fuss.

We were all quite happy to piss against walls and walk through flooded toilets. Sure, there was pushing on the terraces, but that helped generate the unique football atmosphere we loved so much. After a goal, especially, there would be huge surges carrying us up and down, side to side but just as it seemed you might lose your footing, might have the breath crushed out of you, it would subside.

The only problem was, that there would come a day when the thin line that football balanced upon was crossed with disastrous consequences. Today was that day.
Terraces appeared basically safe, as long as there weren't too many people moving in one direction at once. Today's disaster had been caused by a sudden surge of fans coming through an opened gate. Leppings Lane terrace couldn't cope with a flood of bodies, only the trickle that came through the turnstiles.

I'd stood on that piece of terrace on Boxing Day when Newcastle visited in the league. I positioned myself in front of a crash barrier, to avoid the crush as I always did. I'd trusted it to do its job, as had those fans who'd died.

Any accident was bound to happen at a ground chosen as a neutral venue or involve away fans. Home supporters tend to have the same rituals. They had their own time for getting to the ground and were generally more patient than their travelling counterparts.

The very fact that you'd travelled a hundred or more miles to see your team at an unfamiliar venue gave you an adrenaline rush. You searched for floodlights to signal journey's end. Perhaps a visit to a local pub to compare notes with opposition fans, the resultant frantic rush to find the right turnstile, if you were late.

All the time you could hear the buzz of the crowd and this drove you on even quicker. Add on the fact that it was probably the most important game of your season and you had Wembley in your sights, you were bound to try and push your way forward.

Only this time, everybody else was doing the same. Everybody else had been caught in the same traffic jam, tried to find the same parking space or had just one more in the pub.

That didn't bother those in charge. As long as they had your money and someone had told them their stadium was as safe as any other, what more should they do?

At the heart of the Hillsborough disaster was football's tradition. The grounds had largely stayed the same since the war. The only things that had changed were aimed at attracting the wealthy - better seating, executive boxes and restaurants. There was nothing done for the man who blindly followed and gave so much of his life to the club - he'd always be there. That was the cause of the tragedy.

And football carried on.

Saturday 29th April 1989 - Wimbledon (a)

The same day Liverpool returned to footballing action with a charity friendly against Celtic in aid of the victims of Hillsborough, Newcastle were saying their goodbyes to the First Division.

There were still three games to play but things weren't looking good. A run of four defeats had silenced all talk of a revival. The expanse of open terrace at Wimbledon's Plough Lane told a story. There were a thousand fans dotted about, leaning on barriers but most of these were here for a final piss-up in London. It was like a gathering of the clan. Paul came to 'have a laugh'. Propped up on the terrace was Gary. Later, Will managed to find us amongst the rows of metal barriers.

The surprise was that we lasted until the 25th minute. The gentleman of football, Vinny Jones was 'embraced' by ex-team-mate Andy Thorn, the resulting penalty was duly dispatched by the annoying Dennis Wise. Wise had become a thorn in our side and after receiving all manner of abuse about his size, he relished the opportunity to let his feet do the talking (something he didn't always do).

The referee, (an aged hippy called Lester Shapter with an expanse of white hair) later described it as the easiest decision of his career. The match turned out to be the easiest Wimbledon had played in their career.

Wimbledon looked streets ahead of us. Three goals in eleven second half minutes sealed our fate.

The most fight I saw all afternoon came from Kenny Sansom - all eighty-one England caps of him- when he angrily slammed the ball into the empty net after the final whistle. We had given up, the white flag had been waved; enough was enough.

One last look at the scene of my final game of the season showed the depths we had sunk to. The ground held only fifteen thousand and today had held barely five. The stands were barely the height of the surrounding semi-detached houses, a good third division ground at best. The team who had been put together for a pittance eventually finished on the same number of points as Manchester United in twelfth.

The last three games ended in two defeats (against West Ham 1-2 and Manchester United 0-2) and a draw (at home to Millwall 1-1). The last home game saw protests abound. Season tickets were thrown at directors while fans ran onto the pitch to demonstrate their anger. All the time, the Magpie Group was building support as cries of "Sack the Board" became the favourite cry.

The Wimbledon match had also been the last game attended by one of the real Gallowgate characters. After the game, the man who had for seasons led the Scoreboard from on top of a barrier, died tragically that night. I later found out he was called Darren and had been set upon by a gang.

There were rumours about rugby league fans who'd been at Wembley that day but I never heard anything else. The saddest fact was that a personality had been lost. His blond head could always be seen at home matches, bobbing about as he encouraged those around him.

Everyone knew him by sight but as far as Newcastle United was concerned he was just another punter. Newcastle United was his life but the club's predicament overshadowed his death. There was no plaque where he had stood for years, no moment's silence. There would be plenty more to take his place.

Elsewhere, Liverpool eventually replayed their semi-final, beating Nottingham Forest to reach Wembley where they beat Everton to win the FA Cup. Arsenal won the league, thanks to a last minute goal at Anfield in a game postponed to after the end of the season.

Our return to the top flight would find a completely different league with a new name, awash with cash. Satellite television would have taken over and the Hillsborough disaster would have instigated massive changes - the near-extinction of terracing and the rise of the all-seater stadium.

Fat Mick and the girl from Naarwich

It was the end of May. The season had finished and the prospect of a long, dull summer beckoned. For the first time in nearly a year, I was actually out on a date. Unfortunately, my lack of practice was showing.

Struggling to make an impression, my attempts at small talk had been risible. Obvious questions had been hastily asked, stilted answers given.

In ten minutes, I had discovered she was from Norwich, (home of Bernard Matthews and Sale of the Century), training to be a teacher and we both agreed it was nice weather (it really was) but that was it. I was desperate to fill in the long silences, while we waited for a train to take us to Richmond (Surrey) and an overdue pint.

There was nothing for it. I was going to have to talk about football. The cardinal rule of first-date conversations was "avoid football", but I was desperate!

I blurted; "...and Norwich were second and we beat them 2-0...but, we were relegated in the end..." the train arrived to rescue me. With alcohol to help, things got better and by the end of the night, we were able to have lengthy conversations without mentioning the weather and she even warmed to the odd footie tale!

After a year of the world being against me and muttering "Nobody understands me", things were looking up. A string of knock-backs and "let's just be friends", Newcastle's relegation and maths re-sit exams compounded my miserable state of mind.

My ineffectual chat up line of "Will you go out with me?" needed modification. I had been using this line on and off since I was twelve with an amazingly high failure rate. It also suggested a plea, the air of desperation had to go. Instead I would try and look as if I wasn't that bothered, (in which I failed miserably) but showed enough coolness to convince Sarah (otherwise known as the girl from Norwich) to at least risk a drink with me.

A firm believer in destiny (when viewed with hindsight), I had been destined to have a shit year so that I could appreciate the good times ahead. I had something to do when I wasn't at football now instead of wallowing in my own mis-fortune. It was my idea of heaven - both football and the girl.

The dark Goth music that had dominated my record music gave way to more light-hearted punk music. Transvision Vamp and the permanently pouting Wendy James, Carter the Unstoppable Sex Machine, the under-rated (some might say crap) Pop Will Eat Itself and The Senseless Things among others took over to lighten my listening tastes a touch. At least they don't want to kill themselves, I'd tell friends as proof of my brightening mood.

Newcastle had signed proven strikers Mark McGhee and Pompey's Mick Quinn, plus Kevin Dillon (also from Pompey), Wayne Fereday and John Gallacher.

The only cloud on the horizon was the continued boardroom battle that had disrupted the club so much the year before. The Magpie group had been joined by a new group "United Supporters for Change". They called for a boycott of the first game of the season to protest at the board's resistance to a share issue. There was talk of picket lines being set up around the ground to turn fans back.

A moment's hesitation as to whether I should cross picket lines or not was just that, the thought of missing a game proved unimaginable and I took my place along with twenty four thousand other 'scabs'.

Saturday 19th August 1989 - Leeds (h)

A warm August morning started with the news that up to sixty people had died in a disaster on the Thames. They had been aboard a riverboat disco that had been hit by a dredger. The news was too close to home since (re-sit exams permitting) I would soon be back to college and the traditional opening-week riverboat piss-up.

I remembered previous trips and how I'd assumed we were in safe hands. Again, it seemed that the people in charge weren't to be trusted. As with Hillsborough, trust had been misplaced. Of course, we still went to football and aboard unsafe boats because, as everyone knows, disasters happen to *other people.* Also, these events were just too good to miss.

The thought of an afternoon spent dwelling on what might have happened, persuaded me that to stay at home would be a mistake.

Threats of a picket line had been greatly exaggerated and my fears of being jostled entering the ground amid cries of "scab" proved unfounded.

I was no longer able to pass for an under-sixteen, so paid fifty pence extra to stand in the paddocks (£4.50 as opposed to £4 for the Gallowgate). I was older and wiser now and realised it was time to join the more mature and restrained fans who enjoyed the superior side view.

I met up with another London exile called Yorkshire (Paul) whose dad was from Newcastle. He had been slightly taken aback when I grabbed him whilst celebrating a 2-1 win at Coventry the previous season but hadn't held it against me convinced that romance was the furthest thing from my mind. The talk around us concentrated on Mick Quinn and his resemblance to ventriloquist Bob Carolgees. Mark McGhee was compared to his sidekick Spit the Dog (thanks, mainly to his canine smile). The mood was far from positive and the words "fat bastard" seemed to be popular ones.

The narrow Leazes end had been taken over by Leeds fans and there was a complete contrast in the ground to the doom and gloom of the previous year. Indeed, after eighteen minutes new boy Gallacher won a penalty which Mick Quinn confidently buried. This led to a Gordon Strachan-inspired Leeds storming back as goals from Bobby Davison and ex-Newcastle man Ian Baird gave them a half-time lead.

For the first time in a long while, I was able to talk to someone at half-time about the match. My present image meant I was ignored by most fans so unless I took a friend along, which was rare, I was usually on my own and had to pretend to bury my head in the programme, trying to convince those around me that I enjoyed my own company.

The conversation had revolved around how many we were going to be stuffed by, but this temporary gloom had disappeared two minutes into the second half as Quinn stooped to head in. The Leeds fans who had been so cocky at half-time were silenced. Two more goals from Quinn and another from John Gallacher sealed a memorable win.

The cries of "Sack the Board" were for once absent as we sang Quinn's praises. "He's fat, he's round, he's worth a million pounds, Micky Quinn...", and the comparisons to Bob and Spit evaporated (for the time being). He was the first Newcastle player to score four since Keegan had done so against Rotherham in 1982 and the first player to score a hat-trick since Michael O'Neill against Luton Town two seasons ago.

I felt sorry for my friends from Portsmouth who had lost Quinn's services, but he had given Newcastle fans pride in their team again. The problems with the board were still under the surface, but for now everything was smelling of roses.

Wednesday 13th September 1989 - Oxford Utd (a)

With re-sit exams passed, I could relax and enjoy the last two weeks of the holidays. A trip to Norwich to stay with Sarah was combined with a trip to Carrow Road. Sarah enjoyed the game (a 3-3 thriller against Southampton). The Norwich fans we stood amongst didn't seem quite so adept at swearing as Newcastle fans, which made me relax.

Whenever I dragged girls to football (which wasn't often) they enjoyed the match wit and even the odd bit of swearing added in for effect but it was a case of having too much of a good thing. When almost everyone was doing it, I'd feel duty-bound to buck the trend and be Mr Clean. You could see other couples in the same dilemma. Mr 40-f s-a-sentence man was virtually speechless. He'd swear under his breath (or when she couldn't hear) while desperately trying to draw her attention to something else, the match, the players even the police horses. Anything.

A man accompanied by his son would still swear his head off but after each utterance would follow it up with the words: "Don't tell your mother!" Young girls present were apologised to before the swearer continued, unabated.

Sarah's enjoyment of the game meant her future attendance was inevitable, this had been a gentle introduction to football but it would be some time before she was ready for a Newcastle away day. Her idea of a good day out might not have been being crushed by a multitude of swollen, sweaty stomachs but mine did.

From Norwich I set off for Paul's house. He lived in Slough, which was handily-placed for Oxford, Newcastle's next game. The plan being that he'd drive us both to the Manor Ground.

There was a difference between Paul and me, in that he had a season ticket with his dad in the seats at Arsenal and I stood on the terrace with Gary or Will. This contrast in spectating companions drew a direct comparison with the presence of girlfriends/wives at the match.

His dad started taking him when he was 10 and although he heard swearing all around him, he couldn't comfortably join in. Taking part in this football spectating tradition would result in either a disapproving stare, verbal reprimand or a thick ear (or all three). But when you were amongst like-minded individuals, to swear was seen as an art-form. The higher the frequency of expletives, the higher your social standing.

Paul enjoyed watching Newcastle, if only to have the freedom to swear every other word. There weren't any paternal disapproving looks, only the admiration of a terrace full of like-minded individuals. He also enjoyed trying to pass his patronising Gascoigne impression off as a Geordie accent. Unfortunately, he only knew selected phrases such as "why aye" which he repeated ad infinitum.

Gazza's accent was something that countless impressionists made a lot of money out of. It wasn't just the accent but the whole mentality that Gazza promoted, the happy-go-lucky Geordie who only lived for beer, laughs and sex. Although a lot lived up to this image on Tyneside, after a while the stereotyped joke wore a bit thin.

The blame lay fair and square on the shoulders of the British (and mostly Southern) Comedy Industry. Harry Enfield seemed to start the ball rolling with his character "Bugger-all money" and after that, everybody in the country thought they could do the accent whilst waving a £10 note in our direction.

Fans from Sunderland and Middlesbrough were disgusted at being banded with their local rivals but as far as most of the South was concerned, we all came from the same wilderness that existed between Edinburgh and Leeds.

All was well when we set out in Paul's 1981 Opel Cadette. He was confident it would get us there, but it did have *a* tendency to conk out if it wasn't moving. This didn't seem to be a problem, as long as we didn't run into a traffic jam.

This proved to be the fatal flaw we'd overlooked. As we approached the outskirts of Oxford, the six o'clock rush-hour traffic stood waiting for us.

At the sight of the traffic ahead, the aged vehicle started to shudder, as if anticipating its' fate. A combination of slow driving, high revs and a reluctance to stop inched us nearer to the ground but kick off was approaching quicker.

My mind flicked to Star Wars. Like Luke Skywalker speeding along the Death Star trench, we were racing against the clock. The Cadette was our trusty R2D2, ancient but still running.

As we approached a packed roundabout, our R2D2 stuttered and gave up the fight. Paul frantically fought to revive the ailing machine but it wouldn't go.

At 7:15, we bailed out, and much to the Oxford commuters annoyance, tried to push it towards a nearby garage. There were only 15 minutes to kick off. We weren't going to make it!

Our luck changed, as with ten minutes to go, the little car became Han Solo swooping out of the sky to save the day. It spluttered into life and hopes were renewed.

The police kindly let us leave the car behind the away supporters' buses in view of the dire situation we found ourselves in (i.e. missing the kick off). We raced through the maze of alleys that led to the ground.

The crowd's roar became audible as the game commenced without us and then stopped, just short of the turnstile as the away fans erupted. The barely-audible tannoy credited a goal to Mick Quinn and although I had to be glad we were ahead, I cursed my luck that I'd missed it.

The narrow terrace was packed and this, combined with a thick perimeter fence that towered above half the terrace, meant that our view of the action was extremely limited. Newcastle was attacking towards us and so once the ball entered the penalty area, our reading of the game was pure guesswork.

Worse was to follow as Newcastle's Kevin Scott and Ray Ranson combined to deflect the ball into their own net five minutes before the interval.

We had paid the exorbitant price of £5 for the privilege of being here and all-in-all there wasn't that much value-for-money.

Newcastle, had dominated the game and spurned chance after chance, I managed to glean from Yorkshire who we met at half time. He had been able to see as much as we had of Quinn's goal. The only difference being that he had been in the ground trying to make out the action behind the obscuring fence.

Paul helpfully joked that we'd probably lose 2-1. Unfortunately, he had watched and heard me moan about too many Newcastle games and knew that this was the likeliest outcome.

True to form. After surviving numerous missed chances, Oxford did score the winner. The details were unclear. We relied on the other three-quarters of the crowd to confirm the goal. Twice in a week (here and at Bournemouth) Newcastle had scored early on and ended up losing. Quinn had set up a new Newcastle scoring record when he hit the target in the first five games of the season, but that was of no consolation.

I hated Paul's prediction accuracy. His presence seemed to unsettle the team but I always hoped they would earn his respect by turning in a performance to amaze him. It was like bringing a girlfriend home to meet your mum and dad. You wanted them to like her, but even if they didn't, you know *you'd* still like her... only their approval made you feel so much better.

Unfortunately, Newcastle never amazed Paul. We were his poor relations he enjoyed honouring with his presence.

I didn't even have the comfort of witnessing our only goal. It had been like Christmas without the presents. The lads had showed me up again and it was becoming an all too familiar scenario.

At least R2 managed one last run back to Slough before being condemned to the great scrap-heap in the sky - which was some consolation!

Saturday 7th October - Ipswich (a)

With the major distraction from essays and lectures being Neighbours (including the daily repeat of each episode), it was no wonder cheap alcohol from the student bar proved a big draw. The continuing love affair between Scott and Charlene was enough to turn anyone to drink

Instead of frequent visits to the bar, I tried to spend my money on gigs and footballs. Before today, I rarely sampled the traditional pre-match drink. I'd walked past numerous pubs joining in the drunken chants on the way to grounds up and down the country, but it was a day-time tradition that was unfamiliar to me.

Travelling on my own, I was usually eager to find the ground and find someone I might know. Combined with my student status, I tried to only spend money on the essentials of travel, programme and entrance. My introduction to Yorkshire widened my match experience, after all he was the only person, I knew who worked and could therefore afford to drink and watch football.

Yorkshire and I travelled to Ipswich on the train, where we were going to meet up with his friend Ian. Ian not only had a job and the all-important salary, but a company car (another novelty for me) in which he was going to drive to London to see his long-suffering girlfriend.

We were to meet him in the pub opposite Ipswich train station, which was (originally) called The Station. A pint before the game seemed a productive way to pass the time. This period was my maturation as a fan. I was now able to witness the grooming process all the bellies that crushed me had to go through. I observed that the supping process required as much time and devotion as the team did. It was unsurprising to find so many devoted drinkers in one place.

For the first time I was able to talk to the people from the other side of the football fence whose parentage I regularly questioned along with their sexual preferences. The fences that normally separated us weren't in place here and incredibly we didn't want to pulverise each other. This fact would have amazed Maggie Thatcher and the rest of the Tory government who were still convinced we were all animals.

The absence of away fans before Newcastle home matches had kept me ignorant to the fact that there were thousands of like-minded fans all over the country. It was this national ignorance that probably contributed to the trouble that afflicted football.

Most fans appreciated the presence of away fans because it generated the atmosphere we all thrived on. The fact that the roles would be reversed with us as the hosts generated a mutual understanding and a desire to avoid the situations that tarnished football's name.

Trouble usually occurred when there was an important cup-tie or local derby because this attracted the meat-heads, along with their own blend of entertainment. No other spectator pass-time prompted so many people to travel in such numbers so it was due to the general good nature of the regular travellers that more violence didn't occur.

This afternoon, while we were waiting, we drank. I was enjoying the constant stream of ciders that ended up in front of me. I also failed to notice that my conversation had become the utmost drivel or that I was chanting louder than everybody else. Conversation was difficult to achieve without spraying them with cider. Therefore, my conversations were short and rarely to the point.

By the time we left the pub, I was visibly staggering. The fresh air and some chips sobered me up enough to get me inside the ground but once I had found a barrier to lean on the atmosphere carried me away.

I became the sort of fan I hated. I propped both elbows on the shoulders of people in front of me and shouted streams of abuse at anybody not standing nearby. Like anybody who has been drunk at a match, I considered myself the ultimate in terrace wit.

I took particular delight in joining in the various farmyard animal noises and tractor jibes that seemed obligatory whenever we played a team that came from a rural town.

A first half that featured two Ipswich goals compared to a solitary Newcastle shot made me more embarrassing. Gestures and abuse aimed at a jubilant Ipswich contingent went unnoticed by police and home fans alike. The fact that I may have been happily chatting to them only an hour or so earlier was irrelevant and forgotten.

The second half whizzed by and my aggressive celebration of McGhee's late strike hardly endeared me to Paul and Ian but, by the final whistle the alcohol had taken its toll on me and I was completely subdued.

The thought of further alcohol was unappealing. I declined Paul's offer to come for a drink and headed back to college.

The excesses of the afternoon only made me feel miserable and forlorn. I had spent most of my money for the week on alcohol, made an idiot of myself and felt gloomier for my sins.

Lying on my bed, I watched the room spin. My hall of residence was deserted, thanks to the weekend exodus. I wallowed even deeper, blaming everyone for abandoning me each weekend. Even Sarah, who was away with her friends for the night, came under fire.

I took to kicking my football around the room. This only made me angrier due to my lack of co-ordination and control. I cut out the middleman and just kicked and punched the door, sink and any other immovable object. This action only damaged my foot and eventually I gave up and collapsed on my bed, tantrum over and energy spent.

I woke up next morning sore. Reflecting on the ripped programme that littered the room and my pounding head, fist and foot, I came to the conclusion that yesterday hadn't been a success.

I wasn't the sort of person who could drink a lot. In future I would have to admit defeat in the macho stakes. If I spent money going to a match, being able to remember it seemed to be a definite advantage. I would have to stick to the one and risk the sneers and laughs at my expense. Going out for a drink with friends in the evening was one thing but combining football and large amounts of drink was a recipe for disaster. An adverse result combined with a sloppy performance was guaranteed to put most fans into a bad mood but combined with a lunch-time drinking session, the situation seemed ten times worse.

I was so glad there hadn't been anybody around to witness my tantrum. Although being on my own made troubles ten times worse, I'm sure if Sarah had witnessed any part of my drunken ramblings and actions I would have been feeling a lot lonelier.

Saturday 21st October 1989 - Brighton (a)

Because results hardly ever went our way, when they did I felt an intense need to make the most of them. This would usually take the form of boozy evenings mixed with drunken stupidity.

So it was that my first (and last) trip to the Goldstone Ground ended in the kind of match never before experienced. The fact that Brighton was sponsored by NOBO couldn't have helped them much as Quinn scored a hat-trick in a 3-0 win.

Yorkshire's mate Ian had driven us there and back. This meant that by 7pm I was back
at college and looking to prolong the euphoric feeling.

For a casual football observer, such a victory may generate mild interest but when you mould your life around supporting a team, for whatever reason, the adrenaline boost it gives you allows you to forget all previous depressions and massacres. Life looks rosier and your normally forlorn expression is replaced with a warm glow. The longer you can keep out the real world, the greater the affect this 'drug' has on you.

A drunken evening spent reliving every minute with like-minded people prolonged the up-beat mood. The only person who could appreciate this was another fan, in my case Arsenal Paul.

Once again, my idea of the ideal evening differed from Sarah's. Chanting the Blaydon Races to a night-bus filled with London's nocturnal population didn't appeal to her. Similarly, her view of the type of person who enjoyed such activities contrasted starkly with mine. Whereas I admired, she despised this behaviour. It was inevitable that our joint night out was doomed to failure.

By the end of a fractious night out, Paul and I had been 'dumped' by Sarah and her more 'sedate' friends who failed to share our amusement at, among other things, the constant repetition of Brighton's sponsor, NOBO. Although it was a juvenile attempt at humour, it was also part of an exclusive language that gives football fans self-importance and assumes the rest of their world holds the same great fascination in football as they do.

Because football was an alternative world to the everyday one, it developed its own language. Words like off-side, tap-in or set piece were freely used among fans but had little relevance to everybody else. Fans also used their own dictionary of names to describe all aspects of football. A player described as a Keegan would be a charismatic leader or an intelligent and skilful striker whereas a Wayne Fereday would be extremely fast but crap.

Similarly, to describe a stadium as an Old Trafford would be a compliment, as opposed to being called a Brunton Park.

Whenever fans met up, they slipped into their alternative language, excluding those who didn't follow football. Sarah and her mates had no intention of joining us on planet football and so we were on our own, happily engrossed in Mick Quinn, away wins and NOBO embarrassing ourselves to Black Box's Ride on Time. The arguments could wait.

Saturday 27th January 1990 FA Cup 4- Reading (a)

For the second year running, the draw for the FA Cup had given me a match close to London. An away win at Hull had set up this clash, unable to get a ticket for the Newcastle end, I had to put on my best Southern accent and rung up for one in the home end.

The idea of watching a Newcastle match amongst the opposition fans was a strange one. I found it hard to picture the mixed terraces before the 70s brought in segregation.

I expect this move encouraged fans to chant abuse at each other, safe in the knowledge that both police and fences were there to protect them. It wasn't a situation I wanted to revive. After all I spent every day with Southerners and welcomed the opportunity to stand amongst "my own".

Arriving early, I managed to convince a steward that letting me move from one empty terrace to another would be a good idea. He must have decided it was better to keep me away from the home fans for their own safety and so I set off along the side of the pitch.

In these situations, two ideas come involuntarily into your head. One is to wave to the crowd in the manner of a returning hero (risking the jealous cries of "dickhead"). The other is to run onto the sacred turf and slam any available ball into the empty net. The chance to be more than one of the masses carried a high price in the way of fines and expulsion from the ground, which managed to lose it its appeal.

The average fan dreams of just stepping on their hallowed turf. It holds the same reverence as a film or pop star. You can't touch or step on it, yet you have paid so much for its upkeep. The fact that your idols regularly appear upon it gives it the air of mystique. You remember spots where great goals had been scored and long just to touch the ground they had walked on. The fact that you can only smell it adds to the illusion. I resisted temptation and my reward was a spot with the away fans.

I was able to give my pitch-side report to Yorkshire when I met up with him and Ian. Of course he showed no interest in my excursion, barely lifting his head from his riveting match programme.

In the previous round, Reading had disposed of Sunderland and expected to complete a North East FA Cup double. Newcastle even tried to give them a helping hand. First, with Newcastle 2-1 up, Quinn passed the ball back to goalkeeper John Burridge only for the ungainly Trevor Senior to intercept and score and then in the final minutes, leading 3-2, John Gallacher repeated the trick to gift Michael Gilkes the equaliser and a replay.

The local Journal said neither player could have had any complaints if they had been fined a week's wages. It seemed destined that last year's misery against Watford was to be repeated. Was it in every Newcastle team's make up to try and gift the opposition a cup run at our expense or was it to be an example of good things come to those who wait?

In this case, it amazingly turned out to be the latter. Two goals from McGhee, one from Quinn and another by substitute David Robinson secured a 4-1 win and a plum-fifth-round draw at home to Manchester United.

Sunday 18th February 1990 - FA Cup 5 - Man United (h)

My trip home to watch the Reading replay and a 1-1 draw with Sunderland had combined with my lack of a match ticket to maroon me at college in front of the TV. Sarah had cried off with an essay to do so I sat watching with some unknown girl's boyfriend.

Quite chatty at first, I predicted an early Manchester goal, followed by constant Newcastle pressure (if I was lucky) and then a clincher late on. I even resisted the temptation to ask him if he was from the North West.

The early goal duly arrived, courtesy of Mark Robins, a header which in my unbiased opinion, never crossed the line. My companion, who hadn't uttered a word was then subjected to an intense grilling.

It started with the goal and swiftly moved onto his place of origin and lack of attendance at Man United's matches. It was music to my ears when he confessed to having never been to any as it proved the stereotypical fan of the Reds. My interrogation was broken when Mark McGhee fell over Steve Bruce's outstretched leg. While I was celebrating the resultant penalty, my victim escaped.

I was joined by a Birmingham City fan who had my respect for admitting as much. There was no way you could call him a glory hunter. He distracted my attention while the Manchester fan returned. Feeling magnanimous after the goal, I left him in peace

The gloom descended once more when Danny Wallace put the visitors back in front. I made sure he knew of my displeasure, though. A further twist sent me screaming around the room as McGhee fouled goalkeeper Jim Leighton and Quinn headed in. The joyous sight of Manchester players complaining to the referee made the afternoon complete. It wasn't to be our day, a late winner from Brian McClair silenced my near-hysteric delight.

At the final whistle there was a great sense of anti-climax. Instead of the normal utter despair at our annual FA Cup defeat, I felt nothing. The atmosphere in the small TV room was sadly lacking. The Birmingham City fan had left (to finish an assignment), my victim had long since departed, probably to listen to the match on the radio in the security of his girlfriend's room. I was sitting on my own.

I had experienced a watered down, sanitised match, without queues, crushes, aching legs, bad language and dodgy toilets. All these elements made going to the match the experience I loved.

Football was about like-minded individuals sharing a common interest. If you made the effort to travel somewhere, the sense of occasion was greater than if it was presented before you. The shared passion was missing, replaced by varying degrees of interest, mild or otherwise. Interest alone could never re-create a match atmosphere.

There was also no gently easing yourself back into the real world. No shared joke at a team's ineptness or train journey spent pouring over an uninspiring match programme. Instead, the real world returned as soon as you had to avoid Songs of Praise by turning the television off. The only benefit it had was allowing you to watch something you weren't able to attend. The only objects that needed my attention were my room and a long-avoided essay.

Monday 16th April 1990 - Stoke City (h)

The Cup defeat gave Newcastle a renewed sense of vigour. They won 11 of the next 15 games, drawing two and losing two. They also won away at Port Vale and Wolves to set up the chance of catching second-placed Sheffield United.

It was the Easter holidays and Sarah had come up to Newcastle for a few days. Her first Newcastle match beckoned. Life was going extremely well, both on and off the field.

It was a proud moment for me as we walked up from Monument Metro station, past Top Shop towards Gallowgate. Sarah shared my amusement at the number of young lads who had chosen to follow the latest fashion for wearing flared jeans. As a result of the recent interest in the Manchester music scene (nicknamed Madchester), adolescents around the country had taken to listening to bands such as The Stone Roses and Happy Mondays, dancing like Neanderthals and wearing oversized clothes. The highlight of the season had to be the sight of hordes of Newcastle 'lads' charging towards the central station, intent on attacking visiting Sunderland supporters, being impeded by their flapping flares.

I was on my best behaviour but there was barely a tense moment to be had as first Dane Bjorn Kristensen headed in and then Mick Quinn scored his 31st league goal of the season to beat Charlie Wayman's record of 30 in the 1946-7 season.

I didn't know who Charlie was but I had been present when a Newcastle player beat a record that had stood for 43 years. Sarah on the other hand lacked my enthusiasm but thought it was interesting. When Bjorn slotted home the third in the second half I was convinced we were going straight back up.

Sarah was more concerned about why everybody insisted on hugging her but she had "quite enjoyed herself and wasn't averse to attending future games. This was important because the more she liked football, the more I could talk about it without boring her and being nagged to "change the record".

If somebody can't talk about their passions to their nearest and dearest then the relationship to me seems doomed to failure. Most couples go through a stage where they get to know each other's passions. This doesn't mean that I'd want a girlfriend to come to every match, merely take an interest in order to humour me. Luckily, Sarah had no intention of doing this. And so it was as we neared our unexpected first anniversary.

Wednesday 16th May 1990 - Playoff SF 2nd leg - Sunderland (h)

Stoke had definitely been the high point of the season. If we could have stopped the season then, Newcastle would have gone home happy. But we didn't. One win and two draws saw us slump back into 3 spot. To make matters worse, local rivals Middlesbrough had crushed us 4-1 on the last game of the season and in the process avoided relegation to the third division.

As our 'reward' we had to play Sunderland in the playoff semi-final over two legs. Over the two league games, the Mackems had looked the better team with Eric Gates and Marco Gabbiadini not only frightening defenders with their pace but also their grizzled looks. They were not the best looking forward line in the league.

The Roker Park game again ended 0-0, complete with customary violence, especially after John Burridge had saved a penalty in the closing minutes. Unable to attend either game, I rang my dad every quarter of an hour for updates. Each time he commented on the level of his paternal devotion to me.

The return at St James' was just as tense. The ugly brothers did the trick. Gates and Gabbiadini struck and McGhee and Quinn couldn't reply.

A pitch invasion by Newcastle fans at the end failed to alter the result and Tyneside went into mourning.

Sunderland went on to the final at Wembley and cheered us up briefly, by losing 1-0 to Swindon Town. Our delight at this result turned to disbelief when Swindon were stripped of their place in the 1st Division and relegated to the 3rd Division. All thanks to Lou Macari's betting syndicate two seasons before who had bet on key games, including a certain 5-0 Cup defeat at Newcastle.

Sunderland was promoted instead of Newcastle as playoff finalists, and a season that promised much ended in failure.

One man cries and the country loves football again.

When New Order's World in Motion announced England's participation in the 1990 World Cup, nobody realised how football was to grip the country from early June to July.

Recovering from the lost promotion battle, something was needed to dull the pain of Sunderland's success at our expense. Why not a successful England side?

There was mild interest in the group matches, a 1-1 draw against Republic of Ireland followed by a 0-0 draw with Holland and a 1-0 Gascoigne-inspired win against Egypt.

Paul and I had bought tickets for a New Model Army gig on the same night as the Holland game. Setting a video to record the match, we felt certain that we could avoid hearing the score at the concert. After all, we'd be in Brixton, away from football grounds and therefore football fans. We'd be listening to songs about depressed England, piss-heads, dodgy governments and their contribution to our doomed lifestyle. Apart from the piss-heads, there wasn't even the remotest connection to football. The plan was simple, get in Paul's car (the tube was too risky), turn the music up and pray we didn't knock over any manic England fans intent on sharing their viewing with us.

Everything went according to plan. The roads were virtually empty, as empty as London roads ever get, and we made it to the Brixton Academy Dance Hall blissfully ignorant of the score.

Our ignorance lasted one song into New Model Army's set. After a typically fast introduction, the lead singer rasped; "The football's 0-0..."

Our evening caved in on us. A quick check of our watches to confirmed that he had just ruined our post-gig entertainment with the full-time score.

Thankfully, we had no time to dwell on our misfortune as we were flung into a flailing mass of sweaty long-haired and bare chested bodies; all thoughts of the World Cup were temporarily suspended.

Videoing matches, with the intention of avoiding the score, is a stressful business. We thought we'd be safe going to a concert and if the lead singer had stuck to saying "Cheers", "Ta" or "Nice one" after each singer as they normally do then we'd have been alright.

As it was, we sat watching the game afterwards knowing that there was no chance of a goal which took all the expectation and unpredictability out of the football. We hoped vainly he'd been mistaken, but knew otherwise. At half time, we ended up fast forwarding through the rest of the game and despite a moral-boosting performance by England, Paul and I had been robbed of 90 minutes of tension. We were sick.

Things were still going well with Sarah and after the Egypt game we moved in together. We were sharing a house with our landlady and her Yorkshire Terrier, Randy. The idea being that we had free reign upstairs and she lived downstairs.

Throughout the World Cup, an advert was repeated which featured a man sitting in his girlfriend's flat, after casually throwing a ball for her Yorkshire Terrier to catch, he watches in disbelief as ball swiftly followed by dog disappear out an open window. The caption "Time for a sHarp exit..." appears as he stares out at the dog's lifeless body as his girlfriend asks him "Have you met Randy?"

We had moved in with Randy and his mum. Every time we left, we had to run his gauntlet and the thought of throwing a ball for him out of the window was extremely tempting. His owner was an old lady who spent the majority of her time sitting on a stool in her kitchen watching television. She loved telling you about everyone from their star signs and talk shows and soap operas guided her views on life. If you let her she'd sit for hours telling you how to put the world to rights, which as always entertaining and usually involved locking people up or sending them back home.

The down side of our new residence was the poor television reception. The days leading up to the 2nd round game against Belgium featured a good deal of heated discussion. Panic consumed me. In desperation, an over-priced booster aerial was acquired. This fact alone resulted in "discussions" of expense and despite Sarah's attendance at Newcastle and Norwich matches she failed to appreciate my argument "...but it's the World Cup!"

As David Platt acrobatically leaped to score in extra time and Cameroon were crushed by Lineker, the investment was entirely justified (in my opinion). However, Sarah's assertion that we had previously had a decent picture (apart from the shadows and 'snow') didn't cut any ice with me!

Everywhere you looked, there were England shirts, posters and flags. Previously England's performances had quelled such hysteria. Even their World Cup song was number one in the charts and the weather was hot. The South was experiencing a heat-wave and the new British pass-time had become pub football. The population flocked to watch tiny pub screens to share the communal feeling that England's success had generated.

The secret that had been English football's... Paul Gascoigne... was now, international! The fact that he was no longer a Newcastle player hurt Tyneside but he was, after all, one of us and it wasn't his fault Newcastle lacked ambition. The nation eagerly awaited England's first semi-final since the year we won the World Cup... whenever that was.

The actually evening was electric. Three ex-Newcastle lads (Beardsley and Waddle making up the trio) intensified the interest on Tyneside. A goal for Germany only sparked the England team into life. With less than ten minutes to go, Lineker spun and scored to send the nation mad. Watching Lineker score the late equaliser sent shivers down your spine. A Gascoigne booking in the 96th minute meant he wouldn't appear in the final if Germany succumbed and his resulting tears wooed the nation.

Extra time and then a penalty shoot-out held us all spell-bound. There was national mourning followed Waddle's missed penalty but it wasn't long before Gazza's face appeared in every street window and men were given conclusive proof that it was alright to cry (as long as you were a footballer). T-shirts, posters and books appeared with photos of Gazza holding his sweat and tear-stained England Shirt. Even the Tyneside institution that was Viz comic printed a souvenir cut-out crying Gazza (just add washing up liquid bottle). There was no escaping him!

The numbers of people watching football in the pub had also given the marketing men something to think about and despite the crowd trouble that had dogged England, football had presented itself as a very marketable product.

Saturday 25th August 1990 - Plymouth (h)

For the first time in three years, Newcastle were changing their strips and, much to public disgust, had decided to experiment with the traditional black and white shirt. On Tyneside there was uproar as the new home shirt featured thin stripes on one half of the shirt and thick stripes on the other. Umbro had committed heresy.

I, however liked the new strip. For the last six years I had looked enviously at other teams' strips and longed for someone to jazz up our own black and white stripes. Unlike other clubs, the sponsor's logo never appeared on the replica shirts. My Tottenham mates had Holstein splashed across their chests in the football strip equivalent of fuzzy felt, (the magic felt I'd never had as a child). They could even buy a new strip every couple of years, up to date - the latest in essential football wear, complete with the pointless lines and squiggles that were sweeping the league.

Of course, it was blatant consumerism; ripping off the loyal fans but we loved it. At least we had more opportunity to show what loyal fans we were.

After two years, previous Newcastle shirts were covered in clicks and the hem had dropped down and to top it all, they lacked the finishing touches that emblazoned the player's shirts, a big star and picture of the Newcastle skyline. I didn't care that the shirts were made on the cheap and sold at a vast profit. All I cared about was looking the part.

I welcomed the new jazzed-up image and the chance to wear the sponsor's logo, albeit not of fuzzy felt but cheaply printed on.

The only problem was, that on the day it was released, I was stuck in London and despite an extensive search (with an incredibly patient girlfriend) through every possible sports shop in London I only found one shirt and that was too small.

Why did so many adults still get excited about wearing a football shirt? Whenever a new shirt arrived there would be great discussion amongst the football-supporting fraternity. Even at the tender age of 20 and only one year off qualifying as a teacher I had the same thrill at spending £25 on a new shirt as I did when I was 13.

Non-footballing friends would ask what was wrong with the old one. It wasn't the state of the shirt, it was the statement it made about you. There was a huge element of football snobbery involved. Wearing the new shirt proved your commitment to the club.

You were only a true fan if you had done two things. The first was to have travelled a ridiculous distance to see your team and the second was to wear the new shirt. If you wanted the appearance of being a true fan, you could wear the shirt and lie about the travelling. Nobody would have been any the wiser.

Living in London, it gave me identity, a sense of belonging and individuality (after all, how many people actually wanted to admit supporting Newcastle on Tyneside, never mind in London). Even though the vast majority paid no attention, it gave me a sense of pride. I belonged to not just not the team but the area as well.

For the first game of the season, quiet optimism had replaced May's gloom and with a virtually unchanged team, Bjorn Kristensen started the ball rolling with a goal after just 2 minutes. We couldn't believe our luck. This was followed by a Mick Quinn effort and though not quite as spectacular as last season's 5-2 win over Leeds, it still sent the 24,000 crowd home satisfied.

Saturday 1st December 1990 - Leicester (a)

We were doomed to failure the minute Paul said he fancied a day out. Newcastle hadn't won when he'd graced them with his presence, why did I think it could change? I was desperate to show him that a leopard could change its spots.

The reason why this leopard wasn't going to change was that since winning three of the first four games, they had only won two out of the last 15. On top of that, the share issue that John Hall had promised the fans flopped. The minimum number of shares to be sold wasn't reached and the issue called off.

The incentives to buy shares however weren't great. If you bought 250 shares then you were given a free fixture card. 50,000 shares earned you a discount card for the club shop, two season tickets and some exclusive glassware. The fact that crowds had averaged about 14,500 over the last four home games pointed to a distinct lack of interest in the club. The business community decided that Newcastle was a dodgy investment and probably preferred to buy some lovely electricity shares instead. After all the 'leccy board hadn't had two of its top directors staging an open war with each other.

The only plus point was the signing of Gavin Peacock a striker from Bournemouth. A devout Christian, the hope was that we might at least have God on our side. Well you could hope, couldn't you?

After meeting up with Ian and Yorkshire, the usual trail for a pub saw us enter the first pub that was populated by Newcastle fans. Unfortunately, there was a Mexican stand-off taking place. The Newcastle fans were grouped gingerly around the snooker table, eyeing the Leicester fans suspiciously, while their counterparts returned the compliment. After ordering, I was quite surprised to see the others swilling their beers down and making for the exit.

It was unlike me to be unaware of potential trouble spots, usually I'd walk into a place and spend the first few minutes assessing it for possible dangers, then let my imagination took over. I'd seen it so many times before (on television), the accidental stick in the eye, the lost turn on the table, the missed shot...all potential flash-points.

That I had never witnessed a pub fight had more to do with the number of pubs I'd been in as my ability to sniff out dodgy atmospheres.

My stomach took over at this point, and instead of searching out another pub, Paul and I headed for food while the others continued to satisfy their thirst for alcohol.

Not having to peer through immense perimeter fences had improved my enjoyment of matches no end. Since the Hillsborough disaster fans around the country could actually see goals going in and be able to comment knowledgeably on play, without having to add the phrases "I think" or "It appeared". Terrace supporters had always envied their counterparts "in the seats", who not only had superior positioning but were able to see both penalty areas unobstructed.

As always, I tried to put Paul's Newcastle record aside as Mick Quinn headed a Kevin Brock lob past Leicester goalkeeper,

Mike Hooper. This confidence disappeared when Geordie Terry Fenwick equalised to be followed by beanpole Gary Kelly giving Leicester the lead. It was business as usual. Newcastle had missed chances galore and were still behind.

In the second half, matters worsened when Leicester scored two more to lead 4-1. The cries of "What a load of rubbish..." were just forming on our depressed lips when Quinn shimmied then superbly lobbed Hooper. At least we had seen a great goal was the consoling thought before large lad Liam O'Brien headed in to make the score 4-3.

One of the most satisfying moments in football is when home supporters, who have been so confidently declaring your imminent relegation are silenced. As obvious and moronic as it is, there is still a great delight at crying "You're not singing any more..." or some such witty reply.

When any goal of significance is scored it is one of few opportunities to be undeniably superior to someone else. You, yourself have done nothing more than follow the right team, however, just in doing this you feel you are fully justified in basking in their reflected glory.

Teams that regularly win (Arsenal for instance) hardly ever feel the ignominy of being inferior and if they do, they rarely experience it for long. This allows an arrogance to form in which goals are readily available, not celebrated so vigorously and fans don't feel the need to support their team so vociferously.

The North East teams have not experienced success in any competition since 1973, when Sunderland beat Leeds 1-0 in the FA Cup Final. The passion for football in the region was arguably stronger than in any other part of the country and so any small victory was greeted with extreme enthusiasm.

It was partly the reason Paul enjoyed coming to Newcastle matches so much. Any goal resulted in bedlam, whereas Arsenal fans were complacent about winning. The only significant games we seemed to experience were against relegation that encouraged relief rather than celebration.

Even though, we were still behind, we had three goals (away from home) to cheer for the first time in over a year. One more goal and we would have clawed back a 3 goal lead. No wonder we were buoyant.

In true Newcastle tradition, it was thrown away. Under no

pressure whatsoever, Roy Aitken (nicknamed The Bear and it was then I realised why) played a disastrous ball to Beanpole Kelly who merrily skipped towards John Burridge in goal and duly scored to make the score 5-3 to Leicester.

The usual jokes about having a fiver every time one of our players did that bandied about the away end as our buoyancy was popped.

With the clock ticking away, Mick Quinn handled the situation nicely (in more ways than one) and completed his hat-trick. Desperate minutes ticked by as the Leicester goal became a castle under siege but to no avail as the full-time whistle blew.

The gloating home fans made their way home as the tannoy reminded us to remain behind for 'a few moments' while they cleared the streets. It only provided us the opportunity to dwell on another suicidal back pass.

As over two thousand fans emerged from the seats and terraces onto the deserted streets, the mild winter night gave little consolation. As usual there was an incomprehensible mounted police officer informing the coach travellers where they should go and everybody else was forced to walk towards the train station, whether they wanted to or not. Fans who were only metres from their cars, would have to walk to the station and back again.

Luckily, we were station-bound anyway, unluckily the next train to London wasn't due for an hour or so. The delights of Leicester awaited. It was whilst returning to our favourite Burger King that a bar opening out onto the pavement gave a group of Leicester fans the opportunity to gloat on their victory. This was taken in good humour with a polite wave and we thought nothing more of it.

As we returned from our sumptuous meal, the same occupants of the open bar repeated their banter, only with increased venom this time. A torrent of spit rained down as the phrase "Geordie bastards" filled the air and the bar momentarily lost its custom as our 'mates' inside left their relative comfort to continue their abuse.

We needed little prompting to quicken our steps as they pursued us. The steps turned into a sprint, as we made a bee-line for the station, followed by a barrage of objects. The irony wasn't lost on Paul as we reached the police-protected train station. At least he could tell his London mates about the time he was nearly lynched for being a Geordie.

My knowledge of the inside of various train stations across the country swelled over the next few years as it became the only place you could guarantee safety in distant towns. Unfortunately, British Rail hadn't built their buildings or timetables to accommodate the travelling fan. There was rarely anything more to do on wind-swept station platforms than drink hot chocolate (alcohol was usually too expensive or restricted by police) or dully spot train numbers. On top of that, the timetable was usually arranged so that the first train out was due to depart an hour after you'd reached the station.

The attraction of getting lost in a dark and hostile city rarely appealed. Added that it was at a time when the only inhabitants not Christmas shopping usually bore some sort of grudge against you and your team - the train station's steel girders, shattered glass and brickwork that sheltered you from the elements became a home from home.

This was Paul's last jaunt outside of the capital to watch Newcastle. He preferred his convenient life at Arsenal, a drive to the ground, relaxed walk to the stadium and seat in the stands. There was no half-hour wait after the game, police escort to the station or being attacked by home fans. He could enjoy a good night out after he'd been home for tea. Easy life!

Tuesday 1st January 1991 - Oldham Athletic (a)

It's seven o'clock on New Year's morning. Waking from the previous evening's festivities you stand on the remains of last night's pizza. Feeling your bruised ribs you remember moshing (a mix of dancing and fighting) to The Pogues and punk outfit Stiff Little Fingers. A quick check outside informs you that it is indeed as cold as the snow on the ground suggests. The last thing on your mind is travelling across the country to watch football.

I had woken up on Ian's sofa in Heaton. The debris from the previous evening surrounded me. Vague memories of Roy Chubby Brown videos and punk music filtered through. After half an hour spent trying to wake myself, I remembered that our bus to Oldham was due to leave in just over an hour and there was no public transport today, the one day we needed it most.

Alcohol and the cold had combined to deprive me of a good night's sleep. The Newcastle shirt I had slept in was still soaked with drink and basically I stank. The thought of sitting on a hot bus filled with the cream of Newcastle's drinking fraternity and the sights, sounds and smells they provided didn't appeal. A surfacing Ian was in similar state.

Re-tracing our snowy steps into the city centre, we rediscovered bits of pizza that we had used as finishing touches for our ice sculptures. What a state we must have been in. Had it been funnier than farting loudly in a silent room? The jury was out on that.

The shambling bodies that waited by the Haymarket round multi-storey car park probably had similar stories to relate and odours to share with the rest of their respective buses. What made matters worse was the 1 pm kick off that had been foisted onto us. Not only did the early kick off mean an unwelcome assault on the senses but it had been decided to make the match all-ticket.

Newcastle had been so keen to sell their tickets that they had sent them back to Oldham before Ian had managed to get us any. After being assured that we could buy some from Oldham we booked coach tickets.

Standard practice for coaches was for a police search and ticket check. The former was extremely brief and the latter comprised of a request for any ticket-less fans to put their hands up.

They obviously weren't expecting any and confusion set in when Ian and I put our hands up. It was like being back at school again. We were the only ones who hadn't done their homework and would probably get blamed for the graffiti in the toilets.

Our coach was forced to wait as advice was sought. Everyone stared at us as we sank lower and lower into our seats. We were depriving them of their play-time and they weren't happy.

Eventually, a senior officer came on the bus and demanded to know who the two without tickets were. Once again we sheepishly raised our hands, the groans and tuts ran around the bus. There was no alternative, to avoid a lynching the officer told us we could buy tickets at the ticket office. Everyone charged out the bus, too eager to escape the rarefied atmosphere to clout us.

The police's motives for not telling us earlier seemed to be to make us sweat, make an example of us so that nobody else dared to travel ticket-less in future.

The long queues at the ticket office made a mockery of the whole idea of having an all-ticket match. A large proportion were obviously Newcastle fans in a similar situation to ourselves.

A relieved duo entered a compact Boundary Park and its pitched roof stands. Since it was one of the highest league grounds in Britain, it felt like one of the coldest and windiest the open terrace behind the goal to our left had previously been the property of away fans and offered some protection but Spain it definitely wasn't.

In 1927, the roof behind the far goal had been blown away but today I was just thankful to have the lingering atmosphere from the bus and previous night swept away. New Year at Boundary Park was certainly a sobering experience: at least it hadn't snowed.

On the field (or plastic pitch in Oldham's case) Newcastle was drifting in the middle of the table whereas Oldham was second and seven points clear of Middlesbrough in third.

Our record of never having won on a plastic pitch didn't look at first glance to be threatened today. Newcastle amazed us by dominating the opening moments, with Mick Quinn running the show. Oldham was rudely awakened as shots rained in on their goal. At half time, the score remained 0-0. Half time analysis, based on pessimistic Newcastle form suggested a resurgent form from our hosts.

Instead, a flick header from Kevin Brock dropped into Mick Quinn's path. Instead of blasting his shot over the bar, he controlled the ball and from outside the penalty area slipped it under the keeper's body. Nearly a quarter of the crowd unexpectedly celebrated, our group by the side being joined by a larger group standing silently amongst the Oldham fans on the open terrace.

As the final whistle beckoned and victory seemed imminent, our gloating increased. "We can see you sneaking out" and all the other favourites were rolled out. We should have known better.

An aimless cross landed at our Jason Donavan look-alike Mark Stimson's feet. Our celebrations ceased as we held our breath. Every team has a player the fans love to blame for everything, just like every classroom has a pupil nobody wants to sit next to.

Comments about him revolved around his perfectly blond hair, usually immaculate appearance and his frequent defensive lapses. This was to be his crowning glory. He neatly side-footed the cross past an unbalanced John Burridge and into the corner of the net. An own-goal of dazzling proportions.

If one moment made you question the wisdom of away travel, it was this.

The only consolation was that I would not be freezing on Oldham Werneth's barren platform waiting for a non-existent train to arrive. A short walk to the coach and I would be able to thaw out. There were some advantages of coming by coach -at least it was warm, if only from bodily emissions. Some comforting thought.

Saturday 19th January 1991 - Millwall (a)

Gavin Peacock brilliantly scores with a volley as he falls majestically to the ground and the afternoon is complete. The Den and its un-welcoming barbed wire fences and terraces are the same, only this time we are the ones smiling.

Yorkshire and I enjoy this rare moment of supremacy as a place in the playoffs seems possible. A night's drinking beckons, only Sarah would probably have tea on the go. "I'm sure she wouldn't mind another mouth to feed," I assure him confidently.

Wrong! Sarah has spent all afternoon preparing both herself and tea. She looks gorgeous and the meal tastes as good. Yorkshire is an unwelcome inclusion to her plans. Blinded by the prospect of an elaborate and lovingly prepared meal, he is unaware of the frosty exchanges between us. She has made 'other arrangements for tonight' I am informed as my lasagne is slammed down in front of me.
This is the first Saturday we have had a chance to spend together since November she informs me, a fact that had escaped my notice.

Since moving in together, Sarah and I had avoided major arguments but today represented a gulf between us that an argument would fill. I failed to spot the warning signs, the short answers and sighs on the phone, the time and effort spent preparing and the lack of enthusiasm at our description of Gavin Peacock's strike.

The situation failed to invoke an argument. She gave me the silent treatment and even my apology seemed to fall on deaf ears. My only crime seemed to be not reading her mind.

After a kiss on a distinctly cold cheek, I left with Yorkshire to go for a drink in nearby Putney. He told me men will never understand women and their strange moods, it's all down to PMT. I wasn't going to argue with that!

It's at this point, I switch off and run through previous disagreements Sarah and I'd had and reasons for them, mostly about money and my ability to spend what wasn't mine. Football had only once sprung up. Ignoring Yorkshire's sweeping PMT generalisation, I decided to blame it on our ongoing final teaching practice which was leaving us both drained and fed up.

Millwall had presented me with the opportunity to vent my frustrations at bolshy children and teachers whereas Sarah had sat at home preparing for a night of romance that Yorkshire unknowingly gate-crashed.

I decided that as a fully paid-up member of the easy life crew when it came to relationships, the best option was to say it was my fault and set about enjoying the rest of the night.

Sarah had come to a similar conclusion after a similarly enjoyable night. There were apologies all round as we made up, the stresses of teaching put into perspective. Perhaps she should come with me to the next London match, if only to avoid future arguments.

Saturday 9th March 1991 -Watford (a)

Teaching practice was definitely taking its toll on Sarah and me. The nights spent preparing work, writing up lesson plans and marking books combined with the school day to make us both argumentative. We'd both passed with flying colours the previous practice but this time I was struggling in Shepherds Bush.

Put into a cardboard box of a classroom with 30 children, I spent a great deal of my time trying to control one lad in particular who fancied himself as a bit of a smart Alec. I had hoped he'd be on my side since he was from Wallsend but he had no interest in football and his idea of a good time was practising wrestling moves on the rest of the school.

With the final week of teaching beckoning, a trip to Watford drew me like a bee to a honey pot.

I had either forgotten or ignored my experience at Ipswich the previous year and after meeting Yorkshire and Ian ended up paralytic before the game had started.

The frustrations of the previous ten weeks couldn't be forgotten and as I drank, I complained about everything from the teacher whose class I was taking to the tutor who was supposed to be helping me.

Their helpful suggestions varied greatly. Had I tried hitting them when they talked? Even in my intoxicated state, I didn't think that was the successful recipe for a prolonged career. What about tying them up? Could I give them detentions? The answer was no.

The only way out seemed to get even more drunk, which I duly did and managed to eventually forget about teaching and children.

The turnstile operator missed my glazed expression and flanked by Ian and Yorkshire, I managed to avoid the attentions of the local constabulary.

The only part I remembered of the afternoon after that was trying desperately to keep on my feet as I stood on the cow-shed-like covered terrace. John Anderson may have scored the first with a strike topically described as an Exocet missile after the recent Gulf War but Newcastle's 2-1 win was a blur as was the journey home. My conversations with Sarah even more so.

Hungover, the next morning, I could barely concentrate on writing lesson plans. I didn't have a clue how I was going to teach the things I'd planned. Sarah had spent her Saturday preparing and was happily making some extra work cards for her class.

The more stressed I became, the more my brain refused to function and the more I pigheadedly refused Sarah's offers of help.

The Watford match had been my release valve, but instead I was spending my Sunday recovering from unexpected drinking binge. A visit from an examiner loomed and I hadn't a clue what lessons I was going to show them. If I failed this practice, I'd have to repeat these ten weeks in September and wouldn't be able to graduate or get a teaching job for a year.

A tense and traumatic week began. I was desperate to win promotion from student to teacher. In the end a lesson that had started out well ended with a young girl hiding herself in the cloakroom, refusing to come out and my 'friend' from Wallsend having a blinder on the misbehaviour front. I was failed, subject to an appeal.

If I'd thought about it in football terms, it was like having to win the last game of the season. After going a goal up and seemingly promoted, conceding two late strikes to send me into a possible playoff. I thought back to the previous season's failed attempt at promotion, only now it had happened directly to me. All the work I had put in would be in vain. Typical Newcastle, really - I suddenly found myself sympathising with Mark Stimson, if only I had the perfect hair and looks.

At the appeal a compromise was reached. It was my tutor, who was a Leicester City fan, who stuck up for me, showing the kind of faith directors of football clubs rarely showed their managers after a run of bad results. The compromise was I would confidently teach a new class for two weeks. Then, as long as my exams were passed, I would be allowed to graduate with the rest of my group.

Again the comparison with football was uncanny. Here I was, in the playoffs. Graduation/promotion was three games away. In the meantime I had three essays to write and exams to sit.

I had needed to re-sit maths exams in the first two years of my degree but sitting in the pub watching the rest of the year celebrating their success while I was in a kind of limbo made me numb. Equating my life to football seemed to be the easiest way forward, but for once I couldn't.

I'd put in the effort, but nerves had got the better of me. Was this really the job I wanted for the rest of my life?

Sarah's accomplishment at passing was scant consolation to me. I sat alone, watching the River Thames passing under Putney Bridge and thought only of the Tyne and Tynemouth Castle where Burg and I always sat dissecting the world. The bright lights of the pleasure boats would have been out of place on the Tyne.

Everywhere I looked... laughter billowed out of packed pubs. True, it was Friday night but why couldn't everybody else be miserable, if only to feign sympathy for me. Of course there were thousands of people who had worse problems, but they weren't here with me.

The last thing anybody who thinks the world's against them needs to hear is somebody else's woes. On the other hand, I didn't want people trying to cheer me up. I had to go through my mourning or anguish alone. I still wanted them to be prepared to boost my ego if I needed it, but under no circumstances did I want their opinion.

How many people had reminded Mark Stimson that he didn't really want to score that own goal? He had responded with a blinding strike to knock Derby County out of the FA Cup. If Jason Donavon could do it - so could I!

After all, there were still the playoffs!

Saturday 23rd March 1991 - Portsmouth (a)

Realising you have had no time to get any of the recommended books for an essay tends to lead to worry. When all signs of them in the libraries and book-shops of the North East have been suspiciously eradicated this brings on panic stations.

A 2000 word essay had to be written on children and computers. Unfortunately, I had only learnt a few basic facts on computers in schools
1. children always argued about whose turn it was to use it
2. they argued about who was going to type on the keyboard
3. there were very few computers in schools anyway so the children hardly had any time to do the above
4. once they'd finished arguing, it was just as likely to break down, making the children even more frustrated and argumentative.

None of these facts I thought would help me in my attempts at passing the essay, therefore a reference book seemed essential.

It was at this point that Newcastle came to my rescue. They were playing Portsmouth that Saturday and Ian would probably be driving there. The perfect excuse presented itself - catch a lift, get the book and enjoy the match. How could I possibly be faulted when I was willing to go to such lengths to write an essay.

The first two went like clock-work: the night spent with Randy (not literally) was followed by a successful book expedition into Central London. The last point proved the most challenging. A sparse away following grumbled their way through the game. Even when Kevin Brock's lob presented the lead, discontentment lingered at a lifeless performance from both teams. Newcastle was only seven points off a play-off spot with a game in hand on sixth placed Millwall, and yet there was little enthusiasm from the terraces. Even I had found it hard to shout about anything.

The dull fare on offer, had created apathy on the mostly empty and exposed terrace. Both sets of fans shared this disinterest in proceedings, yet the Pompey crowds of a few years ago had been enthusiastic. It wasn't the ground I had visited frequently two seasons ago. I was now an outsider. The only familiar sounds were the occasional shouts of Big John, ably accompanied by a ship's bell. Only now he was performing near match-long solos.

Full time was greeted with shrugs, even though we'd won our sixth away game, it had lacked passion and ingenuity. Lonely chants of "Smith out" disappeared into the chill Winter air, the terrace emptied within seconds. Largely indifferent fans preferring to search for warmth. Conversation never reached beyond a murmur.

My only consolation was the purchase of the book that would enable me to write something about computers. An air of inevitability hung over the Newcastle fans. If some Pompey fans had attacked them, you suspected most would have thought it was just desserts for following such a lifeless team.

On the way back, news started to break that Jim Smith had resigned. It was hard to fathom why. Perhaps the drop in support, home support averaging about 15,000, prompted him to go, but he had never seemed a quitter. He'd said he wasn't going to stay at the end of the season. Why was that?

Since joining, he'd witnessed relegation, a boardroom battle for shares between John Hall and then chairman Gordon McKeag which ended with Hall being elected to the board. There was the share issue flop and Hall stepping off the board to be replaced by his son Douglas. Now George Forbes had become chairman, a fan "who knew Stan Seymour".

The feeling of being in the dark was strong among the fans. Forbes seemed to be there to appease us, so that we could see one of our own as chairman. But how many people who stood on the terraces knew ex-Newcastle Chairmen? Not many, if any.

The excitement John Hall had brought with him had faded. Millions hadn't been spent and now we'd no manager Last time we'd needed a new manager, we'd been relegated.

It seemed like divine intervention was needed, how about Cliff Richard for Chairman? After all, Watford had done alright with Elton John. This was as likely as Harry Secombe leaving Highway and singing on the Gallowgate each week.

How could I concentrate on computers with all this unrest?

Wednesday 24th April 1991 - West Ham (a)

Out went The Bald Eagle (to be assistant coach at Middlesbrough) and in came Ossie Ardiles and his 'diamond formation'. Nobody had a clue what it was and evidently in the first two games neither did the players. Two defeats in his first two games were followed by victories over high flying Oldham (without any Stimson howlers) and Sheffield Wednesday. Draws against Oxford (2-2) and Ipswich (1-1) put us in confident mood for the visit to leaders West Ham.

Ossie had brought in young blood with Czech goalkeeper Pavel Srnicek, local boy Lee Clark and Andy Hunt. The languishing 'Bear with the sore head' (Roy Aitken) stepped down, as did John Burridge and the gurning Mark McGhee.

17-year old local lad Steve Watson had been in the team since November. As United's youngest ever debutante he had received rave reviews for his performances in defence. The youngsters were back in the team.

I put exam revision to one side for the day and set out across London to take in the East End.

Yorkshire and I met in a pub near Bank Underground station. It was filled with London's yuppie fraternity, talking loudly into mobile fans and ordering cocktails any self-respecting Tynesider wouldn't be seen dead with. We were due to meet up with Carl, one of Yorkshire's mates.

It wasn't hard to spot him due to his striped Newcastle top which stood out as much as mine. He hadn't lost his accent at all and took great delight at laughing at anything in a suit, which added spice to the evening. Yorkshire duly arrived, wearing his suit, since he had just finished work and became the butt of all the 'yuppy jokes'.

One of the hottest days of the year contributed to our sunny disposition. To-a-suit we were ignored and categorised as obnoxious nuisances. We preferred to think of ourselves as happy-go-lucky souls and the previous drinking session had helped instil this belief.

The Hammers fans on the tube were actually pleased to see us, if only to relate in great detail their boisterous appearance in the FA Cup Semi-final when despite being beaten 4-0 they sang "Billy Bonds claret'n blue army" for the whole second half. I lost count of the number of times I heard the phrase "...without missing a beat when the fourth goal went in..." There was also the small matter that they were top of the table added on for good measure. Evidently, we were only there to witness their glory.

In arguably their best game of the season, Newcastle dominated and when Lee Clark crossed from the right, Gavin Peacock dived to head in. He was making a habit of scoring the type of goals that you dreamt about, overhead kicks, diving headers and beating goalkeepers one-on-one and we lapped it up.

After the usual scuffle at the back of the terrace, when home fans made their assault on the open gateway that joined the sections of terrace together, we started chanting "Ossie Ardiles' black'n white army." This repeated chant lasted throughout the first half and after a half time break continued well into the second.

We couldn't bear to be out-shouted by anybody, especially when the lads were playing so well. Despite being only mid-table, over the last few games, the lads had played the type of football we loved. After watching too many goal-less draws, attacking football was back and there was hope for the future. Promotion of any kind was beyond us now, but we had our pride back.

Two more 1-1 draws followed, defeat at Charlton and a humiliating reverse at home to bottom club Hull, but there was nothing at stake so the form was just put down to complacency.

My thoughts left football as I took and passed my final exams. Determined not to let my 'play off' opportunity slip, I worked especially hard, along with my Leicester City supporting tutor to win through.

By the time I'd finished my teaching course, college was deserted and my last night as a student was considerably downbeat. A quiet meal with Sarah (who'd gone back to Norwich to get a summer job) then packing up, ready to return home.

It was goodbye to Randy the Yorkshire terrier who I never did see floating out of the window in pursuit of a plummeting ball. Never again would his television-bound mum be able to advise me about my life by referring to my star sign or what she had seen on the box.

It was also a goodbye to student life. Thanks to Ian's car and London's proximity to Division 2 football grounds I had visited 14 grounds but I'd seen very little of St James' Park. Newcastle accounted for the bulk of my overdraft. Students spent a good deal of their (or the bank's) money on alcohol and since I usually only drank with Yorkshire and the others, I managed a saving there. Bizarrely, I never drank snakebite and black again.

Earning at last

Like a young apprentice coming to the end of his training with his club, I was looking for a pro-contract, I had been overlooked by all the education authorities applied to. A dream move back to the Northeast was non-existent, the only teaching jobs I could hope for were in London. The raw enthusiasm was there. All I needed was someone to show faith in me.

A school in Baling wanted talks, they'd read that I'd coached football in a Wimbledon school. I decided to talk to them, after all they were the only ones interested.

There were no contract talks, no agents present or signing on fee. It was simply - here's a job, we know you're desperate.

The head turned out to be the best I could have asked for - loved football, talking about it, watching it, he was even willing to listen to you when you were having difficulties. The one drawback was his team - Man United. He was a rarity, a United fan who was from Manchester and so could be forgiven his loyalties.

Could I work for a Man United fan? Course I could, this wasn't the time to put pride before money.

In anticipation of my first wage packet, I bought my first car. It was a dream come true. The new car accessory for football fans was the mini-strip in the back window. To prepare for first day of ownership, a mini-strip was bought in advance and ceremoniously placed in the rear windscreen before it was even mine.

Away travel had instantly become easier and cheaper. Proudly I would drive, scarves flying out of the windows to pointless away games in my Fiesta Popular 1.0, fill it with empty sweet wrappers, cassette cases and most importantly all manner of black and white memorabilia. I drew the line at fluffy dice but everything else was fine.

"These young teachers who can afford cars, I didn't have one when I started..." the head would say. I indeed felt proud to be at last one of society's earners and a car owner to boot.

There was also a change in my living arrangements. After a year living with Sarah, Randy and his mum, I had felt claustrophobic and in need of space.

I realised I wasn't ready to commit myself just yet but I still wanted the security of our relationship. It was a case of having your cake and eating it. I wanted to do my own thing without having to consider anybody else.

A cramped maisonette flat with a yappy dog and his owner wasn't conducive to a blossoming relationship so perhaps we'd done well just to survive. A little bit of space would do us the world of good.

Living with others was cheap and easy so I set about looking for just such accommodation. Sarah meanwhile had found a shared house in Kingston, only a drive away.

Sunday 18th August 1991 - Charlton (a)

It was my 22nd birthday. I travelled down to London the previous day to move into my new digs, sharing with a West Indian family in Greenford, West London.

Newcastle was playing on the Sunday because Charlton had moved from Crystal Palace's Selhurst Park and its expansive but empty terraces to West Ham's cramped (but also empty) terraces. Charlton were the proverbial nomads and at the time seemed
forever destined to wander.

Newcastle had made only one signing, the mercurial Franz Carr. The Gallowgate songwriters had obviously been working flat out with their original composition for him. "He's here, he's there, he's every fucking where, Franzie Carr, Franzie Carr" we shamelessly chimed.

A virtually unchanged team lined up (apart from Lee Clark sporting a completely shaved hard-lad haircut). Surely on my birthday, the boys would turn in a blinding performance?

My hopes were dashed when Charlton strikers Robert Lee and Carl Leyburn netted. A dreadful performance was brightened by Franzie's late strike. It was too little, too late as usual.

Had losing to Hull at the end of last season been a foretaste of things to come? I pondered as I sat alone in my car outside Baling Broadway station eating take away pizza.

Happy birthday. I thought to myself when the rain started to hit the windscreen and the condensation built up a wall to protect my solo birthday celebrations, I started to wonder whether I did want my space after all. Would my bachelor pad live up to my expectations or
would isolation drive me mad?

Saturday 14th September 1991 -Wolves (h)

When the share issue folded, the club thought of an ingenious plan to get their hands on applicants' money. If you gave the board £100 you would receive a Premium Support Bond.

This carried no say in the running of the club, not even a share in the club, but it carried other benefits:
1. A decorative certificate
2. A free day at the match with buffet
3. A tie (or neck scarf for the ladies) and lapel badge
4. 10 per cent discount at the club shop
5. 2 newsletters a year
6. A prize draw.

Cynically, most saw this as just an attempt to rip off loyal fans, desperate to help out the club they loved. Why had the fans who'd wanted shares not been able to buy them in a private flotation? It made you wonder if the club had wanted fans to own shares in the first place. They would probably be blamed for not supporting the venture, but had it been the failure of London's money men to buy that had wrecked its chances?

Two people who'd decided to help the club were my granddad and his wife, Monica. Unfortunately, their willingness to help the club was tarnished somewhat when they received only one lapel badge. A bitter battle was put on hold when they received letters inviting them to the Wolves match.

He was visiting his first match in over ten years, while Monica was making her first ever visit to the ground at which her father had been a regular. She had loved hearing the stories he told of days gone-by. Of children being passed to the front, of Jackie Milburn and more importantly the now-unheard-of tradition for winning trophies

My Granddad had been a season ticket holder during the fifties, sixties, seventies and early eighties. He had similar memories, but the attraction of watching Second Division football wore thin and he gave it up, just twelve months before Kevin Keegan revitalised the club.

The day started with the ground tour, which even included a chance to 'smell' the hallowed turf. After that the group of about 20 'Premium Supporter Bond' Holders (the words 'Bond Holders' became a phrase which would strike fear into the hearts of fans just a few years later) were treated to a "wonderful" sit down buffet.

Entertainment was presented by the amiable face of the board, George Forbes himself, chatting and actually thanking them for their support. If he'd played The Blaydon Races on the spoons, that would have been the icing on the cake. Their seats gave them an excellent view of the match, which proved to be the only drawback of the afternoon.

Newcastle's performance represented poor value for their £200 donation as they yet again failed to win at home (a run of 3 games). Wolves won 2-1 to add to Ossie's woes. The team slipped to 4th bottom, one place off the relegation zone.

Meeting several of the players was a plus but had they really been rewarded for parting with their money to support the club? Their day had been and gone. The team had dampened proceedings and might have contributed to the long and drawn-out fights over who should get the pin badge.

Early September 1991 -Downe Manor U12 v Horsenden U12

It was my managing debut; the school day had passed extremely slowly. My group of 9 and 10-year-olds had played up all day, sensing my mind was somewhere else. It was now four o'clock and thirteen 11 year olds sat before me.

The head-teacher had picked the team, acting as caretaker manager until I felt able to take full charge, get my feet under the table so to speak. Faces stared at me as I explained what I wanted from each player. It would be a solid 4-4-2 formation I explained. They exchanged blank looks. Keep a defensive line, I continued, more blank looks. "Just stop them scoring". Some realisation dawned but I wasn't overconfident.

For twenty-five minutes the ball bounced around, eventually ending up in our net. Half time, I tried to pep them up, but hadn't a clue what to say. "Just enjoy yourselves, have a few shots." This did the trick. A cross, followed by a half scrum and we'd equalised. I danced jubilantly on the touch-line as I shouted "Yes" and "Get in that bag". My Manchester-following head looked at my over-enthusiasm and commented: "Suppose you don't get to see many of those, do you?"

The leaves that blew on to the pitch, and the sky that darkened as the Sun dropped below the mixture of 70's school buildings and prefab huts darkened the mood. My boys were tiring and trying to cling on desperately to the draw.

Twilight made the goals and ball hard to make out. Two late shots followed as our hosts eased their way to victory. There were three cheers for both sides and then thirteen pairs of young eyes looked at me for some consolation.

I was gutted. I had expected that just watching football all my life would make me a good coach, knowing how to get the best out of them. It was going to be a lot harder than it looked, "Never mind lads, there's always next time" I chirped. They were a long way off the diamond formation and so was I.

Sunday 17th November 1991 - Sunderland (a)

The devastation that was Sunderland's promotion to Division 1 turned to delight as Denis Smith's men struggled and were eventually relegated.

This was the most eagerly awaited fixture, revenge for the playoffs was on everyone's lips. Their back door promotion hadn't gone down well.

Newcastle had picked up form after their early wobbles had seen them drop to bottom place and now we were only four points behind Sunderland, seven places above us.

On the way in, all away fans were given a slip of paper advising us that we would be held for "a few minutes after the game". No reason was given, but we were assured that it was for our "own safety".

What it really meant was that we would held for over half an hour while the Sunderland 'boys' got their ambushes ready and would then be marched to the station.

It was nice of them to write to us, though.

Each derby match at Roker ran to a script. The Roker end would be packed with Newcastle fans, pushing for position or just to get a foothold. This was usually followed by the 'parting of the way' in the Fulwell end as the Newcastle 'boys' attempted to cause as much damage as possible before they were dragged out.

The frog-marching along the touch-line coincided with the packed paddock's exchange of loose change (who said Newcastle and Sunderland fans didn't look after each other). These fans would then be treated like conquering heroes by the hordes already fighting to stay upright as we were forced to accommodate them amongst our ranks.

So it was today. The next part of the script was one that deviated from the previous year's norm. The turgid 0-0 draw never materialised. Instead, Sunderland swarmed all over us. Goalkeeper Tommy Wright had taken over from Big Pavel and he was having a stormer.

The first League goal in a Roker Tyne-Wear derby since 1979/80 season arrived courtesy of a Peter Davenport shot that bounced off half the Newcastle defence. For the first time, I heard the 'famous' Roker Roar - much ridiculed by Newcastle fans as "no bigger than a squeak".

Defeat looked a distinct possibility and the potential humiliation of thousands at workplaces and schools across the region. It was then a piece of history was written in Tyneside folklore. A tussle in the Sunderland half was followed by a ball bobbling towards their penalty area. The packed Roker End wished the ball into the path of lanky Liam O'Brien, who took it all in his stride to produce the most exquisite chip.

Behind Tony Norman's goal, we held our breaths as the ball drifted towards us. Memories of Beardsley scoring at Liverpool were conjured, this time the ball was floating directly along our line of sight. Liam O'Brien's worried gurn could be spotted in the background, as the ball grew in size. The beautiful sight of a Sunderland keeper clutching at thin air contributed to the final landscape.

The resulting bedlam of bodies with every fist punching the air in delight had been a year and a half in the making and a moment to savour.

One of the most exciting derbies for years finished all-square. Sunderland may have started favourites and dominated for long periods but having the last laugh was the most satisfying part of the day.

True to their word, the police did let us out after a few minutes. The twelve o'clock kick off allowed us to march to the station in daylight. In the streets around us from time to time, shouts could be heard which indicated trouble. Apart from the occasional rush as lads, anticipating action, pushing their way through, to join in, (or more likely just watch and later pretend they had had a part to play) there was very little to entertain you on the return journey to Seaburn station.

Talk centred around big Liam and his imminent knighthood, the Playoffs had been a necessary evil to spice up the games between us. The struggle the team had had to contain Sunderland was forgotten as bravado stepped in, league tables were temporarily forgotten as we made our way back to Newcastle.

The four-hour Sunday train journey back to the smoke would positively fly by, once the buffet opened for sales of light refreshments and alcoholic beverages.

Thursday 26th December 1991 - Middlesbrough (h)

Since my last visit to St James, things were afoot in the boardroom. Sir John Hall, who had formerly been named only as vice-president had now re-joined the board, along with his son Douglas. Gordon McKeag who had fought him for control in the late eighties was 'retired' to vice-president. Ex-chairman and enemy of the fans 'Fat Stan' Seymour had left the board to be replaced by Derek McVickers and Freddie Shepherd.

No in-fighting this time, instead a silent coup, the 'driftwood' being transferred to other duties. There was no doubt who was in charge — Sir John — Mr Metrocentre himself. If nothing else, we thought he might be able to put a shiny glass roof over the Gallowgate to protect us from the elements.

However, nothing had materialised so far, on or off the field. The man who at one time had been the hero of the fans was keeping his hands firmly in his pockets. The team was struggling at the foot of the table, too many drawn games were causing concern. Ten games had been drawn and only six won, not the best of times to play a local rival that was chasing for the championship.

Middlesbrough seemed to have a hoodoo over us. We hadn't beaten them since Mirandinha decided to play a bit in 1989. Visits to Ayresome Park usually ended in a tonking and the angular Bernie Slaven jumping on a fence in celebration.

Our only victory had been in the Littlewoods Cup when we won 1-0 at home. Unfortunately, this had followed a 2-0 first leg defeat and counted for nothing.

Why did the fixture computer have to ruin our Christmas by setting us up for humiliation from our second-nearest neighbours? Derby matches at Christmas were only ever fun if you won, otherwise they were torture and quite frankly pointless. I went to football to get away from the agony of family get-togethers only for some idiot to decide it would be nice to have a football family shindig during the festive period.

I would be all for it if you could be guaranteed to stuff your nearest and dearest every time but given our respective form, for Newcastle fans it was as unlikely as a hangover-free Christmas.

An unexpected lively start from Newcastle faded and when the lean but useless Boro forward, Paul Wilkinson set off past an invisible Newcastle defence nobody expected this Christmas turkey to even reach the penalty area.

As he dashed across the half way line in his unusually white cycling shorts, bets were laid as to which blade of grass or divot was going to tackle him. The bravado vanished when he lashed the ball high to Tommy Wright's left.

Stunned, we watched him run to the Boro fans packed behind the goal. At least there was no fence for him to celebrate on.

It was scant consolation. Boro went marching on as we slipped further into trouble. Ossie's diamond formation seemed to have everyone confused, from the players to the fans. About the only people who shared Ardiles' enthusiasm for it was the opposition who enjoyed the easy pickings.

Saturday 1st February 1992 — Oxford (a)

The view from the away end was bad enough, without the fog that enveloped the ground. We knew that bottom-placed Oxford were 1-0 up because it happened right under our noses, but a second goal was invisible and assumed from the cheers of the crowd. Newcastle's fight-back through Kevin Scott and Gavin Peacock provided some return on our admittance but Oxford's final three goals were a fog-bound mystery to us, which is probably just as well as we slipped to second bottom.

What was clear was that Ossie's days at Newcastle were numbered. The friendly face of Newcastle, George Forbes was now Vice-chairman and Sir John Hall, Chairman. There was no doubt he wanted his own man in charge so Ossie was surplus to requirements.

You had to feel sorry for him, because he had been given little support from the board. The money to buy players had been scarce and his most expensive signing of David Kelly at £250,000 from Leicester hardly represented a major investment.

As it was, Ossie's memory was hardly given time to linger before the new man swept it all away.

Tuesday 10th March 1992 — Cambridge (a)

Keegan was back. In typical fashion. He and Terry McDermott swept into town and gave Newcastle their first win in six games, 3-0 against Bristol City. Despite losing to a David Speedie hat-trick at Blackburn and at home to Brighton, the mood was definitely upbeat. Nearly 15,000 had been added to the previous home league gate of 15,563. Every goal clip on television seemed to end with Keegan and McDermott leaping about performing acrobatic scissors kicks.

My previous memories of Keegan had been an overweight superstar trying to perform in a testimonial for Kenny Wharton (a faithful terrier of a player). Kenny's only moment of glory had been that he had sat on the ball, during a 4-0 routing of Luton Town, simply to annoy the opposition.

His testimonial, during our relegation year had been hyped as Keegan's return. There were reports galore in the paper of him working out to be fit for the game. In the end, he unsuccessfully puffed about the field, giving up at half time.

I was extremely sceptical that he could make the difference and was amazed to see the coverage his first game received. Living in London, I had forgotten how fanatical the fans could be and how popular Keegan really was.

With car-assistance, I was able to leave school and my argumentative Year 5s at 3:30 and be in Cambridge by 5:30pm. There was time even for food before meeting Yorkshire and Carl outside the ground.

It was literally a breath of fresh air getting out of London. I could forget the stresses of my new career for an evening standing at the base of one of the floodlights that loomed above the few steps representing Cambridge's away end. We were able to get a great view over the perimeter fence at the action. For once I was able to witness two new signings (a rare occurrence). Both came cheaply and while one had a "sweet left foot", the other resembled the lion out of the Wizard of Oz. Kevin Sheedy arrived from Everton on a free transfer, while Brian Kilcline arrived on loan from Oldham.

Newcastle was a completely changed side. They confidently tore Cambridge apart. When Peacock scored it seemed the perfect moment to leap from our vantage point onto the fence and in the process cover ourselves in grease designed to hinder any would-be pitch invader.

A first half spent laughing at the poor sod whose job it was to wander around the pitch dressed as a giant moose offered further joy as Kelly rifled in a shot, to further endear himself to the travelling group. Once more the fences were jumped upon. The half and full-time whistles were celebrated in a similar manner, with the fences packed with overweight and balding men showing no sign of embarrassment.

We had beaten an in-form Cambridge side who had become our betters. Their strike force of Steve Claridge and Dion Dublin would move on to better things, and so it seemed, at last, would we. My image of an overweight Keegan had been replaced by a vision of a shining star, admittedly with a dubious perm, but I wasn't going to hold that against him.

Saturday 21st March 1992 — Grimsby (a)

When Keegan arrived he had been promised money to spend on players, but the wealth at Sir John's disposal remained as inaccessible to Kevin as it had to Ossie.

Unlike Ossie, Keegan managed to change the millionaire's mind by resigning. In a bizarre aftermath to a 3-1 victory at home to Swindon, Keegan won and money was duly promised.

The fans loved the fact that Keegan had so much power, because they knew he wouldn't betray them. It was part of the reason so many fans were now flocking to games and today was no exception.

After standing and shivering at Peterborough and Grantham stations for well over an hour waiting for connecting trains, I eventually arrived in an unusually warm Cleethorpes to find the town crawling with Newcastle fans.

I made my way through the narrow back alleys that led to the away end. There was hardly a Grimsby fan to be seen. Mind you, there was the possibility that I could have mistaken some of the black and white Grimsby scarves for Newcastle ones, however the longest queues were definitely for the away end.

The reason for this soon became clear. Four police horses had formed a line across the narrow entrance that led to the turnstiles. They would turn from time to time to allow fans to enter a 'courtyard'. Unfortunately, with kick off only 10 minutes away, the huge crowd outside was becoming impatient with the turnstile operators' efficiency and the police found themselves swamped as the area around them filled with supporters desperate to get in.

I mistrust horses at the best of times, but when I found myself staring at the back end of an increasingly agitated one, my instinct was one of survival. Those nearby who shared my view and misgivings pushed themselves further into the cramped courtyard and suddenly, memories of the crush at Tottenham filled my head. I had lost all control of my feet and legs and my main aim was to stay upright.

The newly arrived fans at the back added their weight to the crush in the absence of any instructions from the horse-bound police (who had their own problems controlling their mounts.

An elderly couple was finding the struggle hardest and those around them tried their best to divert some of the pressure but it was proving an impossible task. Chanting inside the ground increased the pressure being exerted by the fans at the back and as expectation rose, so did the numbers near the turnstiles. It was evident there just weren't enough to ease the crush.

Unexpectedly, someone answered everyone's prayers. A double gate that had remained tightly shut swung open Instantly fresh air-filled gasping lungs along with a mixture of grass and mud. The weight of the crowd pushed me towards the bright light at the end of a tunnel. Reaching the end, I was dazzled by the sun.

By the time I had registered where I was, I was already standing in the centre circle. Ten thousand sets of eyes were trained on the most unlikely set of pitch invaders you could imagine. Grandads adjusting their caps, confused young lads, women trying desperately to avoid the flattened and un-ironed look and men still carrying the cans they had been clasping outside.

Once realisation had dawned that we were not going to be nicked for trespassing and that the chants of "Geordies here, Geordies there, Geordies every..." were being directed at us, bravado set in. Hands were raised to applaud our audience and we slowly strutted towards them, pretending to score imaginary goals, nutmeg invisible defenders and generally act like a bunch of complete dickheads.

Any street cred we might have had went out the window, but the fans in the 'pens' behind the goal lapped it up all the same, probably wishing it had happened to them.

It made me think of the 'boys' at Roker Park who made their trip along the touch-line from the Fulwell End to the Roker. Although not of my making, here I was doing exactly the same things they did without the violent introduction. The Grimsby fans simply watched bemused as "Kevin Keegan's black and white army" roared around us.

Once in the 'pen' my glory was over, but I was on a high and if nothing else it had lifted the away end as a 90-minute party ensued. Surges were the order of the day and after months of supporter apathy, Keegan's return had created optimism. Despite a Shaun Cunnington early goal, the fans kept singing as they had before I had moved down to London.

When the Grimsby goalie clumsily dropped the ball and then picked it up again, an indirect free kick was awarded. Kevin 'misunderstood' Brock laid the ball off to new-boy Sheedy who lashed a shot past the eleven players clustered on the goal-line to up the tempo a few notches.

A late Brock 'goal' was disallowed for a foul on the keeper, but that didn't dampen proceedings as the party back to London carried on at Grantham, Peterborough and finally Kings Cross station at 9 o'clock, five hours after Sheedy's strike.

We hadn't won the league, or even the game, but at least we weren't as crap as everyone (including ourselves) thought we were.

Monday 20th April 1992 — Derby County (a)

The draw against Grimsby was followed by the first victory over Sunderland since January 1985 and Peter's hat-trick. An unbelievably popular David Kelly scored what he later described as a "spawny-arsed" goal, but as one wise scholar once noted "They all count" and this one counted double.

Alas, that was as good as it got. Defeats against Wolves (humiliating 6-2), Tranmere (unbelievable 3-2), Ipswich (spawny 3-2) and Millwall (depressing 1-0) sent Newcastle back down to 21st, one place off a relegation spot. Nearly six thousand had been knocked off the attendance for Keegan's first game and things were
looking bad. Not the day to visit fourth placed Derby County and Mr Good Looking himself, ex-Mackem Marco Gabbiadini.

The 2,000+ fans that packed into the seats in the Osmaston Lower Tier were expecting a miracle. Keegan was going to wave his magic wand, sprinkle fairy dust in the air and "Hey presto," we beat a Derby team that had lost only one of their last seven games at home, this was all in spite of our form of four straight defeats.

Unfortunately, it seemed like Kev had used up all his magic. Nobody wanted to believe it and we were intent on winning the game through fan support, a tactic that had had mixed results during the eighties. The home fans were mute compared to the cacophony that greeted the mags.

The warm weather should have warned us that it wasn't to be our day and that we should've stayed in the park outside, playing football with the local lads. Miracles usually happened on dark and dismal days when we least expected them, the warm air perhaps sending the lads to sleep.

True to form, there was the pre-match hype, the individual player chants and the now-customary Keegan worship and then it was business as usual. Derby's first attack of note ended up with Kevin Brock fisting the ball off the line. Penalty and Kevin Brock sent off!

Paul Williams stroked the penalty home but the abuse was saved for the referee, a Mr Lynch, and he would have been if the hordes screaming for his blood hadn't been stopped by the rapidly growing number of police and stewards that barred any entry to the pitch.

As taste of things to come, our seats, which were two rows from the front were subjected to a hail of coins from behind. It made me wish that more cricketers followed Newcastle, or in the very least coin throwing should be a compulsory subject at Tyneside schools. Next, Steve 'usually unflappable wonder-boy' Watson was dispossessed and before you could say "he'll never score", Paul Kitson did just that. Again the coins drifted our way (if only I'd brought a cap or a striped hard hat).

A quiet afternoon from "our favourite ex-Mackem" ended in Gabbiadini lying pole-axed on the floor and mild-mannered Kevin Scott joining Brock for a pre-halftime cuppa. A lone chair back whistled past, as disgust at Mr Lynch grew.

Half time was an unnerving experience. The atmosphere was turning distinctly dark. The sun slowly disappeared behind the black clouds that had formed above us. Even the elements had realised the seriousness of the situation.

Everyone was constructing elaborate plans to get even with the new public enemy number one, and for once it wasn't Mr Good-looking Sunderland 1989.

Thoughts of violence were swept away as the nine black and whites tore into a bemused Derby County. A header from Kelly was pushed into the path of Gavin (God's on our side) Peacock who drove the ball in. It was like re-discovering the chip butty.

We danced, sang and roared as our heroes enacted their own version of The Alamo. David Kelly stared as John Wayne's Davy Crockett holding off the Mexican Army. Texan independence may not have been as important as Second Division survival, but the comparison was there for all to see. All we needed now was for a whirlwind to conjure a sandstorm out of thin air and force the match's abandonment.

But 'Davy' Kelly had other ideas, he lashed a header goalwards that seemed destined to complete the fight-back but somehow stayed out.

Before we knew it, Derby's Craig Ramage had found acres of space to embarrass Tommy Wright through his legs. An annoyed Liam O'Brien lashed out at an otherwise anonymous Tommy Johnson and became the third and final player to leave the field early. The fight was lost. Ramage's second goal ensured the victory beyond any doubt, but still Kelly's heroes battled on.

The seat-projectile in the first half had been a foretaste of things to come as grey and black objects hurtled onto the pitch from unseen hands at the back. We took cover beneath requisitioned projectiles as all available official manpower was concentrated on avoiding a battered referee. The barrage ceased long enough for an enraged Kelly to tear his shirt off and fling it amongst twenty pairs of grabbing hands who failed to notice that the destruction of the seats had recommenced.

Oxford and Plymouth had both won to further deepen our plight and we had dropped into the bottom three, with only three points separating us from bottom-placed Brighton. Was this to be Keegan's and Newcastle's Little Bigg Horn, a glorious fight to the death or an abject surrender without a whimper. If Two-gun Kelly had anything to do with it, it would be the former.

Saturday 25th April 1992 — Portsmouth (h)

25,989 fans nervously shouted on the frustrated Newcastle. Yorkshire, Ian, Carl and I stood tense and silent in the Milburn Paddock as rumours whizzed around us. There was a nervous hubbub and from time to time, the shout of "United" drifted around the ground.

Sarah was amazed by the haggard and drawn faces that stared forlornly at the action on the pitch. She couldn't have chosen a more straining weekend to come up to Newcastle than this one.

From the moment she stepped off the train, she knew something was up. All match mentions were banned. The words Newcastle, match or Portsmouth resulted in an instant stiffening of the back, annoyed snap and change of subject. Uttering words about student days spent watching Pompey achieved a worse result.

She wondered why she'd bothered coming up. Just when we were getting on so well she was subjected to this.
From my viewpoint, and most of Tyneside, it was like waiting for the sky to fall in on you. The battle at The Baseball Ground had been just that, a battle we had fought bravely in but well beaten, it had been our last stand.

The last three away games had been against the three teams at the top of the table, we had lost our easier home fixtures and it looked like luck had deserted us.

Relegation seemed inevitable but still a crowd of 25,989 turned up to watch the last rites.

The score was locked at nil-nil and Oxford above us were drawing as well. We'd be stuck in the bottom three with only a trip to third-placed Leicester City to secure an unlikely life-line.

What hope did we have, Portsmouth had taken Liverpool to an FA Cup Semi-final replay and penalty shoot-out, while we had been knocked out by Third Division Bournemouth in the third round. They were two points off a play-off spot, while we were two points off the bottom. To top it all, Jim Smith was their manager and would probably have loved showing us what we had missed out.

I saw more of my shoes than I did of the match as I constantly kicked the barrier we were leaning against, sighing every so often and avoiding any eye contact with Sarah. I didn't want sympathy, I wanted three points.

The appeals in the press had been for the fans to get behind the team and be patient. Nobody dared berate the team but it led to a surreal atmosphere. The noise on the attack rose sharply, but when they broke down, there was a still as frustrated emotions were bottled up.

Half-time conversation was muted and Sarah's highlight was the conversation she'd had with women in the toilets who'd also been dragged along and promptly ignored by distracted husbands and boyfriends. She came back to see a row of bowed heads gazing at their scuffed shoes.

The second half dragged on with more muttering, silent cursing, shoe scuffing, fist clenching, nail massacring and general stomach-churning tension until... substitute Quinn deftly headed the ball into the path of born-again Kelly on the edge of the penalty area. In one motion, Kelly hit an unstoppable shot that screamed into the top left-hand corner of the Gallowgate net.

Relief poured down from nearly every corner of the ground. The frowns of the previous week were replaced by near-hysterical laughter. Sarah was grabbed by every bloke around her but managed to fend off anything more amorous than a hug. Knotted stomachs had been replaced by unexpected relief while Sarah found herself once more the centre of attention as I waxed lyrically about Kelly's blockbuster. Her annoyance at my Jeckyll and Hyde treatment of her failed to register as I jabbered away excitedly.

The final whistle blew and every face carried an inane grin. Nearly 26,000 Cheshire cats partied away from the ground. The job wasn't over yet, but all we had to do was go to Leicester and win to guarantee Second Division survival.

The fact that we hadn't done that since the opening day of the1984/5 season didn't cross anyone's minds.

Why spoil a good feeling?

Saturday May 2nd 1992 — Leicester (a)

I had always been envious of teams that had something to fight for on the last day of the season. It meant that there was a possibility of a season finishing on a high. The thought of a possible low never entered into the equation. Coventry's never-ending fights against relegation held the country's imagination each year, as did Arsenal's 1st Division Championship victory in the last minute at Anfield.

As Michael Thomas slotted home the clinching goal in '89, the footballing country went berserk one way or another. My own memory of embracing Bevan Bedward, a Birmingham fan was one I long to forget.

It was probably why the FA Cup Final appeared so romantic to so many. Here was the last game of the season and the whole world was watching just two surviving teams. Everybody else's achievements were forgotten for a day.

For only the second time in my supporting career, Newcastle had something more than pride to fight for on the last day. Most seasons had dwindled to mid-table security and drabness. Nothing to get excited over, battles already lost or won —safety assured or relegation unavoidable. Even my first full season ended with a passionless and uninspiring 0-0 bore.

This season was different. After seemingly heading for the sleep-enhancing positions of mid-table, Newcastle had decided to commit suicide and here we were on the last day needing to win away at promotion-chasing Leicester to guarantee survival.

Unfortunately, it was a case of the grass is always greener

on the other side. It was like being jealous of the sympathy given to a hospitalised friend and thinking what an easy life they've got until it happens to you. You discover first-hand the pain, the frustration and depression at being imprisoned within four dull and crumbling walls.

Here I was, on the last day of the season with the 3rd Division looming but, instead of revelling in the drama, it was unbearable torture. The outward calm offered no indication of the inner turmoil and sense of foreboding. To make matters worse, there was nothing I could do but shout and sing my encouragement.

Newcastle had never visited the 3rd Division, a fact that Sunderland weren't able to match. The great delight at seeing them relegated in the playoffs looked like coming back to haunt those Newcastle fans that had cheered on Tony Cascarino and Gillingham.

The only consolation about possible relegation was that we'd stay in the 2nd Division. The reason being the creation of the new FA Premier League to replace the old 1st Division. The knock-on effect turned the 2nd Division into the 1st Division and the 3rd into the 2nd. It was little comfort.

Match tickets were like gold-dust. Luckily, Ian had managed to come up trumps.

At 9:50, a phone call from Sarah had delayed my departure. She had something important to say and could she see me after I got back. I promised faithfully to meet her at Acton Town station at 11pm and she could stay over so we could talk. I was intrigued, but the lads were calling.

A 10am pick up followed. I met Yorkshire and his friends Dave and Carl outside my local Tube station and set off, black and white scarves flying for a midday ticket rendezvous with Ian at Leicester Forest East services.

For the princely sum of £7 a highly-prized unreserved seat ticket for the East Stand (a barn-like stand that ran along one of the sides of the pitch) was in my possession. There was just enough time to hear the hard-luck story of some ticket-less lads in a transit who'd had their crates of lager confiscated by the Leicester police en-route before we set off to finish our journey.

In a convoy of two cars we entered the town centre. Remembering our less-than-enthusiastic reception the previous year, scarves and dangling strips were removed from the car, in an effort to look inconspicuous. The mass of black and white-shirted bodies was a bit of a give-away, though.

A party atmosphere greeted us. Blue-and-white covered fans surrounded us wearing tasteful afro-wigs and plastic fox masks in honour of the club's nick-name —The Foxes. This was the cup final I had dreamed of.

As opposition fans our only role was to act as observers to one of Leicester's greatest achievements. It hadn't even occurred to the home fans that we might actually put up some resistance. All they needed was to get more points than Middlesbrough that day and they were into the soon-to-be-opened Mecca that was The Premiership.

Coloured confetti and balloons greeted the two teams as they entered the fray and nobody, least of all the 1800 Newcastle fans expected anything but a home victory.

Early frantic defending from Newcastle kept Leicester at bay and when Newcastle threatened to take more than a supporting role small skirmishes broke out in the main stand. United fans buying tickets from touts were blamed and the problem fans swiftly removed.

In a tense half, Newcastle were unexpectedly giving as good as they got. Bad news filtered through. Plymouth was 1-0 up against Blackburn. A goal for Oxford (playing Tranmere), and we'd be in the bottom three.

The home fans were still waiting for a score at Molineux where Wolves were entertaining Middlesbrough.

Half-time approached and the much-maligned tranny army was in great demand. There were rumours and counter-rumours. At the moment we were safe, but what if Leicester scored, then Oxford would jump above us on goal difference. Nails were being whittled away, soon there would only be bone left to chew at.

Out of the blue, Leicester's Steve Thompson passed back to his goalkeeper, unaware of Gavin Peacock standing behind him. The linesman's flag shot up and just as quickly shot down. The ground held its breath as he bore down on the hapless Carl Muggleton in the Leicester goal before coolly chipping the ball over his groping fingertips.

I grabbed hold of the complete stranger who had sat nervously next to me before projecting myself gracefully across five seats, landing on top of the jubilant forms of Ian, Yorkshire, Carl and Dave before plummeting downwards head first.

I would later proudly identify my legs sinking beneath a mass of bodies on the end-of-season video. In an instant, all other results became meaningless. If we could only hold onto this gifted lead, safety would be ours.

The silence around us barely registered, as did the referee blowing for half time. Striped bodies were still jumping along the touch-line and waving from the fence as both teams left the field.

In one fell swoop, Gavin's goal had changed the whole atmosphere in the ground. The last thing the home fans (and the away fans for that matter) expected was a Newcastle goal and it had killed the party atmosphere stone dead. The good-humoured banter had been replaced by a more hostile attitude towards us.

A walk to the toilets at the end of the stand became inadvisable. The low fence that separated the Leicester fans behind the goal and our fans in the seats became the focal point of the next confrontation. At first, only threats passed between the two pens but it wasn't long before missiles replaced words. My desperation for the toilet subsided as I watched coins and stones ricochet off the box-like stand walls. Self-preservation became the order of the day.

My concern about brewing trouble was forgotten when I returned to the others. Clustered around a tranny-man, the score came through that Plymouth had conceded two goals in the last minute of the half to Blackburn. Our league position was becoming rosier, if not our personal one.

The news filtered across our section and our further celebrations seemed to annoy our hosts considerably as more police and stewards dashed to disperse any potential trouble-makers from the latest flash-point.

The scorer of the two Blackburn goals that had brightened half-time had been diminutive David Speedie, (once of Chelsea where he had formed one of the most potent strike-forces in the country with Kerry Dixon). He had been a player we loved to hate, his over-competitive spirit (some might say dirty) and ability to score against us hardly enhanced his reputation, but just for now: he was a saviour.

All this was forgotten as the teams re-emerged. Any remaining confetti and balloons was pushed skywards, but an air of tension hung around most of the ground.

Leicester charged forward and all the Newcastle defence could do was hopefully hit the ball up field, only to see it swiftly returned.   The home fans roared them forward and for the next forty-five minutes, we watched as time dragged itself along.

A flurry of goals at Tranmere resulted in a 2-1 lead to Oxford, we had to hold on. No news was available from Plymouth. Anxiety seeped from every Newcastle fan. Constant requests for news were greeted with shrugs and blank expressions.

With just under 30 minutes to go, the confined ground erupted. Middlesbrough was 1-0 down. The Leicester players responded and Tommy Wright was subjected to a barrage of challenges, crosses and shots. A draw for Leicester would be good enough to see them up.

On the terrace behind Carl Muggleton's goal, the fans seemed to have pushed themselves further up the fences. The red and white plastic stripping that served to block the steps onto the pitch were bulging with the considerable weight that was now pushing forward on them. A pitch invasion seemed imminent.

The more Leicester pressed, the more space Franz Carr and Kevin Sheedy found on each wing. After every effort, the crowd appeared to inch further forward.

The enthusiasm of the crowd was quelled somewhat by an unknown event. We only guessed that Middlesbrough had scored as the buoyant mood fell flat. A noticeable rise in the abuse directed at our small contingent seemed to act as confirmation. We were to be the sacrificial lambs if they failed.

Our main concern was still on the pitch as full time approached. An irrational fear, not for my safety but of relegation swept over me. I sensed the animosity, but couldn't care less. The results were all that mattered.

The crowd's support for their team dropped even further as Middlesbrough took the lead. Only a Leicester win by 11 goals would do, and the chances of even one goal was looking remote.

Our situation wasn't quite so clear cut. Nothing more had been heard from Plymouth. Rumours of equalisers were rife. Were they ahead now? Nobody knew.

It was then that it happened. The ball bounced around the Newcastle area and seemed to be drifting out when it was returned into the six-yard box. In all the confusion, Steve Walsh firmly headed home.

The fans perched on the steel fences poured onto the pitch, delighted at the opportunity for fresh hope.

As more poured from the terrace, their thoughts turned to the ones who had contributed to their desperate mood. Since both teams had made a hasty exit, we represented an outlet for their frustration. Coins and anything solid were directed towards our seats as half-time's border skirmish spread.

The rain of objects surprisingly could not compare to the despair that had swept across the stand. The lack of news had created paranoid uncertainty. One minute we had completed the great escape, the next an ignorant void. Objects flew about us in both directions as we desperately hunted for news without success. Ducking every few moments and keeping a generally low to the ground posture, we searched for information. Oxford we knew was still leading, but the lines from the West Country were worryingly silent.

The storm died down as the hordes were pushed back off the pitch. The officials had only succeeded in pushing them across the touch-line and reminiscent of the Wembley in 1966, pressed ranks were massed behind the line.

The sickening sense of doomed failure filled me. Only Newcastle could do this, set us up only to throw it all away in the last minute. Of course lots of teams were capable of it but I was convinced that Newcastle were the masters of it.

The match re-started and Newcastle pressed desperately forward. Steve Walsh headed weakly towards his own goal and saw Peacock dash towards it. He rashly stuck out a foot and only succeeded in diverting it past Muggleton, to be stopped by the massed ranks of feet standing on the goal's netting.

Peacock leapt for delight, but cut short his celebration as the hordes once more engulfed first the penalty area swiftly followed by the whole pitch. Walsh was consumed by sympathetic fans, patting him on the cheek, telling him it wasn't his fault, but that of the Geordie bastards they were about to teach a lesson.

In our seats relief poured out. Standing on the steps, where

I had found myself, with tears welling up, a complete stranger wrapped himself around me, screaming as his weight pulled us both down. The emotions experienced in those two hours had drained all energy from me.

I struggled back to the others who were standing, staring at the figures disappearing down the tunnel, oblivious to the mass of blue wigs and shirts that was heading straight for us. No words were necessary. No matter what anybody else did, we were safe.

The second invasion, despite being much larger and more violent, only heightened our new-found sense of hysteria. Seats complemented the array of objects that we nonchalantly dodged, we laughed, danced and sang even louder, convinced of our untried indestructibility.

With the situation worsening, the police took the unprecedented and unheard-of decision to hold the home fans back and provide us with a head start.

Remembering my promise to meet Sarah, I favoured heeding the police's advice.

We turned our backs on the violent but ecstatic scenes happening below us and headed for the exit.

The streets that enclosed the ground were silent and empty. A few hundred Newcastle fans headed away from the lion's den, having made unlikely escapes both on and off the field.

The roars in the distance were another world away as the sun beat down upon us and the birds sang happily above. Even nature was on our side.

My main threat was from Ian, who had cautiously removed all signs of his Newcastle allegiance and was demanding we all follow suit.   My failure to do so resulted in him trying to rip it from my back, after a brief scuffle I agreed to take my shirt, despite my protestation that we were the only people in Leicester who weren't secure in the stadium.

Escaping through deserted streets felt surreal. My own usually cautious nature had been forgotten as a result of the 'high' I was now experiencing.

On safely reaching the car, we awaited confirmation of both our last goal and Plymouth's result. On hearing of a Speedy hat-trick to defeat Plymouth and that our last had been credited to Steve Walsh, all arguments evaporated. Scarves were unrolled out of each window and shirts donned once more. The feelings I had experienced had been everything I had expected of a cup final at Wembley. The uncertainty about other results had generated the same buzz as being amongst a crowd of 80,000.

The only drawback was the sense of anti-climax afterwards. Driving away, the buzz died down and we each reverted to our own thoughts. A celebration drink was a necessity so we headed to my London local. Our black and white outfits made us stick out like sore thumbs but to my annoyance we were mostly ignored by the regulars. It was just a usual quiet Saturday night out for them

Our great escape had measured zero on the country's Richter Scale, only on Tyneside (and Wearside) would the news have registered, with differing reactions. I imagined what it would be like in Newcastle, bars heaving with Newcastle strips, all drinking Steve Walsh and Gavin Peacock's health.

The stream of drinks soon made up for the lack of atmosphere as we wallowed in our triumph. A quick check of my watch told me it was only 10 o'clock and there was time for a curry before meeting Sarah and we headed off for nourishment.

On the few occasions that I checked my watch during the meal I never worried that my watch still indicated an hour to go to my rendezvous. The evening was going well, so why worry.

Yorkshire happened to mention, after we'd paid the bill that they'd have to get the tube. Rubbish, I replied it was still only ten. His announcement that it was in fact 11:40 had me sprinting out the curry house towards Acton Town station.

In a reduced state of awareness, I bounced my way along using lampposts, dustbins and walls to keep me in the general direction. The cider and curry that was sloshing about inside threatened to make an unwelcome re-appearance each time, but luckily I made it in one piece to the station.

It was by now ten to twelve and Acton Town was covered in semi-darkness, the street-lights providing a glow which lit up the entrance.

Only a few homeless old men were sifting through the rubbish bins and casting envious and angry daggers towards a darkened shape that had stolen their favourite bench.

Fears that Sarah had gone home or been kidnapped were quelled the moment I focused on the body curled up on the seat. My introductory hello was viciously cut short with the rebuke "Where the hell have you been...?" I tried to explain about the watch (incidentally a present from her), our escape from the jaws of death and my presently reduced state of accountability (it just wasn't my fault!) but the look and storm off told me she wasn't having any of it.

I trailed after her, hoping Newcastle's successful fight against relegation would appease her, but this seemed to make things worse. "I could have been raped, murdered..." I realised silence was the best policy, bar the occasional apology, as I concentrated on following quickly behind her, without ending up in a dustbin or the road.

She had calmed down by the time we reached the house I shared with four others. A cup of tea later, she had managed to put her experience to one side. She had said she wanted to talk so I lay back and listened.

We had been getting on really well she commented, which I agreed with. She got on well with my house-mates, again I nodded. Perhaps living in a cramped flat with an elderly telly addict and a dog called Randy hadn't exactly been conducive to a blossoming relationship. Again I agreed. It might be a good time for us to live under the same roof again. She'd like to move in.

This was out of character for her to take a lead on such issues. I'd pushed for us to live together and then decided that it was time for some space and I felt it was the perfect end to a perfect day. I was floored and not only from the drink.

It was the equivalent of having a girl asking you out, which had never happened to me. I could only think of nights curled up together watching match of the day.

I didn't even want to avoid lonely nights after football because I'd enough people around me to limit these. The added incentive of having meals made for me and a more regular laundry service did appeal but they weren't major factors.

I'd matured. Perhaps my life was going somewhere. Newcastle under Keegan looked like they were going places and Sarah and I were moving in together. What could be better?

A place in the Premiership?

The last days in London

The summer had whizzed by. I was playing happy couples with Sarah in Acton along with an Italian couple who enjoyed testing their rickety bed to its limit. There were two Polish lads who were friends of the landlady, a Spurs fan who had turned armchair football into an art-form and an Irish girl who hated all forms of televised sport.

The only down-side was the landlady's husband who made a point of checking-up on the state of the house just as one of the female members of the house was exiting the shower or bath. It wasn't long before they changed their daily routine to avoid his fascinated glances.

Sarah and I had both survived our first year of teaching. The appearance in a cup final of the year 7 team and winning the year 6 championship had endeared me to the head and made up for any shortcomings I may have had as a newly-qualified teacher.

Newcastle had retained Keegan's services and signed John Beresford from Portsmouth and two ex-Mackems in Paul Bracewell and Barry Venison.

The latter arrived with a disgraceful array of dodgy suits that put self-styled fashion gurus such as Mick Quinn to shame. To compliment the image he had long-flowing locks that ran onto his shoulders to complete the 80s new romantic image (in the style of Duran Duran).

Allowances were made for his appearance since he'd arrived from Liverpool with excellent pedigree (if you ignored the Sunderland connection).

Beresford complemented the 'nice hair' gang that was growing at Newcastle with well-manicured blond hair in the Mark Stimson mould. Stimson could have been so much more popular if he had only done a 'Clarkie' and had it all shaved off. In an instant he could have earned the admiration of the majority of Tyneside. They wouldn't have forgiven his own-goal at Oldham but they might have forgotten it sooner. The jury was out on whether Beresford would go the same way.

All had arrived for just over £1 million pounds and looked money well spent. Season ticket sales were heading towards an all-time high and far out-stripped Sunderland who had launched a television and newspaper campaign claiming that you could buy two of their season tickets for the cost of just one at Newcastle. The phrase "Get your season ticket now" was repeated endlessly and bore all the hallmarks of a desperate campaign.

Newcastle on the other hand kept on quietly filling up the

ground and at the first game of the season found out that I was the only member of our band who hadn't bought a ticket. As a result I was unable to stand in the paddocks which were rapidly becoming season ticket only.

It was back to the Gallowgate and my roots!

Saturday 22nd August 1992 — Derby County (a)

Sarah joined me on the drive up to the Midlands. The plan being that we would make an extremely long round trip to visit her family in Norwich.

It was a return to the ground Newcastle fans had tried to demolish. Predictably we weren't allowed near the nice shiny plastic seats they'd brought in to replace the ones that had been hurled onto the pitch. We were to be housed in a terraced pen to the side of the pitch.

Derby had been taken over by our fans and Sarah surprisingly didn't fancy being clamped amongst groups of sweaty beer-guzzling Geordies in a pub somewhere so we opted for chips near the ground and an early entrance into the stadium.

We walked through a park that led to the ground only to meet a pair of eight-foot high locked gates yards from the ground. Sarah suggested finding an alternative entrance and was sceptical when I suggested we could climb them easily.

Her patience at this point started to wear thin, especially when a helpful group of intoxicated fans proceeded to half-lift and half-throw her into my arms on the other side. Her embarrassment at being flung over was taken out on me and didn't share in my grateful thanks to the lads (who were only trying to help) as she stormed off.

Her mood calmed as we found a quiet spot, backs leaning against a barrier with a good view of the pitch.

Our quiet spot gradually filled and by kick off we were being shoved about in a tradition that I'd forgotten existed. Sarah failed to share my sentimentality as she protected herself from hands grabbing at any hand-hold after each surge.

An action-packed first half whizzed by as Sarah's continued attempts at avoiding being groped were proving a real struggle.

At half-time I promised I'd find a quieter spot as I ventured towards the toilets at the back of the stand.

My journey was halted by the sight of fans wading through growing pools of liquid to get to the toilets. Preferring to wait, I headed back to Sarah. As I glanced down at my feet I observed that the 'unidentified' liquid was gushing down the terrace. This discovery failed to humour her mood and as the second half started she was beginning to boil.

A quick goal from Gavin Peacock brought back happy memories of the scoreboard crushes in the Gallowgate. My partner's mood on the other hand had swung in the opposite direction. In celebration, an enormous bloke with tattoos covering both arms and neck (and beyond) flung himself (and his friends) on top of her.

His delight at the goal was cut short by Sarah's sharp elbow to his groin. He could only gasp and stare at the back of her closely-cropped head, trying to comprehend his current state of agony.

His bemused and pained expression gave way to anger as he launched himself towards her. Panic rushed through me. Should I jump in to protect her?

Thankfully, my mind was made up for me. She turned around seconds before he managed to reach her. Glancing at her female form he gasped "It's a lass!"

Seizing the opportunity, I dragged her to safety and as I did so Lee Clark cracked the second goal in. Mr Tattoo's pain was instantly forgotten and in the confusion, we slipped away to stand amongst the puddles which were being ignored by the majority of the delighted fans.

The rest of the game drifted away. I tried to look unperturbed but the prospect of a silent drive across the featureless and barren Norfolk Broads held little relish.

Standing in pools of the residue from flooded toilets; being jumped upon by all and sundry was all part of the terrace life for me. Although not particularly pleasant, it added the spice that other past-times couldn't compete with. Sarah had absolutely no desire to bond with anyone but me (and even that was decidedly unlikely in the stony silence of my car) and had enjoyed none of it.

She had been thrown over railings by well-meaning

individuals and tossed about on the stormy seas of celebration. She had stood in piss, was mistaken for a man and almost attacked. She was feeling a little tetchy. I thought it prudent not to plan any more football away days for her.

The terraces were a male domain in which women were welcome but would have to give as good as they got. They would have to be prepared to stand up for themselves but at the same time not rock the boat. They would have to accept the conditions, the lack of women's toilets and just be grateful to be allowed to join in.

We all enjoyed it so why couldn't they?

Was it the case that we had unwittingly become accustomed to the poor treatment and facilities, felt secure amongst the masses to ignore the crushes and discomfort?

I'd been standing on terraces for nearly ten years now and felt certain that this was only way to watch football but Sarah was used to being able to move about freely and losing that was not her idea of fun.

Saturday 5th September 1992 — Bristol Rovers (a)

Four victories out of four and 2nd in the league suited us just fine. The cobwebs of the previous years had been swept away. We had beaten title challengers Derby County and West Ham with crowds of nearly 30,000 cheering Newcastle on.

Today's visit to Bath's Twerton Park required only a short drive along the M4 from London and a quiet day out. Our stroll up the league had gone largely unnoticed by the press outside of the Northeast since every paper had focused hugely on the greedy boys of the Premiership.

Twerton Park was as far removed from the big league as you could get. Rovers were sharing the ground with Bath City after their ground had been condemned and its capacity was just over 7,000.

Low shed-like roofs hung over the seats at the side with small uncovered banks of terrace at each end which the neighbouring houses towered above. Any decent clearance from a defender or shot from an over-zealous forward resulted in a lost ball in some-one's garden. From time to time honest souls would throw balls back over which would land on the pitch, confusing the players.

Food was made under the main stand and carried on hot trays along the touch-line, without any risk of salmonella poisoning at all.

The announcer was a white-haired individual who allowed his locks to flow down his back and obviously fancied himself as Bath's answer to Peter Stringfellow. His remark about one of local rivals Bristol City's players Junior Bent "...and I bet he is" hadn't really gone down well and he lost his job.

The fans were always friendly and the cosiness of the ground always made you feel welcome. The match programme cover featured a painting of an eighteenth century (or thereabouts) pirate ship instead of the usual football-related photos that other clubs preferred.

This was to be our last visit to Twerton Park and as a thank-you Newcastle put up the worst performance all season and one man won the game for us —goalkeeper Tommy Wright.

With the score at 1-1 after Kevin Sheedy had equalised after an indirect free kick in the12th minute, Tommy spent the afternoon diving from one corner of his net to the other. Every shot ended up in a save. Newcastle hardly looked capable of stringing a few passes together, while Tommy seemed to be keeping for fun. He could have worn a red nose and juggled with one hand and still kept Rovers out.

With play firmly lodged in the Newcastle half, Rovers momentarily went to sleep and a quick break resulted in Liam O'Brien heading in a David Kelly cross. It was the ultimate kick in the teeth for our hosts and added to the protracted celebrations that followed.

Still Rovers didn't give up. The most miraculous save most had ever witnessed occurred six minutes from time. A Carl Saunders shot seemed to be deflected onto the post by Wright and landed at the feet of one of the Rovers' players. His shot was destined for the opposite corner before Tommy flung himself across the full length of the goal to push it out for a corner.

If Tommy Wright had been English he'd have been called Gordon Banks we concluded as we headed up the steep and winding road that led to the M4. We had witnessed the biggest smash-and-grab raid of the decade and for once we'd come out on top. The times they were a-changing.

Sunday 3rd October 1992 — Brentford (a)

The new 1st Division was turning out to be a bed of roses. Who needed the Premiership?

First day attendance in the new Premier League had been 25% down on the previous season and very few people had bought satellite dishes to watch the Sunday and Monday doses of top-flight footie on offer. Even pre-match entertainment such as the Red Devils, dancing girls and some free fireworks couldn't pull them in. The £340 million Sky had paid to broadcast football was not looking like a sound investment.

ITV had pounced gleefully on the chance to show 1st Division action and virtually every Sunday we were treated to a local match.

In London, I was able to watch the exploits of Charlton, Watford, Millwall, Brentford, Southend and West Ham. However, they rarely gripped my enthusiasm, somehow.

The juggernaut that had become Newcastle was thrilling the whole country. Keegan had won the 'Manager of the Month' award for September and we were three points clear at the top of table. A Newcastle programme had carried an article rubbishing the greedy Premier League because Newcastle weren't in it!

The club that had been in the doldrums a year earlier was now sprinting away with a 100% record (played 8 won 8). Today's visit to London represented the nation's first opportunity to witness the lads in action, live and free on ITV!

Prior to the game I'd woken up to Keegan answering questions on BBC's Saturday morning children's show — Going Live! The programme had been essential viewing for teachers anxious to know what the children in their classrooms were talking about when they should have been working.

Suddenly my class's patronising comments about my 'Norven' background changed to respect in one go. All thanks to Wor Kev's appearance!

Brentford were the closest league team to me now and a few of the children supported them, although the majority had never heard of them. The majority of football fans in school were Arsenal or Man United fans but sadly had never been inside any football ground. The Brentford fans had my respect for venturing outside of the norms of boyhood by supporting one of the lesser teams.

Predicted scores had been bandied about for weeks beforehand, loudly on the playground and using sign language and whispers in the corridors on the way to lessons and assemblies. I had to constantly remind myself that I wasn't one of the kids any more and resisted the temptation to shout any of my repertoire of Saturday afternoon ditties.

The maths lesson on the previous Friday had been spent working out the relevant probabilities for goal scorers and scores but I stopped short of taking bets, preferring to keep my job.

I'd convinced Sarah that we'd have a quiet day out that day, promising none of the Derby disasters would occur. We'd meet up with my mum and dad who were down for a few days, go for a scenic walk, quiet lunch and drink... then off to the match. What could be nicer?

Early that morning we visited nearby Kew Gardens. I appeared interested in the wide array of flora and fauna. Took part in articulate conversation with Sarah and my parents and never mentioning football once. Appreciative noises were made at the giant pagoda and various greenhouses and I generally acted the role of an intelligent and horticulturally sensitive man.

That was until I caught sight of...Andy. "What the ---- are you doin' here?"

Andy was one of Ian's mates and one of the group I had been standing with at away matches. Our joint shock at meeting each other in the horticultural world that was Kew Gardens resulted in all polite mannerisms dropping. An instant return of my match accent followed as we both questioned each other's presence in such middle-aged surroundings.

He claimed he was doing research for work, my excuse was non-existent. I was to all intents and purposes out for walk with my girlfriend and parents.

It was like being spotted by the school style police. All my credibility in the group would be gone. Visiting botanical gardens was not one of the past-times listed in the footie fans A to Z of acceptable activities. The only safe place to be was an alehouse.

Why hadn't I been in the pub since it opened, spreading Geordie cheer to the Brentford regulars? After all Brentford had a pub on each corner of the ground.

What was I doing here in leafy Kew? I should be breathing in stale cigarettes and beer not smelling exotic fragrances in a well-cultivated greenhouse. My deviance from the football norm would have led to raised eyebrows and bewildered stares. It wasn't something I would be discussing later with the others if I met up with them.

We promised not to divulge each other's presence to the others and carried on our separate ways but guilt had started to set in. It was twelve o'clock... the time for culture had gone, all thoughts were now on the match and pre-match tension (PMT) had taken hold. All I could think of was pub, lunch and match.

A hurried lunch was followed by nervous and impatient foot-tapping as I waited for the others to finish. I could hear the ground calling to me and bugger everything else. Parents who'd devoted their lives to me were swiftly and selfishly dispatched with a "Thanks for the lunch..." and Sarah was dragged away to the match.

The compact Griffin Park ground welcomed us in and the shallow terrace promised a quieter afternoon for Sarah. Avoiding contact with any large, tattooed men, I sensed that today would be a more sedate affair, more like Twerton Park than the Baseball Ground. At least we'd avoided climbing any fences.

A competent performance resulted in a two-goal lead and I had to feel sorry for my Brentford pals at school. A late strike brought them back into the game and added a bit of interest but they rarely looked like drawing level.

We had hardly broken sweat. It was a new feeling coming out of a ground after a professional display like that. I now knew how Paul must have felt after watching Arsenal stroll through an easy victory over lesser opposition, although on meeting one of my 'little friends' afterwards I took the opportunity for some non-teacher-like gloating, barely managing to stop myself from adding the odd four-letter word.

The presence of the boy from school had quickly brought me back into the real world. The relaxing evening after the match was deprived thanks to the presence of work the next day, probably the biggest drawback to Sunday games. Saturday was a precious day, the only truly relaxing day of the week. Football and Saturday were made for each other. Morrissey once wrote "Every day is like Sunday". He was nearly right, he obviously didn't like football!

Saturday 24th October 1992 — Grimsby (h)

It'd only meant to be a quick drink to celebrate a colleague's birthday but by the time I rolled out of a taxi at 1:30 am, still singing footie songs to the street. Controlling bodily parts proved to be a challenge.

A night spent in the company of the toilet bowl hardly endeared me to Sarah nor did the journey up to Newcastle that was slowed down by my stomach motions. The last place she wanted to be was St James' Park.

It was supposed to be a momentous day for me. The growing numbers of fans being locked out of home games had convinced me to buy a season ticket for the remaining 16 home matches. The ground was gradually filling up with season ticket holders and the only part of the ground left was the Gallowgate 'L' section; next the scoreboard with a floodlight stood in the middle of it.

Getting up at 7am to get up to Newcastle in time to apply for a ticket and then get into the ground was a forgettable rush. I handed in my application form and paid my £93 without any ceremony and tried to hurry Sarah along but she was in no mood to be rushed. Similarly in my state I hadn't the energy to hurry her.

Watching the first Newcastle victory at Roker Park in donkeys' years on Ceefax whilst constructing a newly-purchased set of MFI shelves had convinced me that I was in danger of missing the Newcastle boat. Tickets had been snapped up by the 18,500 season ticket holders before any of the public plebs had even had a sniff of them. I was determined not to miss out again.

I had no idea why I had convinced Sarah to come home with me but it was the last time she accompanied me to a match. For over three years she had put up with being dragged to matches, in all kinds of weather, watching all manner of appalling displays only to experience my bad moods first-hand. Why had she continued to do this?

There was only so much a girl could do. The alternative had usually been a day spent preparing lessons for the following week but now, even that seemed appealing.

An agonising ninety minutes ended in the unfortunately named Dobbin scoring in the 90th minute to compound the misery.

I wondered why I dragged her along so much? Most of the lads were only to keen to escape their 'other half' but not me.

One reason was guilt. I spent precious little time with her during the week thanks to schoolwork (hers, not mine) and then on Saturdays I'd bugger off for the weekend to get my weekly fix. A home match meant I'd be away all weekend.

I was still escaping from the drudgery of everyday life but now that included Sarah. I wanted her to join me so that she could be a part of the world I enjoyed so much but she was firmly rooted in the real world. The more I became engrossed in Newcastle the further I pushed myself away from her. Sarah became associated with the teaching world I longed to escape each night. Seeing the piles of work she brought home made me guilty. The easiest action to take was to avoid it by going out. It was a vicious circle that was strangling our relationship.

The big question was now, how many weekends would we have together? I was now a season ticket holder for a club that was 300 miles away. My rekindled love for United had resulted in a cooling of my relationship with Sarah.

She was the only reason to stay in London. How long could I carry on this dual life? I was going to have to choose — football or the girl.

Wednesday 4th November 1992 — Birmingham City (a)

The more football I went to, the more Sarah threw herself into her schoolwork. I hated spending hours each night preparing for the next day, preferring to try and do everything at school, an almost impossible task. I'd watched my mum do just that for years only to be pushed out when she wasn't needed any more. I was determined not to let that happen to me.

When not at football, I desperately searched for gigs to go to. The school football matches gave me an after-school escape from the prospect of marking sets of maths or English books but it meant reluctantly the time had to be spent at home.

A quick drive up the M40 to Birmingham with Yorkshire appealed more than a date with fractions or grammar. Midweek games broke the week into easier chunks and made it all the more manageable.

The wisdom of our journey was assured as Newcastle led 3-2 in a see-saw first half. The performance of teddy bear look-alike Kevin Brock in the injured Tommy Wright's oversized goalie's shirt inspired me for the rest of the week. Especially when receiving a kick on the head attempting a save. Physio Derek Wright's role as provider of smelling salts to the diminutive keeper kept him on the pitch, if not fully aware of actions.

Returning to a silent house at half past midnight instantly reminded me that school awaited only eight short hours away. If one thing could be counted on, it was that my year five class would act as the perfect wake-up tonic. The sobering effect of multiple ten-year-olds was unrivalled, but at least there was only two more days to last until the weekend.

Saturday 28th November 1992 — Cambridge United (h)

It was the best example of fan power I had ever seen. Leading 2-1, thanks to two `Ned' Kelly goals and Newcastle were awarded a penalty. Kelly wanted his hat-trick and so did the crowd. "Kelly, Kelly..." cried the crowd as Peacock, the regular penalty taker, and the two-goal hero argued over who was going to take it.

A clear November evening sky, lit by the floodlights, provided a dramatic backdrop to the bitter argument. Ned stepped up with the ball and the cheers faded into the frosty air as a hush descended.

Placing the ball on the spot, he walks away then turns. A quick glance at the keeper, followed by one at his chosen corner. The referee's whistle blows, quick charge then...blam! High to the keeper's right. 28,000 fans were proved right and feel justifiably chuffed.

A final goal for Peacock and the party heads down the hill. The first hat-trick of the year and a triumphant start to life as a season ticket holder.

Meeting up with the lads in Tynemouth, a party is promised and duly delivered. Inhibitions washed away, I re-live 'Ned's' penalty to a group of students. For the first time in my life, there seems to be a female competition for my attention.

After realising I can't keep impressing them if I talk about the match all night, the tack is changed. Like a team used to the long-ball game deciding to 'play it on the ground' when they are 3-0 up, showing an interest in them (as opposed to football and myself) works wonders. I am the caring jack the lad, much to the disappointment of mates who had struggled to hold their attention.

"Call me," I casually slot in after a quick kiss goodbye, unaware that jealous eyes are burning into me.

It is only the next morning that I remember Sarah, my live-in girlfriend.

I had been on such a high to be back home, without having to worry about upsetting anybody else that the evening and drink had carried me on. Living in Newcastle, matches in London had been my alternative life — one where I didn't give a toss about anything but having a good time, forgetting school and exams. Now, the roles were reversed, nights on the town called out to me.

Burg assures me she will call me. Sarah and I had been on the rocks for a while I convince myself. Luckily I hadn't done anything more than a peck on the cheek to feel guilty for but my forthcoming conversation with Sarah spins around my head as the train returns me to Kings Cross. Never having been in the situation where I have had to choose between two girls before, I'm clue-less. I know one thing, my days in London are numbered.

Back home, Sarah greets me with a bearhug and tells me she's missed me. What can I possibly say that doesn't make me out to be a complete git? I decide honesty is the best (and stupidest) policy.

In an attempt to test the water, I ask her how she feels about me. The word love is mentioned. This isn't going well.

I blurt out that I've met someone else. Cue the tears. Trying to make the situation a little better I add that nothing has happened but that my heart's not in our relationship or London any more. I'm homesick and it's all down to David Kelly's hat-trick.

I didn't mention Ned Kelly's part in our break up, I don't think it would have helped my cause. I had been flattered to have so much attention heaped on me this weekend and the excitement generated by a new romance had certainly been the icing on the cake. I didn't even know whether she would ring. If she didn't, it didn't matter because I had made my mind to move.

London had been good for a while but it lacked the familiarity and welcome of home. I'd missed going into shops and actually being able to talk to people I didn't know. There was an air of suspicion that dominated London. Not that everybody in Newcastle told you their innermost secrets, far from it, but if you made the effort to talk to people, they were less likely to ignore you.

The song "Home Newcastle" by Busker was an apt song and one that you could guarantee hearing once a season at St James' and its lines about London wine and the River Tyne kept on reverberating around my head.

The only problem now was how was I going to find a job? My own personal newsagent... dad... would be called into action for the jobs in Thursday night's Evening Chronicle.

Saturday 12th December 1992 — Notts County (a)

My student friend had rung up and I'd promised to see her next home match. Until I found a new place to live, life at the house would be difficult.

At least Sarah was still talking to me. I wouldn't have blamed her if she hadn't, after all we'd lived together twice and each time I'd got cold feet. We'd been together three and a half years nearly but the pressures of work (my dissatisfaction and her diligence) had pushed us apart.

As a means of escape, a trip to Nottingham was a welcome break. It beat joining the Christmas shoppers fighting over Thunderbirds toys (the Tracey Island models had become the Christmas present and parents queuing overnight to get one wasn't uncommon).

Yorkshire and Carl joined me on the trip to a Notts County ground that had seen a lot of change. It was my first visit there and I was instantly over-awed. Black and grey seats and gold steps stretched all the way around the ground. The rows of empty seats were the modern version of the crumbling terraces I'd experienced in the past and the roofed stands would keep the atmosphere in the ground. The corner gaps between the stands allowed clear views of the city and the nearby City ground on the banks of the Trent to remind you that the rest of civilisation carried on.

Here was a club that had looked so impressive both on and off the field as they reached the top flight two seasons ago, spent millions preparing their ground for the arrival of the Premiership only to be relegated before its riches arrived.

As I tucked into arguably the best pie I'd ever tasted at a football ground I had to feel sorry for them. They languished third from bottom with facilities (including the pies) like these and although the ground probably held 20,000+ supporters they had struggled to get half that. The Kop Stand behind the goal however was teaming with Newcastle fans and a fantastic atmosphere built up in our end at least.

The first half passed without incident. This gave Carl and me the chance to enthuse about the County pies experience. Our spirits were unusually high, despite a largely uneventful first half, as we breathed in an atmosphere that had a sweet taste to it. Another deep breath confirmed there was definitely an unusual but pleasant aroma in the air, above the regular smells of pies, burgers and cigarettes.

It was then that our view dropped down to the row directly below us where a Newcastle fan was leaning back as if on some Jamaican deck-chair smoking one of the largest cigarettes I'd seen.

In our hunched positions, with concentration fully employed on the match we had failed to identify the illegal fumes that drifted straight up our noses. The man in front was completely stoned but his joint (it hadn't taken a rocket scientist to work that one out) had carried on smoking away, brightening up the match no end.

Fans on his row clambered over him, in search of pies, toilets or both, but he didn't register a thing. The Geordie choir that celebrated Sheedy's tap-in two minutes after the interval followed by Peacock's clincher four minutes from time couldn't distract him from his smoky haze.

The uplifting smog of the first half had combined with the two goals to put Carl and me in the best possible mood. Our friend had long since collapsed onto the floor as we inspired those fans around us with our determination to embarrass ourselves with two-man Mexican waves and a medley of

Newcastle songs past and present.

As our two-man Conga at the final whistle wound its way down the stairs we finally returned to the real world. Once onto the streets outside, we contented ourselves with joining in with the chants of new favourite "E-I-E-1-E-1-O-up the Football League we go...when we get promotion, this is what we'll sing...we're the Geordies, super Geordies...Keegan is our king" (to the tune of Knees Up Mother Brown).

How much our afternoon's enjoyment had been down to the 'atmosphere' that had consumed us was anybody's guess but the party feeling that had consumed me the previous week against Cambridge had once again become the highlight of a difficult week. Newcastle was the light at the end of the tunnel. I was still public enemy number among the females back in Acton, but that was the furthest thing from my mind as I swaggered back to the car.

Saturday 11th January 1993 — Bristol City (a)

In recognition of devotion to Newcastle, people were invited to nominate someone to become Magpie of the Month. Head-teachers who talked incessantly about Newcastle in assemblies received a special black blazer and their photo in the programme. There were articles galore from the board thanking Newcastle fans for their commitment and telling them how wonderful they were. It looked like the times were changing and at last we had a board to trust.

Standing on the open terraced away end at Ashton Gate I didn't much feel like a devoted fan. I felt lousy. I thought it was just a sore throat, but despite two packets of Lockets I still couldn't sing Keegan Wonderland. My voice disappeared before I could utter "There's only one..."

Even the annual ritual chanting of "You fat bastard" at one of the portly members of the Bristol City supporters failed to inspire. His attendance at previous Ashton Gate fixtures had greatly enhanced the verbal competitions between our respective sets of fans. Perhaps he'd even been the inspiration behind the song "Who ate all the pies..."

Sitting high in the seats away to our left he had been the guiding figure for his peers, who sat unobtrusively about him.

Today was definitely my off-day.

Most of my life revolved around using my voice. If I wasn't verbally encouraging and discouraging children, I was shouting at the match. I wasn't even bothered when Kelly and Scott gave us a win after being 1-0 down, which didn't seem right.

I was silent on the way back but I had no idea why I felt so lousy. By Monday I was squeaking like a mouse with a fondness for sharp objects and a trip to the doctors revealed I had tonsillitis and was assigned a week off school.

This was all well and good, a trip back to Newcastle along with a week watching Anne and Nick or the ITV lot didn't seem so bad and I'd also get sympathy visits from Alison (my student friend) who I'd got on really well with over the Christmas holiday. Would I be fit for next Saturday's match?

Being a teacher, you could describe it as a professional injury — no voice meant no teaching. But, it wasn't an injury I could be proud of. People had sympathy for footballers who had damaged ligaments or hamstrings or even the dubious groin injury (which always made you wonder if they were over-doing their social-life a bit too much) but tonsillitis; just a bad sore throat.

As it was I had tonsils the size of golf balls but now they were like two large red tennis ball knocking about at the back of my throat. I did indeed get a great deal of long-range sympathy from Alison. Could I mention my illness to the lads next Saturday?

Not a bit of it, as far as they were concerned, a couple of throat sweets and I was right as rain, able to drink me usual fifteen pints before eating a couple of vindaloos.

If I'd had a decent injury like a broken leg or arm, then I could have raised a passing interest but my affliction was as macho as having a cold. I'd not heard anyone complaining before a match about 'having a sniffle' so I decided that the best thing to do was keep quiet about it.

Anyway, only lasses complained about being ill — being a football fan meant being a man. The ultimate injury to brag about would be a groin strain but there wasn't any chance of that for me.

Saturday 20th March 1993 — Notts County (h)

The split between Sarah and I had been completed. We'd settled our differences when I moved out of the house in Acton to move to a shared house near school, a sad end after nearly four years together.

At least the Newcastle board was still being complimentary about everyone. A picture in a previous programme featured a fan who'd hitch-hiked to Italy for an Anglo-Italian Cup game only to be robbed in France. Douglas Hall, Freddie Shepherd and Fletcher offered him a lift home on the club-chartered plane with the team.

He wasn't offered a black blazer as Magpie of the Month (probably because of his long hair and tattoos) but plenty of fans were — just one big happy family!

The team was fifteen points clear at the top of the 1st Division with only 11 games to go.

Keegan was allowed to do what nobody ever dreamed a Newcastle manager would be allowed to do, and that was spend a massive £1,750,000 pounds on Bristol City striker Andy Cole. Not only that... but £700,000 was spent on Scott Sellars from Leeds and £450,000 on Mark Robinson from Barnsley.

Not since being relegated in 1989 had so much been spent and most of that had come from the sale of Paul Gascoigne to Spurs. We'd not sold anybody but the board had finally come up with the cash.

It was a bolt out of the blue and finally confirmed the belief that Newcastle was a sleeping giant about to wake up. Supporters had maintained that if there was a decent team to watch the ground would be packed out each game and now it was going to be put to the test.

Andy Cole became our most expensive player by a long streak and what's more he was black. Newcastle had never had a black player who had totally won over the fans until now. Howard Gayle's stay had been short, Tony Cunningham had grafted and been respected but had never really won everyone over while Franz Carr had had his moments but was never consistent enough to win over the bigots.

I felt certain that Cole would finally silence the minority of fans who went on about `darkies' and made monkey noises whenever black players were on the field.

Living in London had opened my eyes to racism and I knew that though it had nearly been stamped out, Newcastle fans were an easy target for National Front propaganda because no black players had totally endeared themselves to them.

Alison came too. She'd attended quite a few matches already that season and surprisingly loved every minute of it. There was no coaxing, she was desperate to go and I wasn't going to argue with that.

Andy Cole was given the number eight shirt and the crowd was willing him to score. He looked promising in the first half but like the rest of the team had nothing to show except a solitary Rob Lee goal.

In the second half it all changed. Two goals in nine minutes from 'Ned' set the stage for Cole's finale. A pass from Ned presented Cole with seemingly nothing on but he controlled the ball, swivelled and drilled the ball into the net. A St James' carnival commenced as the new boy became the golden boy.

Most were pleased to welcome such a great player to the club but I thought back to my friend Hassan who had stood listening to the racist abuse being handed out to Wimbledon players and I knew that Andy Cole was going to change all that.

The carnival carried until the Sunday as the Central Station was filled with fans who had stayed the weekend and were now about to return South. Cole was the buzz-word on everybody's lips.

I had felt ashamed at times about being a Newcastle fan due to the treatment they had historically handed out to black opposition players but for once I was proud of the reception handed out.

I almost felt that everybody else shared my view on the racist fans, now we could point at Andy Cole and say that that black player is giving his all for us and all Newcastle fans should support him for it. If we abused other blacks, we are abusing him.

As I waited for my take-away back in Kings Cross, I wanted to shake the hand of the nearest black man and tell him that Newcastle was no longer a racist club, thanks to one moment of genius. The predicted cool look and possible threats of violence persuaded me otherwise.

Saturday 17th April — Millwall (a)

Charlotte was the kind of girl male football fans dreamed of but was extremely wary of. A shirt-wearing season ticket holder in the liveliest section of St James' seats, she drank like the proverbial fish and had turned swearing into an art-form.

Her forthright feminist views and sharp tongue meant conversations with her had to carefully avoid any hint of sexism or risk the inevitable verbal and physically battering.

Her sense of humour made her a popular member of Ian's growing group. I had met her a few times and managed to successfully avoid an ear-bashing so far.

She was present along with a full complement at the specified meeting pub before the game. London games always meant a meet in the same pub, just off Covent Garden tube station.

The combination of a few pints and a balmy spring day lulled us into a false sense of security. Sweat-shirts and jackets were abandoned in favour of black and white shirts.

Visits to the East London clubs of Millwall and West Ham usually necessitated the covering of visible colours. Bearing in mind historical altercations between ourselves and the aforementioned clubs, it was viewed as common sense rather than a cowardly act of club betrayal.

On packed tube trains, it would have been easy for a would-be attacker to do their worst and disappear before you could react, whether that be to collapse on the floor thanks to a gaping stab wound or try to retaliate.

Today was a complete contrast. The care-free attitude was helped by the presence of train-loads of similarly-attired fans. There wasn't a Millwall shirt in sight as we stepped onto the platform at a crumbling New Cross Gate station.

Relaxed supporters wandered towards the ground as if on a Sunday afternoon trip to the local park. The cracked and crumbling masonry on the terraced houses either side of us combined with the rotting woodwork to suggest this wasn't exactly one of the most desirable districts of London.

However, the sun was shining and we were still top of the league (if only two points ahead of 2nd placed Portsmouth) what could possibly happens to us?

The complete absence of police (or anybody else for that matter) had helped conjure up the ideal football world that we now lived in. It was a world where violence didn't exist, Geordies were welcomed by everybody (except Mackems). All thanks to the entertaining brand of football that Keegan's boys excelled at.

We had visited usual trouble-spots in large numbers and been welcomed as peaceful fans. All one happy footballing family!

Except Millwall, as we soon found out. Our ramble down quiet suburban terraces came to an end as our ranks met up with those of the home fans pouring down from the pubs on Old Kent Road.

Our following at previous Millwall games had numbered about 1,000 but today, five thousand Newcastle fans were set to converge on the least friendly ground in the Division. Many hadn't the slightest inkling how unpleasant the afternoon could get and those who had were lulled into a false sense of security.

As we began to merge with the main body of fans, the temperature seemed to drop, just as did when a particularly dark storm cloud passed overhead. Striped shirts could conspicuously be seen trying unsuccessfully to wade across the river of blue.

Our songs about Keegan being our king were dwarfed by the shouts of "We are Millwall, no-one likes us". Someone had undoubtedly stepped on my grave because shivers shot through me. Memories of caged animals clambering up twenty-foot partitions only five years earlier appeared vividly in my now over-active mind.

My sweatshirt was put on as a precautionary measure as I tried to cross the waters. Emerging intact on the other side, I was quick to spot the funnelling fences for the away end and could breathe again. Charlotte and Carl could not.

Unaware of any animosity towards them, they had continued to proudly display their colours and had also successfully reached the far side of the river. Unfortunately, they were ten yards past the away entrance with the weight of the crowd carrying them towards the home end.

Shoving their way back had not proved the wisest option, particularly when Carl had tried to barge his way past the type of immovable object you associate with GBH outside of a dodgy night-club. The object promptly grabbed Carl and was about to exact his own special brand of retribution when he found himself shoved back into the growing mob and told in no uncertain terms to "Leave him!"

In a scene similar to Sarah's pained aggressor at Derby, it took a similar amount of time for realisation to dawn. His anger turned to embarrassment at being caught off-balance by a woman but like a shark sensing a struggling swimmer he charged after the duo, who had taken the opportunity to leap headlong for the safety of the fence.

In the process, they had upset more (by now off-balance and annoyed) fans who joined in the Keystone Cops-like chase. Carl had only his backside to clear over the barrier as the first hands grabbed him. With help, he was pulled to safety but the whole incident had upset the apple cart.

The two young policemen who had quietly minded their own business were subjected to a barrage of coins, masonry, bits of trees and anything else handy. A scene of a quiet stroll had suddenly been turned into a battle zone. Fans pushed past us with blood streaming from their heads while others poured over the fences at every available spot, escaping the rivers of hands attempting to drag them back.

Safety was the dirt path that lead along a man-made valley grassy verge on one side and ten-foot corrugated wall on the other. The surreal nature of the previous ten minutes had us lost for words. One minute... the birdsong in the empty street; the next open warfare.

We'd left the two policemen frantically calling for assistance, glad that we didn't get paid to come to football. That would severely ruin the enjoyment of it all.

The atmosphere inside the ground was once again a complete contrast to the chaos outside. Fans chatted as they leaned against yellow barriers and the civilised process of trading chanted abuse carried on blissfully unaffected by the war zone outside.

The warm day took the harsh edge off the stadium's atmosphere and Newcastle's total occupation of the Ilderton Road End helped the 'homely' feeling. It was hard to imagine the dark and brooding ground we'd visited on November 5th 1989, the splashes of yellow positively gleamed in the sunlight.

Both sets of fans contributed to an electric atmosphere as the game kicked off but the Millwall fans had more to shout about as their team tore into Newcastle. Their position in seventh had given them hopes of a play-off place and the lads were definitely struggling to contain the likes of Malcolm Allen and Jamie Moralee.

It was no surprise when they took the lead. A flukey bounce off Paul Bracewell sent a right-wing cross over Pavel's head in goal. In the Millwall goal, the Yank with the appalling combination of short hair at the side and long at the back, Kasey Keller was having a field day. This combined with Cole's catalogue of missed chances to give the impression that today was not going to be our day.

The fight-back in the second half made this game one of the matches of the season. The element of tension that makes good matches into classics was evident in huge proportions.

Games that had been dull for an hour suddenly became classics if the need to win inspired a team to recover from a one or two-goal deficit to snatch victory. Roy of the Rovers managed it every week but if you were lucky it happened once or twice a season. The rarity of such comebacks made them all the sweeter when they did come. The more pressure you'd had before the all-important breakthrough also served to sweeten the memories.

Today was one of the best. With twenty-five minutes left we were facing the potential loss of top spot. The chances had come and gone. Patience was being lost and tempers were beginning to flare.

Cole, twisting his way through a crowded penalty area bobbled the ball across to Clark who drilled it in. My view of the back of the net was obscured by the security fence making me reliant upon the fans behind the goal to tell me whether the ball I had lost sight of had entered the net or not.

I didn't have long to wait as their reaction was instant. Just eight minutes later Cole again bobbled into the penalty. His toe-poke was headed in the right direction when once again, I lost sight of it. The reaction of everybody else left me in no doubt as to its final resting place.

Millwall's bombardment of the Newcastle defence was resisted and at the final whistle we celebrated the most important victory of the season, complete with balancing acts on the terrace barriers but lacking any Millwall backlash.

Maybe the presence of half of South London's constabulary helped dissuade any would-be attackers but as we strolled back up the still quiet and crumbling terraced street, our mood before the storm returned.

Squeezing into the waiting tube trains on the empty expansive platforms of New Cross Station we bid our final farewell to the Den and hopefully to Millwall. What once must have been a bustling and grand Victorian commuter station had now been left, like every other part of New Cross we'd witnessed on our visits, to fall apart. Streets that had once been proudly kept were now an eyesore, one that Millwall's move to a new ground would be spared any future visiting fans.

A night of drunken celebration in Central London followed and when it was time to return back to my room in Greenford, I remembered that my landlord was holding a party. 'A quiet gathering' was how he'd described it, but as I rounded the corner into my road, the sounds of laughter and music greeted me. He had said I was welcome to join in, but his guests would be 'a bit old'.

Approaching the front gate, the silhouettes dancing behind the curtains were forming bizarre shapes — obviously people, but what were they doing? Opening the front door, I was greeted by a rather large topless 40 year-old with a drink in each hand. "Oooh, it's a youngster..." she cackled as she drew nearer.

Turning tail, I ran out, just catching sight of my landlord dressed as a German army officer and brandishing a whip.

Wandering the streets of Greenford, there were no pubs open, clubs or cinemas to go to, my mind was processing the party.

Sunday 25th April 1993 — Sunderland (h)

Promotion was within touching distance and Newcastle fans were revelling in this new era of fan/board of director togetherness. The release of a new strip, this time made by Asics gave the fans the perfect opportunity to demonstrate their further commitment to the club.

Everybody knew that the shirts represented a fantastic mark-up for the club but if it brought more quality players to the club then the £30 would have been well spent.

Newcastle's dazzling on-field performances had been described by Boro manager Lennie Lawrence as a Juggernaut but we were about to be exposed to their out of control marketing department.

The ground looked like it was going to be filled with season ticket holders next season and the demand for new strips was phenomenal. However, this wasn't enough. In one fell swoop, the board went from saints to sinners.

The introduction of a new club called "The Platinum Club" started the rot. For a marvellous "one-off" payment of £3,000 you were allowed one of 1800 seats in the Milburn stand next to the directors' box. Members would guaranteed their seat for 99 years, have their own bar, with television (colour ones at that!) and the all-important fast food facilities. Members' burgers would contain real lettuce and tomatoes in them.

It was like taking candy off a baby. Nobody wanted to miss out on being a major force in the Premiership. The way the ground was filling up, missing the last boat meant you would be unable to see the team in the flesh.

Worries about next season put aside, the rain that had fallen most of the weekend had left the pitch looking like a swamp. The puddles scattered about the pitch didn't make the game's completion likely. You wouldn't have been surprised if a couple of ducks had landed in them and waited to be provided with bread.

The 30,000 capacity crowd that stared down upon a watery pitch included Alison for the last time. Long-distance relationships never work is the adage everyone offers you when you set out on one and it was beginning to hold true in this case.

The cost in phone cards had become phenomenal and once the early excitement has subsided, the necessity to get on well every time you met created an unreal existence. Barely daring to speak to each other, the grey skies mirrored our moods.

The match may as well have been water polo as players sent spray shooting up with every kick. The players foolishly failed to use water wings, worried about their appearance presumably. Attempts to kick the ball resulted in a deluge for anybody standing by and the number of times players missed the ball as it swam on top of a pool of water made the match a lottery at times.

With eleven minutes gone, one of the new boys was about to be included in a role of honour. A free-kick from Scott "Salty" Sellars curled around the Sunderland wall and as it thumped against the post the thud was heard all over Tyneside as ITV beamed the game across the North East. The resulting spin along the line wasn't quite so audible but the crowd's reaction was instant and vociferous.

Sunderland descent towards the relegation zone had been given a massive help with our first double over them since 1956 in the days of Jackie Milburn. Their manager Terry Butcher had been touted by them as a winner but fallen a long way short despite his England pedigree as a player.

The gulf between the two clubs was massive, it was a far cry from the preseason hype of two tickets for the price of one. In the final reckoning which fans had made the better investment? I don't think there was any argument on that one!

Sunday 9th May 1993 - Leicester City (h)

The campaign started by those fans facing eviction from seats they'd sat in for years fizzled out as the rest of us were too concerned about the team. After all, why should we bother about them, their relocation behind the goal was the view we'd had for years (give or take brief spells in the paddocks), It wasn't as if they'd been kicked out of the ground.

The happy recipients of membership to the Platinum Club were pictured in the match programme wielding an enormous check for nearly £150,000. Although this money was for 44 members of a previously unheard-of Jesmond Racing Club, the number of suits, ties and 'smart blazers' was worrying.

Were these the sort of people who'd scream their lungs out for the team or were they going to be contented sitting back in their padded chairs with built-in ash tray smoking cigars and discussing the 'peasants' sat below them?

For the past few years, the business world had locked itself away in the executive boxes, looking like goldfish but completely separate from the hoi-poloi. But was the Platinum Club going to be filled with 'suits', interested enough to brave the element so that they could feel part of the crowd?

Certainly the fans who'd found themselves deposited in the under-construction Leazes Stand felt that these people would be better off tucked away in their little boxes as objects of fun for the rabble. The dispossessed Milburners' fight had been ignored by the rest, an action we would live to regret. However, today's promotion party was for all of us. Next season was another world away.

A win at Grimsby had confirmed promotion and the title. A goal apiece from our new deadly duo of Kelly and Cole had done the trick. Andy Cole had become the fans' favourite with 9 goals in 10 appearances, an unheard of tally for a present day Newcastle forward. The song-writers had been working overtime to come up with the rhyming ditty "Andy Cole, when he gets the ball he scores a goal, Andy, Andy Cole"

Ahead of us stood the rapidly-rising Leazes Stand, complete with temporary stage upon which aged Northeast 'rockers' Lindisfarne played and were mostly ignored.

The 1st Division Championship trophy was presented by an uncomfortable-looking ex-Chairman Gordon McKeag. We knew that we had reached the big time because Alan Robson the ginger-headed Metro Radio DJ was standing in the middle of the pitch microphone in hand.

His constant shouts of "Make some noise" became nauseous after a while, as did his choice of a pink blazer to go with his otherwise black outfit. Despite his best efforts the carnival carried on as cries of Champions (or its more fashionable Italian translation) rang from every corner of every stand.

This was accompanied by the new favourite ditty "Terry Butcher on the dole" (to the tune of the Scout tune Gingangooly). Not wanting to ignore our nearest and dearest who had avoided relegation at Notts County. Their fans had mirrored the pitch invasion that accompanied Newcastle's clinching winning at Grimsby. Smugly we noted their achievement failed to compare.

Sales of the new shirts had obviously gone well as every corner displayed both the striped home shirt and the new blue away strip. Anxious not to miss out on the great event, I had mail ordered both shirts and they had duly arrived the Wednesday before.

The day they'd been due, I'd raced home at lunch-time like an excited schoolboy to see if they'd arrived and to my delight they had. I proceeded to wear the home shirt to afternoon school, much to my head's disbelief. "...and this man's a teacher!" he muttered. Of course, the children thought I was the ultimate in cool —having a shirt on the day of its release.

It was also a dream come true for me. For years I had waited to see the sponsors logo fuzzy-felted onto a Newcastle shirt and it was like Jimmy Saville had waved his magic wand! Not only did the away shirt carry the felted words "McEwans Lager" (which I couldn't stand drinking) but the home shirt carried the Blue Star of Newcastle Breweries, the symbol of everything Tyneside!

Everywhere you looked new shirts sprang out at you. There were lads standing on barriers leading the choirs wearing them, men in the seats, even women proudly wearing their colours. Asics and the club must have made a killing.

The Leazes end that was to be standing for the last time had been invaded by Leicester fans and for the last time we goaded them with "Sing in the Leazes". They duly obliged and were instantly drowned out. The previous season's game was a dim and distant memory and there wasn't a hint of animosity from either set of fans.

We were to be joined in the top league by West Ham who had finished above Portsmouth thanks to having scored one more goal than the South coast outfit.

It didn't take the team long to enter into the festivities. A control and shot by Ned Kelly after five minutes was saved by ex-Boro keeper Kevin Poole only for Andy Cole to follow it up. Just eight minutes later, a back-heel by Cole put through Robert Lee to score. Leicester had only come to make up the numbers. Next it was Ned Kelly's turn, first with a header then with a crisp drive to add to the fun with only 27 minutes gone. Another for Cole followed by Kelly's hat-trick made this the biggest half-time lead since 1946 when United beat Newport 13-0.

All through the half-time we sang 'the Andy Cole song' but it wasn't until the 67th minute that he completed his hat-trick and the Gallowgate, that had begun to wane, responded vigorously to the goal. Kelly had scored the first hat-trick but Cole was the crowd's favourite.

Finishing the season on 96 points was the best-ever points total of a Newcastle team. The crowd cheered the team for a further half-hour before I had to leave to catch my train to London. Few were leaving as the party promised to go on and on.

I felt like a party pooper as I descended the Gallowgate steps for the last time. The grassy bank to either side of me and its uncovered toilets (well they were just walls really) would be knocked down once the Leazes End was finished.

I was saying goodbye to an old friend who had served me well. It would still be around for a while, but I knew our time together was over, the end of an era. My newly-acquired status as a season ticket holder had to continue in the soon-to-be built Leazes Stand, since half way through next season the Gallowgate would become a building site.

Soon, terraces at St James' promised to become a thing of the past. Although models of the new ground looked impressive, what would it be like? Where would the atmosphere come from? What would happen to the scoreboard...and the corner for that matter?

The party behind me roared on. I stood on the corner of the Gallowgate bus station and took one last look at a sight that had thrilled me from the moment I laid eyes on it. The towering East and West stands were from a completely different era to the two terraces, they were the shape of the things to come.

Glancing at my watch I forced myself to turn away and hurry towards the Central Station — at least they won't try and rebuild that I consoled myself with.

I had lost a piece of me that day, the euphoria of the performance had eased the pain but it was a sombre and anti-climactic journey back to the smoke as past memories filled my head. My first experiences of Gallowgate life, Darren the blond lad who died, Goddard's goal against Manchester United to equal Len White's record appeared in my head. I pictured Waddle, Beardsley, Gazza, even Mirandinha with his black gloves on (the jessie); the joy and frustration they brought with them, the endless rivalry between the corner and scoreboard, inane it may have been but always entertaining.

Arriving back home I missed last orders by a matter of seconds, the barman looking perplexed when I told my team had just won the title. I was in a world that didn't even know Tyneside existed, a world I had to escape. Nothing was doing on the job front but I'd have to pull out the stops and re-double my efforts.

By the time the 93-94 season kicked off, I was determined to have a Tyneside job, after all there was nothing to keep me here anymore.

Converting the enemy

Of **all** the places to end up, Sunderland had to be the last on my list. Durham, South Tyneside, Gateshead, North Tyneside and Newcastle, all areas of Newcastle support, proved dead ends which left an interview at a school behind enemy lines my best option.

I'd hardly enthused when I received the letter asking me to attend an interview, coming as it did twenty hours after failing hopelessly on South Tyneside. They'd hardly hire a Mag to teach their children and run their football team was my reasoning.

Maybe they hoped some of Keegan's glory would have rubbed off on me because out of three entrants I was given the nod.

I had my own pedigree by now. Two Championships won, and three cup finals reached in two short years in London, returns that Arsenal's George Graham or Man United's Alex Ferguson would have been proud of.

Visiting the school, I got the impression that there was some bad feeling in the camp. One female member of staff was keen to give potential newcomers more than one evil eye. This continued on subsequent visits to the school, my every word and step being closely scrutinised.

It turned out she had applied for the job but my pedigree had won through. I was like flash Ron Atkinson, breezing into a new club to find the caretaker manager none too chuffed at not being giving the job.

Her transfer to a Newcastle school avoided any possible run-ins. I could drive up from Tynemouth in my flash "C-reg" Ford Fiesta Popular smoking my impressively large cigars without envious eyes burning into me.

Once installed, I soon found out that there was a difference between the Ealing Schools U11 League — Northolt Division and the Sunderland Primary Schools U11 League. My glory days were over. Like a manager of a successful 1st Division Side I was to find life in the Premiership a lot tougher.

Saturday 14th August 1993 — Tottenham (h)

First impressions of a Premiership ground were breath-taking. Everyone who took their seats in the newly-completed Leazes stand had a view of the ground that had been denied ever since the old Leazes, rickety roof and all had been demolished.

We were now joined in one corner to the East Stand and as a result a giant flag that had been introduced to us at the Leicester party match now passed over us, carried by expectant grabbing hands.

The Gallowgate, still in use, was now the smallest stand in the ground, dwarfed by the seemingly endless rows of seats that stretched behind us. The whole ground had a new character, the use of grey seats on grey concrete was unimaginative but, by the time kick off arrived, the noise made up for them.

Blue and black-and-white-shirted fans everywhere lifted their hands above their heads to applaud the teams as the annoying Alan Robson screamed at us to make some noise. The only effect this had was to silence any impartial voices, thankfully his enthusiasm died away when the match started.

Yorkshire, Ian, Kew Gardens Andy and I (among others) had all applied for seats together and, after complaining about our allocation of paddock terrace tickets, were allocated nearly a whole row of seats in the middle of the Leazes.

We found ourselves surrounded by those exiled from the Milburn Stand, thanks to the creation of the Platinum Club (which looked surprisingly full prior to kick off). Their reluctance to join in any chants was countered by our enthusiasm. It was disappointing to note that requests from the rest of the ground to "Sing in the Leazes" (or as we were later nicknamed — the cheap seats) were met with a muted hush. Still, it was early days.

There were also wry smiles at the sweets handed around amongst their numbers before and during the game, not quite flasks yet but it was only mid-August.

The match itself was forgettable. The team differed greatly from the one that had won promotion. Out of the door went two of the best-loved strikers at the club: 'Ned' Kelly went to Wolves for £750,000 and Gavin Peacock made the long journey to Chelsea for £1,250,000. In their place came the Greek Nicky Papavasilou (from Olympiakos for a meagre £120,000), Alex Mathie (a promising youngster signed from Morton for £250,000), Malcolm Allen, (signed from Millwall for £300,000) and the return of a prodigal son. Peter Beardsley returning to the North East for £1,500,000 from Everton had found himself on the wrong end of one of Neil Ruddock's elbows in a so-called friendly match at Anfield. He was expected to be out for months rather than weeks.

Without Pedro, Newcastle found chances hard to come by. Sheringham scored the only goal at the Gallowgate End to set their fans in what had been "the corner" dancing away. The other forgettable fact about the match was the Spurs manager — Ossie Ardiles, back to haunt us on our big day, typical! It was just the result we should have expected.

A rainy Saturday in September — Valley Road v South Hylton

I'd avoided playing games on a Saturday morning when I taught in London and it was a rude awakening for me. The weekend was sacred — and I'd intended to keep it that way but pressure to play fixtures soon saw to that.

It was my first game and since the other school's teacher didn't fancy being ref, I foolishly obliged. A large home crowd had gathered and I was the object of abuse right from the off... thanks to my choice of Newcastle promotion season anorak.

Two dubious looking lads offered to run the line for me and I naively accepted. It soon became apparent that they weren't entirely unbiased when one ignored every offside and the other was flag happy. My decision to ignore them didn't go down well with the locals.

The fact that I dared wear the enemy's colours, (Sunderland being the only place in the country that didn't enjoy Keegan's attacking football) hardly won me many friends.

My new school (South Hylton) gave me the perfect start by roaring into a two-goal lead. A streak of a lad called Eddie Dodds was pulling all the strings, the midfield supremo in the Gascoigne mould.

It was he who stepped up to take a penalty after one of the home team's defenders had instinctively caught the ball on its way to the net. Of course the decision was met with derision — "You're blind ref," came the call. I had berated referees at grounds up and down the country, only now I found out what it was like to be on the receiving end. The temptation was to respond with a coolly flicked "V" sign but only a wry smile gave my thoughts away.

My smugness disappeared as Eddie's kick sailed over the bar and with it his confidence. Valley Road swarmed forward, pulling one back before half time to send the crowd wild.

I never seemed to know what to say at half-time apart from

"keep it up lads". Not one to throw around the tea cups, preferring to keep my job, there wasn't a lot to do except gee them up. The crowd wasn't what I'd been used to. In Ealing you were lucky if two people wandered past. Here, half of the school had arrived and every bit of the touch-line was packed.

A cluster of lads behind the goal showed disbelief whenever their own diverted efforts were disallowed. Shots that were drifting wide miraculously swerved off their shoes into the goal; more fuel to the shouts of "dodgy ref'

My lads tired and eventually the crowd spurred the home side to a 3-2 victory. There were the traditional "Three cheers" then we trooped off. We'll play worse than that and win I consoled them with.

It had been a rude awakening, but I'd lost my first ever Horsenden school match 3-1 and followed it with great things. There was hope!

Monday 15th September 1993 — Sheff Wed (h)

After losing the first two games (the second away to Coventry 1-2), the lads confounded the critics by drawing at Old Trafford 1-1. A win and two draws later we were still flattering to deceive in the lower half of the table.

Such was the media interest in Newcastle, Sky decided to broadcast from St James' for the second time that season. The annoying effect of this was a blank Saturday without a game (the whole point of having weekends I had assumed) and a Monday night fixture.

Football and Saturdays had been inextricably linked for nearly a century. A whole culture had formed itself around this male-dominated tradition. Saturday was the ideal day to relax in the company of your peers, leaving the Sunday to entertain lady-friends or family. Work was another day away, which meant drunken excesses would not be punished by a working hangover. You could ease yourself back into the real world, wallowing in your own self-pity without a boss breathing down your neck (or 30 screaming ten-year-olds) or having to do little more than slouch in a comfy armchair with your legs resting on the nearest pet.

When television came along and with it Match of the Day, it

provided the non-drinking (and drinking) football fraternity with the perfect way to round the day off, safe in the knowledge that a day of relaxation lay ahead of you to unwind from the stresses of modern-day football.

ITV's introduction of a Sunday highlights programme unknowingly started the shift away from Saturday footie when the odd game was beamed live a day late. If fans then had known that Brian Moore's jovial smile, shiny head and endearing smile would lead to the Sunday/Monday Sky weekends then they might have turned off in their droves. But they didn't!

Admittedly, night matches had their own magic, the glare of the floodlights, sight of steam wafting from busy burger vans and the view across the city sky-line.

Unfortunately, I'd spent all day trying to educate Wearsiders, without my weekend fix of football, followed by a Saturday night tipple at my local hostelry. My nerves were shot, I was impatient and irritable — snapping at the slightest misdemeanour. What fan wouldn't be? Rushing back from Sunderland hardly instilled a relaxed pre-match disposition.

To welcome us in there were the dancing girls and Newcastle's brand new, crazy foam character Monty the Magpie who was intended to be a hit with the kids but probably ended up trying to pull bits of chewing gum and chocolate from his feathers. He disappeared so quickly nobody ever wondered if he'd been real or a symptom of over-active imaginations.

The extra camera angles that Sky prided itself on included the new touch-line camera which spent all its time whizzing up and down the side. It was searching for fans to whip into the frenzy of waving hands, fingers and shouts of "hello mum" that accompanied any public opportunity for a moment of fame.

I assumed this was intended to further immerse the armchair football fan in the Sky football-experience.

Football was presented as a wonderful world, without swearing, terrace aggression or indifferent fans tired of poor facilities and lack-lustre performances.

Everybody was happy, smiling, all-singing and all-dancing. As a novelty, Newcastle fans enjoyed living up to this. We were the happy-go-lucky fans that everybody loved and there was no shortage of fans desperate to perform for the camera.

Tonight was no exception as an absolute cracker was

served up. Andy Cole gave us the lead, only for Andy Sinton to score twice before half time for Wednesday.

There was plenty of opportunity for the side-line camera to capture Geordie ecstasy in the second half as Cole levelled things, followed by a spectacular lob-shot from debutant Alex Mathie. Malcolm Allen completed the scoring to give Newcastle their first Sky victory in four attempts.

The victory was a classic great escape and I set off home in high spirits. Unfortunately, in the back of my mind was the thought that school awaited tomorrow. I could try and wind up the class but since Sunderland were hopeless, they weren't bothered (most preferred Man United). A Sunday in bed and an evening out on the town would have been preferable, but Sky had put paid to that.

The prospect of work would certainly have put a downer on any celebrations that night. Oh, for a sleep-inducing office job!

Wednesday 27th October — CC Cup-3 Wimbledon (a)

The result of the game had been decided at the weekend. Trailing 2-1 at Southampton (two goals of the season candidates from Matthew Le Tissier) Keegan had substituted young North East player of the year Lee Clark.

He reacted by storming up the touch-line, before being promptly redirected by Keegan towards the bench, all in front of the Sky TV Cameras.

They lapped it up and suddenly Newcastle was a club in crisis. Clark found himself in the reserves but it was his pal Andy Cole who caused further ructions.

The day of the cup-tie he went AWOL and in his absence the team looked a shadow of its former self.

An early goal from Wimbledon's Warren Barton was cancelled out by a Scott Sellars shot under the keeper but with twenty minutes left, Dean Holdsworth scored the winner.

We were destined never to beat Wimbledon in a cup competition. The only success being an uninspiring 1-0 extra time win in the equally uninspiring Mercantile Credit Cup, a competition that swiftly disappeared from view due to an extreme lack of interest.

Andy Cole duly appeared the next day, claiming a bout of home-sickness. This was no surprise since the club had given him digs in the County Durham village of Crook, hoping the lack of nightlife in the ex-pit village would protect their star striker from controversy.

Not the sort of place you'd expect any sane individual to place the league's hottest property. He was duly moved to up-market Jesmond while the club promised they would be more attentive in the future.

The next Saturday, Wimbledon visited and with Clark and Cole out to prove a point they were duly hammered 4-0. It was Beardsley who scored a hat-trick who impressed the most with Cole returning with a goal himself.

The away defeat provided yet more pessimistic proof that my dreams of Wembley were set to remain just that.

Monday 8th November 1993 — Oldham (a)

The plus point of the Sky experience was being able to see away matches more often. The fact that it was a Monday night had effectively ruled out my attendance at the fixture so it was the pub football experience beckoned.

Newcastle was heaving with black and white shirts. Most had been out since six o'clock and by the time I arrived at 7:50 the only views to be had were from behind pillars or through windows. The big screen had hit Newcastle big-time!

Three Bulls' Heads, Farmers Rest and Inventions were all full and the match had already started when the George and Dragon was selected.

Its remoteness from the rest of the pubs in Haymarket and Monument meant it was bound to be quieter. The choice of entrance from the smoke-choked and homeless-populated Haymarket bus station or a walk past Old Eldon Square put it off most drinkers' pub-crawl circuit.

Positioned under the Eldon Square shopping centre it had a cavernous feel to it. Shiny metal and plastic dominated — definitely not an olde-world pub, more like a throwback to the eighties.

The absence of a big screen also reduced the crowd but there were enough televisions to satisfy the few punters scattered about.

Since the number of people who owned a satellite dish was still small, the idea of communal watching had been a popular one.

This was United's fourth match on Sky that season. Before that, it had been two in two years. A 2-2 draw with Notts Forest in the

FA Cup covered by BSkyB had seen us blow a two-goal lead and a Mickey Mouse Cup tie at Tranmere had finished 6-6 and been lost on penalties in front of a meagre crowd both at the ground and on television. The number of people watching Premiership matches in the pubs and clubs of the region had turned Monday nights into a continuation of the weekend.

Newcastle carried on entertaining the country. A first half goal from Oldham was about their only shot of note as Newcastle dominated. The goal owed more to new signing Mike Hooper's ability to unconvincingly wave at crosses than any great Oldham pressure.

In the second half Beardsley and Cole worked their magic, Cole's chip over his shoulder just beating Pedro Beardsley's drive for goal of the day.

For a team that had failed every time they'd appeared on live television, Newcastle were making up for it now. Since Keegan's arrival we'd won eight and drawn six, losing to only Southampton in a game we'd dominated.

Although the crowd at the pub had been locked in their own little groups it was still better than sitting at home on your own and there was the added bonus of alcohol on tap.

With ticket prices on the up, this brand of football was to become the poor man's football. All the people on lower wages who had cheered the lads on win, lose or draw would now have to be satisfied with their view from the pub.

The number of people who could get into St James' without a season ticket was set to drop considerably with the closure of half of the Gallowgate. Match tickets were available now to only 2,500 applicants at £9.

The advent of all-seater stadiums meant increased prices - £241 for 19 league matches (£12.60 per match) and £11.50 for cup ties, an increase of £3-£4 on the previous season.

I just hoped there would never come a time when I couldn't afford to support them, I was certain I'd make sure of it. After all I was now one of the earning middle-class, with a good wage coming in and Newcastle were too big a part of my life!

Saturday 27th November 1993 — Arsenal (a)

My Young Person's Railcard was still giving me good service. Having cheaper travel had allowed me to move freely around the country.

Today's trip to Arsenal was a revenge mission. Ever since we'd achieved promotion, I had longed for the chance to rub Arsenal Paul's nose in it.

The previous season he'd come to watch Newcastle beat Charlton 3-1 at Upton Park. His hoodoo on them had been broken. Even then he'd said that the football on offer hadn't been a patch on Arsenal's Premiership fare!

Hearing that made me seethe. His arrogant dismissal of one of the great Newcastle teams would be avenged. I was full of myself when we met before the game. Leaning against one of the squat garden walls that surrounded the Highbury ground I predicted Arsenal's demise.

After all we'd won our last four games convincingly and more importantly were an unheard-of fourth in the league, a point ahead of the Londoners.

I'd enjoyed everything about the day so far, from the packed London-based train, the Newcastle sing-a-long when we stepped onto the Kings Cross platform to out-shouting the Arsenal fans in the confined and caged tunnels of Arsenal tube station. Over four thousand Newcastle fans descended on London convinced today was our day, and that Andy Cole would `do the business' against his former club.

The ground looked superb, the art-deco stands either side of the pitch were packed as was the newly-opened two-tier North Bank. The only eye-sore was the Clock End's two layers of executive boxes above us. I'd always loved seeing tiered stands ever since Subbuteo introduced their own, to be filled with mini-supporters. The fact that to fill one stand you would have had to spend well over £100 proved a distinct drawback to thousands of table football fans. The North Bank was exactly the way Subbuteo stands should have looked (of only you had the money).

The atmosphere in the Clock End made up for its ugliness as the craze for passing huge flags over our head failed to stifle the noise.

Like every dream the bubble had to burst. The recently-installed big screen in the corner of the ground that made our own soon-to-be-removed scoreboard look like a portable television had been entertaining us with goals from Ian Wright and Andy Cole. Alas 'the Jumbotron' may as well have only showed half of the goals since Andy Cole had one of his off-days, as did most of the team.

They were two goals down before they suddenly woke up. A cracker from Pedro gave us something to smile about but it was too little, too late.

Gloomily, I rushed back to get the six o'clock train North avoiding

Paul's smug and satisfied smiles. It was obviously too much to be able to rub his nose in it just once.

To make matters worse Arsenal leapfrogged into third place ahead of us. If we had won we'd have gone second but we just didn't have the necessary class to do it.

I decided not to contact him to discuss the match.

Saturday 4th December 1993 — Tottenham (a)

I had recently discovered that the best kind of relationship was a casual one. Ever since Sarah and I had stopped going out with each other, we had got on better than ever. The occasional day or two spent together ended before any unnecessary arguments took hold.

I was going to spend the weekend with her in London. A gig on the Friday night, footie on Saturday before returning back to Newcastle on the Sunday represented the perfect weekend — music, match and female company.

Rushing out of school at 3:30, I dumped my car in Tynemouth before racing for the 5pm train to Kings Cross, already decked in black and white uniform. The train crammed with business commuters made me feel conspicuously out of place, especially with my gig-wearing army boots and essential kit bag that had seen me through years of pop festivals around Britain and Ireland.

The coincidental appearance in London of The Senseless Things and Newcastle had been too hard to resist. The former took me back to my student days, when having seven bells knocked out of me by an assorted collection of scruffy and hairy wildebeests was considered good clean fun. Although only 23, two years of teaching in London and half a term in Sunderland had taken its toll on me.

Going out during the week had become an effort and my sole source of conversation revolved around children and the various ways I could think of getting my revenge for the last few months of torture. Conversations would start with the words... '35 children', or 'classroom the size of a postage stamp'.

The football crowd that met in the new meeting place of the Bacchus pub before matches had given up humouring me, preferring to let me witter on to myself in a corner. I'd become a conversational cripple. It took a few drinks for me to forget until Sunday evening's school panic set in. No wonder my alcohol consumption at weekends had gone up!

Today, with my headphones thumping out such delicate lines as "Everybody's gone, must have been a neutron bomb..." my mind drifted to carefree days lying in a festival field in Reading listening to unheard-of rock bands, smelling unknown food whilst being trod on by drunken and dread-locked beings.

I may have been the only one at the gig with a Newcastle shirt but nobody minded and the only comments I got were positive "I hope you stuff'em", "up the arse" (the team Arsenal and not an offer) and general anti-Spurs statements. It was still a rarity to see Newcastle fans (or any other team's fans from outside the capital) in London.

Everybody seemed to support whichever team was doing well, usually Arsenal. There was of course the occasional nutter who would scare the living daylights out of you for half an hour about his mistrust of Geordies before saying how much he admired Keegan. Strangely, they all tended to support Chelsea.

The test of a good gig was how sweaty you'd become and how much your ears hummed afterwards. I had sweat and humming-a-plenty but mainly due to fat male football fans putting their arm around my shoulder so they could shout in my ear. Oh... for a female fan to do the same!

With the promise of seat tickets, Sarah had agreed to join me. It had only been just over a year since her Baseball Ground experience and how the two stadiums differed.

Apart from the shelf to our right, every part of the ground was a mass of blue seats. At the far end of the pitch, an unusually high roof had been erected to protect an enormous video screen (big, but not quite Jumbotronic) that would dwarf the two tiers of seats below it.

The ground looked years ahead of the fare in the First Division, only lacking the character of an exposed terrace or the homeliness of a barn-like stand. The whole ground was functional, if not welcoming, right up to the double layer of dark-glassed executive boxes to our left.

It was all very civilised, until the kick-off neared. The whole of the lower tier of the Park Lane Stand (now, a terrace with seats stapled to it) had been given over to Newcastle fans and the full musical repertoire was churned out over and over again.

Since promotion, singing was one aspect of Newcastle matches that had changed. It was mostly down to the chants nicked from supporters of so-called top 1st Division sides such as Wolves,

Ipswich and Swindon.

Years spent listening to boasts of imminent promotion once a winning lead had been achieved against us, (after earlier silence) had increased the number of songs at our disposal.

Our efforts had revolved around the favourites of "Newcastle, Newcastle...", "United, United...", "You fat Bastard", "We hate Sunderland" and "The Blaydon Races" among others. These were changing times, "Kevin Keegan's black and white army" had been replaced by the more manageable "Toon Toon, black and white army". The fact that the former had not been so universally popular was down to its wordiness. The new lyrics proved a popular alternative.

We could also call upon "E I E I E I 0, up the Premier League we go", "Walking in a Keegan wonderland" (an original composition), the variation on "you fat bastard" — "Who ate all the pies...", and the classic "We put Terry, Terry Butcher on the dole..."

Sarah managed to hide her admiration well but couldn't have failed to appreciate the sheer range of musical numbers available to us. We'd taken away grounds by storm, despite a drop in the vocal support at home that was probably down to a settling-in period after the opening of the Leazes (or North) Stand.

The game exploded in the second half when Beardsley volleyed in from eight yards. Despite the obvious advantage of grabbing hold of Sarah to celebrate I preferred to leap about on my own.

Goal moments are unifying moments. Raging arguments could be forgotten in an instant in favour of unashamed displays of emotion and tenderness.

The players themselves either took part in manly group hugs, leaping on top of each other or carried out their own personal (and anti-social) celebrations. The leap was popular and against Brentford, the previous season, Lee Clark had reached the heights of simultaneously carrying two team-mates. Alas one of the great 'leapers' of the team, Ned Kelly was no longer around to entertain us with his athleticism.

It was all well and good for the players... they had an expanse of grass in which to throw themselves about. In the days of terracing, fans were able to show their appreciation by leaping on anyone nearby but, with the advent of seating, this freedom was severely restricted.

Faced by these newly imposed constraints, the options

were limited to a punch of the air or civilised rapid clapping. Bodily contact was now frowned upon (especially between members of the same sex) and only attempted by the brave or drunk.

Grabbing hold of Sarah in order to administer a jubilant kiss might have been an attractive option, but judging by her attempts to fight off a stumbling and incoherent neighbour, the potential for humiliation out-weighed the benefits.

The penalty that handed Tottenham an equaliser didn't go down so well but another super strike from `Pedro' Beardsley restored the euphoric mood. It was an act sadly missed by Sarah's neighbour, who had by now sought sanctuary in the toilets.

The previous week's nightmare at Arsenal faded when the final whistle blew. There would be no skulking back to Newcastle after this match. As an added bonus, Sarah was willing to go for a few drinks in London, the perfect way to follow up the unexpected win.

The best place to drink in London for footie fans used to be Covent Garden. That was until, a few idiots redecorated sections of it and after that, the bouncers had the perfect opportunity to refuse to admit the undesirable footie-shirt wearing fraternity (or so the rumour went). There was to be no more singing in or outside the Punch and Judy for us.

This allowed all those 'beautiful' theatregoers who had been put off Covent Garden to return, but pushed the fans out to the fringes. At the end of Carnaby Street, Sarah and I found an establishment and at the same time a new tradition was begun.

Every London weekend after that finished with the same circuit of pubs, each one crammed with interested individuals who congratulated or commiserated with me. I became a novelty: a practising Northern fan. I had been there and had the shirt and programme to prove it.

Sarah acted as Devil's advocate and since we weren't romantically involved, she didn't mind me acting like an idiot and took great delight in reminding me of my increasingly worsening state.

It was to be our final swan-song together. She had eased my transition to living in Tynemouth by giving me the opportunity to escape south when I needed it. The arrival of a new man in her life put an end to that. Still, there were probably hundreds of women in Newcastle just dying for me to sweep them off their feet.

It was time to move on. I wouldn't be having any weekends in London any more. The first thing to do was to find my own place to live.

Being a 24-year-old living at home wasn't helping my social life, a shared flat beckoned along with easier access to the Newcastle nightlife.

Tuesday 28th December — Chelsea (a)

Sitting alone in a broken down Fiesta, on the hard shoulder of the M1 at 4am, in the middle of a snowstorm, is the perfect opportunity to question your own sanity.

I'd decided to go to an all-night gig (actual finishing time three-thirty) in Nottingham then drive down to London for the game that day.

In my enthusiasm I hadn't reckoned on needing sleep or that the car would break down. By the time help arrived, I was tucked up inside a sleeping bag and unwilling to move.

Once the mechanic had worked out what was wrong, I didn't feel like driving on but was advised that it was in my best interests to make for the next services before resting.

Watford Gap Services may not be a site of natural (or unnatural beauty) but despite the lack of inspirational surroundings, sleep eluded me. The only alternative was to complete the drive to London and an ex-teaching colleague's house.

To further question the wisdom of the journey, we were to stand on Chelsea's infamous home terrace The Shed. The cost was £9, a snip compared to the £25 being charged Newcastle fans.

Allocating the tickets Chelsea couldn't sell (in the East Stand — gods' level) to the away fans was a low trick especially since they were struggling to reach 20,000 fans for most matches. On principle I refused to pay, but there were a good few others who had, and standing on the home end, I wished I'd joined them. My mate, Mark was an Everton fan but luckily lacked a Scouse accent so we managed to talk without bringing attention to ourselves.

Greedily cashing in on a 'big' crowd, Chelsea also upped the price of the programme by 50p to £2, a fact exposed by the box containing them, which had £1:50 sellotaped to the side. Thanks to our league position, we were now considered a big draw but for those who braved the elements, there was to be scant reward.

Played on a freezing pitch the football on offer wasn't worth £1, never mind £25 and when Chelsea scored, my misfortune was completed.

Standing amongst the home fans had virtually silenced me. Football without singing was soulless, an experience I didn't want to repeat in a hurry.

Unable to show my frustration at a crap performance or attempt to cheer the lads on was alien to me, but the worst part of all was hiding my disgust at Chelsea's goal. We had played badly but so had Chelsea. The one player who had had a decent game was former favourite Gavin Peacock.

A change of spark plugs completed, I returned home as quickly as I could. Perhaps New Year might offer a change in my present luck. One thing was clear, I wouldn't be hurrying back to this part of London!

Saturday 5th March 1994 — Sheff Wed (a)

The old adage about not mixing work with pleasure was about to be thrown out of the window like an out-of-favour striker.

I'd taken a shine to one of the female members of staff at school and adopted the role of a predator in order to lure her into my clutches. My interest was aroused by the fact that she was the first teacher I'd ever seen wearing Doc Martin Boots to work and favoured dark colours (such as black). This convinced me that she might favour similar types of music. I'd sit reading the New Musical Express on Wednesdays hoping that she'd show an interest but found myself cruelly ignored.

My next move was to move up to Newcastle so that I could give her a lift to Sunderland each day, the perfect opportunity for casual chat after a stressful day, perhaps the odd after-work drink. There was also the added bonus of living near the City's night-life (if she wasn't too busy).

It soon became apparent that she was quite able to resist my charms. More time would be needed to win her over.

Newcastle, meanwhile, were just emerging from a rocky patch. After winning the first four games in 1994, they then hit the usual rocky patch, losing to Luton Town in the FA Cup, being beaten by Southampton 2-1 at home (again thanks to the pesky Le Tissier) and Wimbledon and Blackburn away.

Goalkeeper Mike Hooper, signed from Liverpool in September, was blamed for most of the defeats and so Pavel Srnicek came in from the cold.

Hooper had gone from hero to zero in six short months. Originally nicknamed Super Dooper Hooper, once his form dipped the label was dropped quicker than his own attempts at claiming a cross.

The team trounced Coventry 4-0 with an Andy Cole hat-trick (his fourth of the season) and with spirits high, the team stepped out onto the Hillsborough pitch wearing a one-off kit of all-green with blue pin-stripes on the shirts.

The kit had been commissioned after the previous meeting between the two clubs, when both had to wear their away kits because both sides' home and away strips were deemed too similar.

It was amazing to the think that Asics had designed a strip that couldn't be worn when required. The cynic within me (along with a great many others) smelt a rat. When the club announced using one-off strip for the game, its eventual launch seemed imminent.

Oh no, replied the club we'll not be selling the strip but... under 'pressure from fans' they 'relented' and the shirts appeared all over Newcastle, mostly worn by gullible youngsters who 'just had to have' the new strips.

It was a sign of the times that Newcastle had learnt how easy it was to drag money out of pockets, all thanks to the appointment of Freddie Fletcher as Chief Executive.

Rumours abounded when he joined United from Glasgow Rangers that he hadn't been popular with their fans, thanks mainly to his eye for making money. On joining Newcastle, the people of Tyneside must have seemed easy targets. The popularity of the Platinum Club had demonstrated this.

As far as the St James' Park regulars were concerned, if he was making money for the club then that had to be a good thing. As long as he didn't come up with any more bird-brain ideas that might affect us attending matches, we didn't care. After all the money to pay for new acquisitions like Ruel Fox had to come from somewhere didn't it?

Carl, Charlotte and I, along with the rest of the fans, sat in the Upper tier of the Leppings Lane stand, but it was proving a hard task finding any value-for-money from either of the two teams on the pitch.

We'd made a cacophony banging our wooden seats every time we looked like crossing the half-way line to no effect. With the ninety minutes up an extremely dull bore-draw had been our reward for our efforts in getting down.

The Newcastle players had blended in admirably with the pitch. No doubt this would be blamed for making passing more difficult. This wasn't what we'd come to expect from the team known as The Entertainers.

That was until Cole was cruelly brought down from behind by

Sheffield's Andy Pierce. His sending off was scant reward for what had looked the only promising moment of the match but when Beardsley's free-kick wriggled through to Cole (through a multitude of legs), we were rewarded as he slotted the ball home.

From doom and gloom to delight, we were desperate to hit the Newcastle pubs, complete with away match programmes jutting precariously from back pockets.

Shirts were kept on for that 'just back from the match' look and although very few were bothered, we felt that Cole's goal had lifted us to a higher plain.

If it had been a goal-less draw, we'd have only changed the expression on our faces from inane grins to disgruntled scowls, everything else would have remained the same. We enjoyed sticking out like sore thumbs amongst the smartly dressed Bigg Market clientele by swaggering around in this way, but it never failed to start conversations.

When I convinced the others to join me at The Mayfair's rock night we stuck out even more, the only ones not dressed in leather or grunge gear. As I bounded about to the sounds of Nirvana and The Sex Pistols, in a small side-room the other two slept with broad smiles on the faces, blissfully unaware of the music thundering over them, Andy Cole the only person on their minds. What a difference a goal makes.

Saturday 19th March 1994 — West Ham (a)

When a group of fans charged onto the pitch to celebrate first Andy Cole putting us 2-1 up, Robert Lee's clinching strike and finally Alex Mathie's icing on the cake they had no idea how much they'd incensed the home fans.

Not only had we been given the whole of the newly opened Bobby Moore stand's lower tier but we'd had the cheek to desecrate their sacred turf. There was also the small matter of our 4-2 victory in one of the most exciting games of the season.

I'd become so used to wandering out of away grounds, colours clearly displayed, singing the lads' praises that I had forgotten the bad old days of football violence. Today it came back with a vengeance as old rivalries were renewed.

Having driven up with another teacher, who supported West Ham (despite coming from Sunderland), we'd parked up a side street and both walked up with our respective shirts on. The warm Spring day in London had meant dispensing with anything more than short sleeves.

Having been promoted together, both clubs considered themselves to be showing the rest of the Premier League how to play exciting football. There was a mutual respect between both sets of fans and the return of hot weather helped improve the good feeling on the way to the ground. For the first time ever, I walked to Upton Park without a backward glance.

The mutual respect disappeared the minute the old favourite about petrol bombing West Ham fans raised its ugly head. I'd sung it when I was a young, aggressive teenager desperate to show a hard edge but now, in the friendly atmosphere of the Premiership, it looked as out-dated as terracing.

Once the 'boys' had charged onto the pitch, rubbing the home fans noses in it, the prospect of a continued amiable ambience was zero.

I hadn't expected trouble, however. I was happily singing "Andy, Andy Cole" on the way out when I split from the main group that was heading for the tube station.

My friend's car was parked in the opposite direction but I still felt safe. My mood turned sour the moment a particularly loud Newcastle fan was picked up, thrown against the wall and told to "shut his stupid Norvern mouth". The satisfied grin on my face disappeared.

Another fan came fleeing around the corner with blood pouring from a head wound and the sickening cry of "We hate Geordies..." chimed out from about a hundred East End voices. The lack of police added to my unease at the situation.

Obviously, they'd accompanied the main body of fans to the tube station, not expecting anybody to go in the opposite direction. The blue star on my striped shirt made me look extremely conspicuous.
The best policy was to remove my shirt (a Mega City Four tour T-shirt underneath saved East London the horrid view of my spindly arms and chest) then fold it up and stuff it into my trousers. At least I might have created some feelings of sexual insecurity amongst some of the fans I was trying to avoid.

The male ballet fraternity had nothing on me as I turned the corner, only glancing up from the ground once to work out how to avoid the mob before me.

My eyes, avoiding all eye contact, continued to study the pavement. It felt like every eye was burning into me, waiting for me to risk a glimpse and give myself away. The bulge in my trousers looked extremely suspicious. By braving the busy main road, I was able to skirt around them and after an age (probably only 30 seconds) I was clear and heading for the safety of my mate's car.

As we exited London I had the uncontrollable urge to cheer in the exact manner that Arsenal Paul had done over six years ago. It compounded my mate's misery and confirmed Newcastle's arrival as one of the big boys. We were no longer a mid-table team, we'd played the two teams that had been promoted with us and after stonking Swindon 7-1 we'd now done the double over West Ham. The gap between us had widened, we were becoming one of the aristocrats of the Premiership, while the Hammers, our once-close rivals, were still treading water.

Friday 1st April 1994 — Leeds (a)

My life had taken a dramatic change for the better. Along with Newcastle's spectacular form (six games won on the trot), the situation with the girl with the Doc Martins had taken an upturn.

An unassuming night out to the indie-rock music club at the concrete jungle known as Maddison's night-club (above the swanky Swallow hotel) had turned into a romantic midnight walk, paddle and freeze on Tynemouth beach. It was the stuff you could tell your grandchildren about (if you ever had any) or Mills and Boon were famous for digging out (apparently). Though not perhaps the lads (and lass) at the match.

The only drawback had been her confession that she was an ardent Middlesbrough fan brought up on the Holgate End (Boro's version of the Gallowgate). Even that I managed to overlook using the old adage that love would find a way (although 30,000 Newcastle fans (and a fair few Boro fans) would disagree).

On the way down to Leeds I proceeded to bore everyone with my sickly tales from the previous night and early morning, omitting the crucial detail of her footballing allegiance. I had simply mentioned that not only did she like my kind of music but that she liked football too. "Where was her season ticket for?" they politely enquired, to which I feigned ignorance.

Although ten points behind leaders Man United we still hadn't given up hope of the championship, taking today's opponents as our role model.

The signing of the long-haired Darren Peacock for £2.7 million pounds had smashed the record set by Andy Cole's purchase by nearly a million. Everybody had said our main weakness was our defence, so the signing was aimed at solving that one.

I returned to the relaxed atmosphere that had been at missing West Ham, perhaps down to my latest trick of dreamily floating everywhere, the un-welcoming industrial estate hardly registered.

Yet again, we had been allocated the whole of an end and Newcastle fans duly filled every available space around the South Stand.

On arriving at the turnstiles, the sight of broken glass and an unusually large police presence indicated that all was not well. I came down from my cloud just in time to see Leeds fans, in plain view of the police, running up to the large queues formed outside the away turnstiles, attacking individuals before running off unimpeded by the luminous green law enforcers all around us.

There was more bother inside the ground with Newcastle fans 'innocently' buying tickets for the Leeds sections. The well-behaved 'fans of the Premiership' dream had been shattered somewhat.

Safely in the ground, a cracking match was transmitted to the nation of satellite dish owners. Andy Cole's goal off a rebound gave us high hopes of a victory, especially when a goal-bound Brian Deane effort was acrobatically cleared off the line by youngster Alan Neilson.

Everything was going for us; my present good fortune was going to see us to victory.

This changed in the second half as Leeds peppered the Newcastle penalty area with shots and crosses. When Andy Cole raced towards goal at the opposite end, victory looked certain but at the last minute he played the ball wide to Beardsley who held his head as his shot sailed high over the bar.

With three minutes to go, I was brought down to earth with a bump as Chris Fairclough knocked in the equaliser.

It looked like a recipe for disaster when both sets of fans were released together onto the streets, but despite a lot of shoving and verbal attacks we returned safely to the car. The late equaliser may have calmed the more aggressive tendencies of some of the home fans but there were still a lot of reports of continued violence from both sets of fans.

Thinking hooliganism was a thing of the past had been a false dawn. It was alive and well and had only been lying low.

Meanwhile, I had a trip to Ayresome Park to look forward to. My new girlfriend had invited me to the same ground I had once thought of as one of the most intimidating spots for a Newcastle fan to visit. A case of entering the lion's den.

Saturday 2nd April 1994 — Middlesbrough v Notts Forest

My only other visit to Ayresome Park had been in Newcastle (and Boro's) relegation year (1989). It had not been a pleasant experience.

On the train there, two ten-year-old lads had been acting as 'spotters' for some particularly unappealing Boro fans. They stared at me for the duration of the journey, making it quite clear what awaited me at the other end.

I must have stuck out like a sore thumb (despite only the neck of my Newcastle shirt being remotely visible). The moment I stepped onto the Middlesbrough station platform, I was bundled into a waiting police transit van along with a collection of nervous-looking Newcastle fans whisked to the stadium.

Fights had broken out throughout the match in the red barrel-roofed South Stand next to us. At the final whistle, not only were we detained for three-quarters of an hour but were bustled into double-decker buses and deposited at Thornaby Station, in the middle of nowhere and well away from any marauding Boro fans.

Newcastle and Sunderland fans wittily called Boro fans smoggies or smog-monsters after the ICI chemical works that dominated the landscape and whose towers always seemed to be billowing various unknown gases.

In return, Middlesbrough fans hated Newcastle (and Sunderland) because out of the three major North-East teams, they were the ones without anything to show for their years of existence. They were the poor relations down the road, too far away from us to be bothered about but close enough for them to feel bitter towards us.

Newcastle and Sunderland matches were arranged so that both sides never had to travel on the same day, but this didn't apply to Boro, whose fans we frequently met on our travels.

On the journey back from Wimbledon, fighting had broken out in the train's buffet car and Newcastle and Boro fans had to be separated — Boro in the virtually empty first class and the rest of the train for us.

A distinctly hyper-active police dog was positioned as guard, a metre from my seat and lunged at anything wearing a black and white shirt. Its aversion to us, the enclosed carriage and the high speed of the train made it extremely aggressive. At one point, the lad sitting on the seat over the aisle and I had to resort to sitting on the two young ladies positioned next to us, as gnashing teeth appeared through the open doorway. In any other situation this would have been a pleasurable experience.

Although my accent wasn't strong I tried to avoid any conversation with my girlfriend on the way to the ground, standing on the Holgate End and on the way home.

The hostility of my previous visit was missing, although there were frequent anti-Newcastle chants.

In total, eleven different songs reached my ears, ranging from the popular "All the Geordies went to Rome just to see the Pope..." to the unoriginal chant about hitting Keegan with a baseball bat.

It was a refreshing change to be standing at a match again and the low, pitched roof above us echoed the noise of the crowd around us.

The closeness of the fans generated an atmosphere of its own and encouraged the type of banter that had been lacking at St James' since the advent of the Leazes seats. You could listen to and join in a myriad of conversations all around you and could guarantee there would be at least one person bursting to have the last word. Being organised in rows of seats only encouraged conversations to either side of you, interacting with another row had become a thing of the past.

A 2-2 draw provided a good deal of excitement with two goals from 'good-looking' local boy Jamie Pollock. There was also my first 'surge' of the year when the first Boro goal went in, an aspect of all-seater stadiums that would be sorely missed by the young and thankfully missed by the old.

The downside was returning to the car, finding a side window smashed, wires lying all over the floor and an empty space where the stereo had been.

Welcome to Middlesbrough I thought.

Wednesday 27th April 1994 — Aston Villa (h)

In contrast to Ayresome Park, the atmosphere at St James' had taken a nose-dive. With half of the Gallowgate turned into a building site, priority had been given to home fans and for most of the year there had been no away fans.

The scoreboard had gone as well, never to be replaced. Most of the noise came from the corner of the Milburn Stand nearest the Leazes End as we struggled to make a vocal impression. There was a lot of noise, but the lack of a concentrated body of singing fans meant choral output was at a minimum.

Tonight, there was a buzz around the stadium. There was a chance to witness history in the making. Andy Cole had scored 39 goals, the same number as Hughie Gallacher and George Robledo, the highest ever United goals tally in a season. Ahead of legends from the twenties and fifties respectively, Andy was on the brink of becoming the highest ever United goal-scorer.

Not since Paul Goddard scored in seven successive matches to equal Len White's record had there been such excitement about one player. Fans who had sat quietly most of the season found their voice.

An early set-back only spurred the crowd on as Bracewell volleyed from outside the area and Beardsley knocked in a penalty but everyone was rooting for Cole.

When Scott Sellars slotted a ball inside two Villa defenders, Cole bore down on the goal. The crowd leapt to their feet and thundered... as if cheering on the final furlong of the Grand National. Taking the ball wide of the keeper's lunge he slotted the ball beyond the thrusting boot of a desperate defender.

Mayhem ensued. Nobody else had ever achieved such a feat in over a hundred years of Newcastle United. The greats of Milburn, MacDonald and Gallacher had never managed it. The jubilation matched the occasion.

The team responded by scoring a further two, 5-1 a fitting tribute to Cole's achievement.

When he'd arrived, I'd hoped that he'd be a success to educate the racists in the crowd. He hadn't changed everybody's attitude but those who still slagged off players with different coloured skin had been given something to think about.

If nothing else, their acceptance of him as an honorary Geordie was the start of a broadening of minds.

By the time the curtain closed on our first season in the Premiership, European football had been secured for the next season. An unheard of third spot and qualification to the UEFA Cup a fitting reward for the players' efforts.

The loss of the Gallowgate was a sad one, but what was to take its place promised to be more impressive, if only in size. How much of the spirit of football would be lost, though was still to be revealed.

The advent of seats in place of terrace would inevitably mean increased prices, a ground that had cost me £5.50 to stand in when Keegan had arrived, now cost £11.50 to sit in. A 100% rise in two years would mean a lot of devoted fans who had stood by the club in hard times being priced out of the market: the end of the working class game.

The naïve hope was that a 100% increase was enough, but by the time season tickets were renewed, it became clear that it wasn't. The only question now was had the entertainment value increased by a similar amount?

Onwards and upwards

Taylor's Turnips had been beaten in the "Battle of the Vegetables" by the Swedes the tabloids proclaimed wittily. The subsequent parting between Graham "Do I not like that" Taylor and the English FA was a popular one but hardly compensated for England's first missed World Cup in my supporting life-time.

England's absence in the 1994 World Cup meant that, despite the television hype to the contrary, the nation's interest was lacking. Ireland's exploits generated mild enthusiasm from outside of the Irish fraternity but that was as far as it went.

If nothing else, the Summer action had both managers and newspapers trying to spot potential players for the coming season, as the rumour mill went into overdrive.

Normally, this transfer merry-go-round passed Newcastle by. There hadn't even been a sniff of an anonymous full-back who had played a few minutes for an equally uninspiring country. That was until now.

The Chronicle billboards were awash with World Cup defender signing stories as the region held its breath. Thoughts of top-class Brazilians, Italians (even Germans) were conjured up but when the new acquisition was revealed to be Switzerland's Marc Hottiger, the first reaction had to be "Who?"

His signing for £500,000 hardly excited but you just had to have faith in Kev's judgements. After all, it was only eight years since Paul Goddard's £750,000 arrival had smashed the previous record signing of £350,000 for John Trewick. Since then, Andy Cole's and Darren Peacock's signing fees had dwarfed that amount.

As it turned out Hottiger was only a taster when Belgium's Philippe Albert joined United. Not only had he taken part in the World Cup, he had actually had enough vision to score. At £2.65 million he indeed represented a mouth-watering prospect. His goal was repeated endlessly as the season approached, much to the annoyance of Sunderland and Middlesbrough fans.

The central defensive partnership of Albert and the Yeti-like Darren Peacock (who inadvisably continued to sport unfashionably long hair (for the Northeast) throughout his stay on Tyneside) had cost an unheard-of (on Tyneside) £5.4million There was no doubting that the club was going places. Our days in the First Division were now firmly behind us.

The marketing of the club had gone into overdrive. To cope with the upsurge in demand for games, matches were being beamed live to the Odeon Cinema and repeated the next day in the pubs and clubs of the region. The green third strip had proved as popular as the first two and the club had bought out their own colour monthly magazine, Black and White.

This last initiative was nick-named "Bland and Shite" by a number of the supporter-produced fanzines. It was a name which appeared unfortunately apt, especially when readers were confronted by Steve Howie's cookery corner. His familiarity with rock bun recipes would hardly set fear into the hearts of the
Premiership's strikers or fans.

Largely unnoticed had been the demise of the Newcastle United Supporters Club. The little shack behind Marks and Spencer had provided the only "town centre" outlet for Newcastle merchandise and had also ran their own travel club, that had provided myself and others many happy away memories.

First they had mysteriously stopped selling official merchandise and then the travel club was disbanded when the shack was closed. The feeling that the enthusiastic set of 'oldies' had been pushed out of the market was strong, especially when the football club included match tickets in their own travel package. These packages were available to anyone and possession of a season ticket wasn't necessary. This infuriated season ticket holders who had been unable to purchase away tickets.

With the amount of money being spent by fans, it was hoped

that the club would not feel the need to raise match-day prices but this wasn't the case. The cheapest season ticket rose by £37 to £278 (a rise of just under £2 per game), not a popular decision, but worse was to follow.

Freddie Fletcher was the catalyst that had led to the over-subscribed Platinum Club and he was at it again.

West Ham and Arsenal had previously introduced a bond scheme that guaranteed season ticket holders a seat in the ground for their lifetime, as long as they shelled out £1500.

With the waiting list for Newcastle season tickets growing by the day, fast Freddie had introduced a similar scheme costing £500 but only guaranteeing a seat for 10 years. The marketing was aimed at convincing fans that they would be showing the ultimate commitment to the club.

In the background, rumours that failure to buy a Bond would lead to the loss of your season ticket filled the local letters pages. All of a sudden, what had at one time been the ultimate commitment to the club, was now the least you could do.

The traditionally-named Leazes had become the North Stand only to be retitled the Sir John Hall Stand. The newly-completed Gallowgate End was likewise renamed the Exhibition Stand. The building work had spelt the end of two of the most vociferous banks of terrace in the country and sent a clear message that there was no place for sentimentality and tradition in the club. It was all about today's board and sponsors. Spectacular it looked but its welcome to its own fans had been spoilt by the dash for cash.

Saturday 10th September 1994 — Chelsea (h)

The big consolation for the St James' regulars (now annoyingly nicknamed the Toon Army) was that the team was doing the business on the pitch. The lads were two points clear of Man United after winning the first four games. Three of them had been achieved without skipper Peter Beardsley, who was attempting to set a record for the number of consecutive seasons he could sustain a broken cheekbone.

The visit of Chelsea saw the only Premiership clubs with a 100% record face each other. It was also the return of Gavin Peacock, whose release was still thought by many to be one of Kev's few mistakes.

The new Exhibition (Gallowgate) Stand coldly towered

before us and in the process spoilt the fabulous panoramic view across the Tyne towards Gateshead. Night games had offered the best sight as street and house lights snaked their way up the river embankments, the perfect backdrop to passionate footballing nights. Although the uncompleted corners allowed a limited view, it was only a matter of time before that disappeared too.

Also gone was the sight of the city's starlings, casting weaving and dipping patterns across the sky. The loss of both these sights was hardly compensated for by the rows of uniform seats. The club's planning department had obviously not taken into account my nostalgic memories when they created the stand, expecting everybody to be too enthralled by the action on the pitch to partake in a bit of bird-watching.

After the pitch had been blamed for United's poor run of form at the beginning of the year, £350,000 had been spent on laying a new one. It appeared to be money well spent, for now, as there was no sign of the quagmire evident the previous season.

Both sets of players enjoyed it as a spectacular feast was served up. An early Cole run and shot from the edge of the penalty area was one of the best goals seen by the new stand but it wasn't long before the returning Peacock levelled. It was a goal that signalled great delight amongst the Chelsea fans sitting in the new away section to our left.

The previous season's ban on away fans due to the reduced capacity had coincided with the most apathetic atmospheres experienced at the ground. Without anyone to compete against, singers became an endangered species. When nearly 2,000 away fans were admitted once more, so the sound level rose. I personally hoped that they would provide more people around us with the impetus to join in with the ditties successfully doing the rounds at away matches.

Further excitement came our way when a Lee penalty rebounded for Fox to drive past Chelsea keeper Kharine. Paul Furlong spiced things up with an equaliser before half-time but the lads showed their mettle with a goal apiece from Cole and Lee.

The pair were having their own mini-scoring contest, Lee having scored five goals in five games and Cole six. Everything Newcastle touched was turning to goal and it made it very easy to ignore all Freddie Fletcher's little schemes.

The only disadvantage of this was that the more we ignored

him, the more audacious his plans would become. This was fine, as long as our own positions weren't under threat because nobody wanted to miss out on watching the top team in the country.

It was a position that Newcastle had held for barely a week in 1984 but this time it would be ours until mid-November. Sunderland was in a completely different world to us, much to our delight.

Tuesday 18th October 1994 — Athletic Bilbao (h)

With the world at our feet, complacency set in. All the years of fighting to escape from the first division, third place in the Premiership had all been for this day, at last the giants of Europe were playing at St James'. The Anglo-Italian Cup had generated virtually no interest whereas this was the real thing.

Unbeaten in the league, five points clear at the top of the table and 3-0 up against the Spanish giants, the second leg a mere formality, self-satisfied smugness oozed out of every section of the ground.

The players felt it as they tried to ignore the delighted Mexican waves coasting about them and in a blink of an eye, our world came crashing down.

The first Bilbao goal was careless, but surely it was only a consolation. The second silenced the party. Delight turned to disbelief. What had we done?

Shocked and stunned we filed out at the final whistle. From party of the year we had been delivered directly to its wake. At least we'd won, we coldly comforted ourselves... but was it enough?

The answer was no. Sitting in the flat I'd moved into with my Boro Girl and her United-supporting flat-mate we listened to the return leg in Spain.

Metro Radio, now the sole broadcaster of Newcastle matches, was running a European Special. The commentators were marvelling at how great the lads were doing, confidently predicting a 0-0 result that would take us through to the next round.

They obviously hadn't been watching Newcastle long as their optimism made you cringe. How dare they be so confident we thought but as the final whistle crept ever closer and we listened to them crow, we started to be sucked in.

Just when we'd started to believe that our complacency at home would go unpunished, we were out. A late goal combined with a Beardsley hitting the post to spread egg well and truly over the presenters' faces.

There was no satisfaction in saying "we told you so" since we wanted so much to believe them.

It wasn't fair but as my mum (and everybody else's mum) always replied: "Life's not fair". If only fans listened to their mum's and not Metro Radio.

Wednesday 26th October 1994 - CCCup 3 -Manchester Utd (h)

Being drawn against Man United in any cup competition in previous years would have meant certain elimination for us after a spirited performance.

Ever since the creation of the Premiership, the League Cup (now titled Coca-Cola Cup) disappeared from their list of desirable prizes. I remembered listening to the midweek commentaries on Radio 2 as a teenager, lapping up the atmosphere generated by Man United or Liverpool (the teams usually featured). A competition that had been so popular for the last couple of decades with a final at Wembley was now just a reserve team outing for the Manchester reds.

Their excuse was that the Premiership and Europe were more important but they had been quite happy to appear in finals galore when they weren't so successful. The truth was that they'd become bored with it. Three visits to the final in four years had given them only one victory.

The excuse of concentrating on other competitions was a popular one amongst fans who've just witnessed another early exit from a cup but for Manchester, it wasn't an excuse. They'd won every other domestic trophy the previous year and their fans had become so spoilt with days out to Wembley, arrogance had set in. The rest of us mere mortals could scrap over a day at Wembley if we wanted. It was beneath them. This attitude helped form the country's disdain towards them. We just didn't like to be looked down upon or snubbed. No matter how many times Liverpool reached Wembley in the 80s they still wanted more.

As far as Newcastle were concerned there'd only been one sniff of success in this competition (1976) and Manchester City had made sure we could smell but not touch

Even though we knew it would predominantly be their reserve side, here was the perfect opportunity to progress at the expense of the biggest name in English football. It would be men against boys — easy meat, we were, after all, still top of the league.

Making his home debut was striker Paul Kitson, signed for over £2million from Derby. A long drawn-out transfer saga hadn't endeared him to the fans when he couldn't make his mind up whether to come or not. He'd made up for this when he threw himself in front of a goalie's kick, giving himself concussion but boosted his standing with us no end.

The rout failed to materialise as Manchester's 'kids' battled away. In particular, Nicky Butt seemed to be everywhere. One minute foiling a Newcastle strike the next launching one of his own. Prospects of a replay at Old Trafford looked ominous. True, it meant nearly 10,000 Geordies could take over Manchester for the afternoon but would the home side relish being beaten in front of their own fans? A stronger side would doubtless be played, if only to avoid losing face.

As the final ten minutes approached Philippe Albert came to our rescue with a stonking header. Thus, confirming his hero status with the fans.

His performances had even inspired an increasingly rare example of terrace wit as wags rhymed his surname with "the Bear", allowing us to shamelessly croon the 'Rupert the Bear' theme tune with "Philippe Albert, everyone knows his name..."

Even the quiet ones about us, who normally spent their time passing around endless packets of sweets joined in.

The best possible finish was provided by our skinny new boy, Paul Kitson when he slotted the ball under Peter Schmeichel's body.

The good feeling from the win barely lasted until the weekend when it was revealed Andy Cole would be out for up to a month with shin splints. Not many had heard of that one before but everybody knew that without him, we'd struggle. The three games he'd missed previously (after walkabouts and injury) had all ended in defeat.

With a league fixture at Old Trafford on Saturday, few expected anything more than defeat...

...and we were right.

Sunday 15th January 1994 — Manchester Utd (h)

Defeat in Manchester was swiftly followed by our exit from the UEFA Cup. As if to rub salt into our wounds, another reverse at Wimbledon dumped Newcastle to third place in the league.

Andy Cole's goal-scoring return against Ipswich gave a

glimmer of hope but a late equaliser put paid to that. In the next nine games, he failed to hit the target. Whether he was still injured or not, the team's performances were heading rapidly downhill.

Scott Sellars and Peter Beardsley in particular were missed as Manchester City ended my Coca-Cola Cup dreams and contributed to a thoroughly miserable Christmas.

The only bright spot was the knowledge that season ticket holders would not lose their seats if they didn't buy a Bond. After demands from the newly-reformed Supporters Club, Uncle Freddie graciously put our minds at rest. Bearing in mind the dire state of affairs on the pitch (despite being 5th — how times had changed!) it was the only thing he could have said.

Robert Lee had kept Wembley hopes alive with a late equaliser against Blackburn but there didn't appear any point even turning up for the replay when a few days later that Andy Cole was sold for £6million plus winger Keith Gillespie.

The mourning faces were evident all over Tyneside. The exodus of star players in the eighties that sealed our return to the 2nd Division was a wound that was still to be healed. After two magic seasons, were we now to see the breakup of the team in the same way?

Fans confronted Keegan demanding to know what he was playing at. Hall didn't escape their wrath either.

When the dust had settled, it had been Keegan's decision and the board had nothing to do with it, a case of "Get out of that one, Kev 'cause it's got nowt to do with us." The latter invoked a good deal of scepticism, but when push comes to shove, you had to have faith in a manager that had turned the club around from the edge of Division 3 (or 2 depending upon the year).

There was no doubt that Cole was going through a rough spell (along with the rest of the team) and as long as the transfer money went towards players, then Keegan would eventually be forgiven.

Too often money had simply vanished or in the case of Gascoigne badly invested. The present board, as fond of taking money off you as they were, had bigger plans. They wanted to make the club one of the biggest in Europe if only to fill their own egos. All the fans wanted was to be able to share the ride and if selling Cole was the way to achieve it, then so be it.

Of course, sitting and watching Newcastle struggle to break down Manchester hardly gave you much faith in the board. No Cole or Beardsley left Paul Kitson on his own up front. The thin man battled away and duly came up with a late equaliser to ease Keegan's worries.

Thankfully, both clubs had agreed not to play Cole or Gillespie so we were spared the misery of seeing Andy score against us.

Even though selling him was the right thing, it was sad to see him go. Singing the 'Cole-goal' song endlessly as Leicester were crushed 7-1, his debut goal against Notts County, hoping that Newcastle and racism would become a thing of the past. I was bursting to talk to the black people about me as I was standing waiting for a burger opposite Kings Cross but resisted the temptation.

How much had he done for racism on Tyneside? He'd started the ball rolling, Ruel's presence would provide another black hero for the people to worship and I felt certain that more would follow. For that, Kevin and Andy deserved praise and respect.

Wednesday 18th January — FA Cup 3r -Blackburn (a)

Never having witnessed a cup victory away from home, part of me was convinced I never would. Nevertheless, I left school as soon as the last of my class had run happily towards their parents or straight towards the sweet shop (depending which was closest). Gill (my Boro-supporting girlfriend) and I were renting a house in South Gosforth so I dropped her off at Heworth, picking up Carl, Charlotte and Gill's friend Lisa.

Gill didn't fancy coming along, the last thing she wanted to do was drive to Blackburn, bearing in mind Boro's cup defeat against Swansea the previous night. Setting off at 4pm, allowed us 3 ¾ hours to reach Blackburn. With Carl as navigator we took the scenic route through Spennymoor and Barnard Castle before joining the A66 West.

This route may have saved us time but at 7pm we were stuck in a mammoth traffic jam following signs labelled "away coaches" which we argued would lead us to a safe place to park.

As we learnt, nearly to our cost, the signs were actually designed to send you via the longest possible and busiest route to a spot where you could just about see the ground. Hopes rose every time the ground appeared closer only to be dashed by a turn seemingly taking us away from our destination.

With kick off only twenty minutes away, Carl once again took over as he used his non-existent knowledge of Blackburn to bring us within gazing distance of Ewood Park.

With kick-off only minutes away, the prime concern was to dump the car asap. It's amazing how little care is taken to secure a suitably safe car park for your pride and joy. Anybody with a cardboard sign and a vacant piece of land could (and did) set themselves up as an "ofishal" car park. Desperate football fans would gladly dump their only escape route out of whichever miserable part of the country they found themselves, as long as they could make kick-off.

It was easy for my passengers to leave the car with a mysterious man in a balaclava and it was surprisingly easy for me too. After all, he did have a neatly written sign.

Reaching the Darwen End, Lower Tier all thoughts were focused on the task at hand. We hadn't won since early December, while Blackburn hadn't lost since November and were top. Hopes weren't high but we'd still packed out nearly half of the stand, more out of desperation than anything else. Nobody wanted to miss out on a famous victory, just in case it happened.

An unusually good performance had blunted Blackburn's 'famous' SAS — Shearer and Sutton.

Just when we least expected it, we had a goal to celebrate. A free-kick was rolled into the path of 'bargain boy' Hottiger, who let fly from twenty yards into the left hand corner. Our staple diet of gruel had been replaced by a Swiss roll. There was a moment for the good fortune to sink in before bedlam. Lisa took it all in her stride, but this was the first time many of us had seen Newcastle ahead in an FA Cup tie away from home — it had to be an omen!

The noise from the travelling army in the second half was reaching a crescendo, along with our gloating when Blackburn equalised. We'd laughed at Shearer's inability to score (a feat he hadn't had any difficulty with before). Carl and Charlotte had regularly shouted "chicken and beans" to emphasise the dullness of both his personality (represented by his choice of pre-match meal) but the goal brought us down to earth with a bump. Our bubble had exploded into a myriad pieces, a winner was only a matter of minutes away. It was the same old script of broken promises.

The fans in the lower tier seats to our left who'd sat silently throughout the game now erupted into life. Their sudden resurgence of life made a mockery of our boisterous support

For the first time in my life, a trip away in the cup didn't end in defeat. Lee 'Jigsaw' Clark (who usually fell apart in the box) found himself in the Blackburn penalty area with only the keeper to beat. We steadied ourselves for the verbal onslaught he was to receive when he blasted high and wide. But no, instead, he had the audacity to score.

This wasn't what we expected at all. Plucky fight and defeat, yes. Dismal humiliation...yes. There was no way we could actually win...was there?

The final whistle indicated just that. This was a Leicester City on the last day of the season, certainly not a Wimbledon away.

Many of us came of age that night. Not only had we won away in the FA cup for the first time since 1982, we'd done it at the Premiership's leaders. It was a landmark in my life. I could marry, have children and grow old happy in the knowledge that I had at last witnessed Cup success.

For the next forty minutes we acknowledged Keegan by singing 'Keegan Wonderland', not only the twelve-inch re-mix but the full length album version. As a bonus, Sky had caught it all for posterity. My friend, the West Ham fan from school would have dutifully recorded it for posterity.

Thoughts of our balaclaved friend and his dodgy car park returned. We weren't even sure if the car park had been a figment of our imaginations, conjured up in our desperation to see the match. On our return, the shadowy figure had gone but there was an array of cars desperate to make a speedy getaway.

We crossed an iron bridge over a canal that the others assured me had been there previously and to add the final cherry on tonight's cake — there was the car — intact, even down to the stereo and windows.

The others managed to stay awake long enough to see the M62 before they drifted into their own dreamlands. Speeding back to the North East and an early wake-up call from an unsympathetic Boro fan, I was resolved in my belief that it had to all mean something.

My first win, the return of form at the right time, it all lead to one thing... Wembley. At long last I would reach my Cup final. I may be less tolerant with my class of Year 4's tomorrow but it will have been worth it.

Looking at the sleeping Lisa in the front passenger seat, I wondered if she realised how honoured she had been. Twelve years I'd waited for this and here she was at her first away match, a lucky mascot indeed.

Our good luck carried on as a Paul Kitson hat-trick saw off Swansea City and two Keith Gillespie 'flukes' against Manchester City put us into the quarter finals for the first time since 1974 and the Wembley flop against Liverpool. All we had to do was to win at Everton. Easy!

Saturday February 4th 1995 — QPR (a)

There were so many times that Newcastle proved a complete embarrassment that memories merged into one. One occurrence that almost guaranteed an abject performance and that was bringing a non-Newcastle supporting friend to a match.

I had arranged to meet an Everton-supporting friend called Mark in London. Since QPR were struggling in the lower half of the table, Newcastle had to stand a good chance of a win.

Surveying the pitch the prospects of an entertaining football, played on the ground looked bleak. The lack of sunshine due to the shadow cast by the stands had put paid to a new pitch. Instead was a perfectly ploughed field on one half and luscious grass (as luscious as any pitches got in February) on the other.

An injury-hit team was promptly torn apart by Les Ferdinand. Forced to play Mike Hooper in goal and without regulars Steve Howie, John Beresford and Barry Venison the travelling army cringed as 'Leslie' contributed to three goals before half time. The lack of any further goals in the second half hardly restored any pride.

Mark left me at White City tube station after describing the match as an experience. Some experience, I mused as stood waiting at Kings Cross for a train to carry me back up to Newcastle.

The previous week we had beaten his Everton team 2-0 and when I desperately wanted them to put on a show so I could bathe in their reflected glory —they'd come a cropper.

The trip hardly represented a good investment. At least, Wembley in May would be a day to savour knowing that I'd witnessed possibly the low point of the season — the mark of loyalty. As it turned out Mark's team would have a bearing on my dreams of Wembley.

Sunday 12th March 1995 — Everton (a)

I'd always thought tales of fans getting tickets from relatives or friends who "had one spare" was an Urban Myth. Everybody knew someone who had struck lucky but details were always vague. Luck had been on my side when Ian had set up my greatest football experience at Leicester but Cup fever had hit Tyneside and tickets were at a premium.

Even though my trips away numbered a paltry five, I had the same chance of acquiring a ticket as the other 30,000+ season ticket holders. They could have sold the few thousand tickets allocated ten times over and it was pot-luck whether you got one or not. Fans who had loyally followed the team away throughout the season had their noses put out of joint when they were unsuccessful, while some of the lucky ones hadn't attended one.

I wasn't one of the lucky ones and when my cheque was returned, my world crashed around me. Phone calls to Mark, the London Scouser, proved fruitless but at least I had the consolation of an afternoon with the box, thanks to those nice people at the BBC. It was scant consolation.

My black and white guardian came to the rescue. The unlikely angel was my sister, whose father-in-law was an Everton season ticket holder and my saviour. His offer of a seat in the main stand was music to my ears: "Tell me mam, me mam, I won't be home for tea, I'm going to Wemberley," I chirped.

The dream was on — my first quarter-final match would lead to the twin towers. After all, we'd already beaten them at home and while we were locked in third spot, they were only two points above the relegation zone. A mental note was made to be sympathetic towards my host. It didn't do to crow.

There was some cause for concern: Peter Beardsley and Steve Howey had picked up injuries but thoughts of defeat were pushed to the back of my mind on the drive across the Pennines.

The Scousers around me showed no interest in my allegiances and after a bright start by Newcastle, I patronisingly felt sorry for them, so convinced was I of success.

By half-time, although we hadn't scored, the match was going our way. My sister's father-in-law had sat calmly beside me, muttering occasionally and cursing his own team. Basically the placid supporter I had expected him to be.

This façade disappeared the instant Drunken Ferguson headed on to Dave Watson to score. He leapt wildly about, showing a distinct lack of sensitivity towards me, in what was a painful moment in my life.

The ferocity of his celebrations took me by surprise. If it had been the actions of a teenager, it wouldn't have looked out of place, but from a father of two grown up thirty-ish sons...I don't think so. It was an unexpected side I was seeing of him and in the process he'd risen in my estimation.

Bizarrely, we were sitting above the Everton director's box and the scene to my left was being repeated by expensively-attired executives wearing beige trench-coats and ties. These were the sort of people I labelled as free-loaders. The business world being treated to a corporate lunch who were denying loyal fans of a place in the crowd and being treated to a slap-up lunch on top.

How dare they enjoy themselves so much! Their delight made me more determined that United were going to rub their noses in it.

But they didn't. At one point, Ruel Fox could have earned with a replay but in true Albert Craig tradition, he fluffed it. An open goal to shoot at and he shot wide.

From my viewpoint, I stood up to honour a goal but in my haste had failed to spot whether it had entered the goal or not. It took me a full five minutes to spot my mistake. My situation had been confused by a group of lads hugging to my left, assuming them to be Newcastle fans.

I couldn't believe my dream was over for another year. Maybe it was a dream and I'll wake up in the shower, anticipating the journey ahead and a place in the semi-finals. Had some-one not read the script — this was our year...my year. After 11 years, I was to get to Wembley.

The daze I was in lasted the journey home. To make the situation worse, the BBC's decision to show the game live meant that it was now 5 o'clock on Sunday evening. School was only 16 hours away. A whole school-full of Sunderland (or just anti-Newcastle fans) would be waiting to rile me. In my weakened state, I would be powerless to resist.

I should have known better when, firstly the BBC chose to show an FA Cup game live and then Pedros was injured. Every significant cup defeat had been beamed to the nation and the most painful had involved the know-it-all observations of John Motson. The number of cup runs halted by the BBC was growing (Liverpool and Tottenham (a), Man United and Wimbledon (h) to name but a few).

My season was effectively over. On reaching home, I discovered there was a message that Will had rung. Since Newcastle weren't going to Wembley would I be his best man at his wedding? Honoured as I was, it couldn't take away the pain.

Newcastle's season drifted away. A final placing of sixth would once have been hailed a miracle, but not anymore. The club considered itself amongst the top clubs in the country and charged prices to match. Our expectations had risen accordingly.

Eight straight wins at the beginning of the season had us clear at the top but then the rot set in. The side slumped to just three wins out of a possible ten and in the process missed out on Europe. One of the wins had been against Arsenal but the satisfaction gained was still tarnished by the cup defeat. An FA Cup final place would have made the season one to remember and would have avoided this end of season limbo.

It was Everton's victory at Wembley that had deprived us of Europe. Sitting in Will's London flat, while he jetted off on honeymoon, eating take-away pizza, Gill and I watched the highlights of the cup final. It was like watching someone walking around your house, drinking out of your Wembley 95 mug and laughing at your misfortune, all at the same time.

She was happy because Middlesbrough had been promoted as champions from the First Division but I had glimpsed the Promised Land, only to have it snatched from my grasp. Her calls of "There's always next season," were distinctly hollow. If only I could believe her.

The French Cavalier and the City Gent

Not qualifying for Europe had been a blow to Newcastle's new breed of ambitious directors. Reaching the FA Cup quarter-finals had whet everyone's appetite and we wanted more. Success was no longer a pipe-dream to be smoked by elderly fans or snorted by the new 'yuppie elite'.

To demonstrate their determination, the board splashed out an unprecedented £14 million on players. No more journeymen from Sheff Wed reserves for us, it was spend, spend, spend. Even more surprising was that this was all done without a rise in season tickets.

In came Warren Barton, a £4 million 'catch' from Wimbledon. Always a pain whenever we played them, his blond locks put him in the same family as the peroxide pairing of Barry Venison and John Beresford (the former having moved

on to play with Graham Souness in Turkey). Luckily, he didn't share their desire for wearing
loud and tasteless suits.

Also arriving was Reading's goalkeeper Shaka Hislop who, despite conceding four goals in the First Division playoff final was still deemed a good keeper, based on his ability to save penalties. At £1.5 million he far outstripped the last big money keeper who had arrived with Wembley penalty experience. We hoped that he would fare better than Dave Beasant.

David Ginola arrived from Paris SG for £2.5 million and although once the season started it was his skills we were amazed by, pre-season it was his blond bombshell of a wife who received the admiring glances of the male half of Tyneside at least.

The icing on the cake was the capture of Les Ferdinand. Immediately nicknamed Sir Les, his award as Britain's Best Dressed Man was forgiven by the fans once his physical presence and eye for goal had won us over. His demolition show against us at QPR the previous season proved that he was the perfect follow-up to Andy Cole and the man to lead us to glory.

There was also an end to the endlessly clicked Asics shirts of the previous season as Adidas took over as our shirt manufacturer. The grandad-style collar on both home and away shirts proved an instant hit as nearly half a million were shifted by the start of the season. The away shirt, with red and blue hooped tops, cream socks and shorts won my vote as the best away shirt and everywhere you looked for the first home game of the season, Adidas was plastered, on supporters and billboards. No wonder the club could spend £14 million.

The ground finished, 36,000+ seated fans were set for a glorious season, there was to be no repeat of the disastrous false dawn of 1988.

Wednesday 30th August 1995 — Middlesbrough (h)

Three wins out of three had lifted us once more to top spot, just the time to meet newly promoted Middlesbrough.

I was still living with Boro-supporting girlfriend Gill and wedding plans were in an advanced stage for the following Summer. An early-season meeting between our respective clubs would avoid any of the tensions that accompanied a relegation or championship battle. An early-season outing to test out the strength of our relationship.

I was feeling quite benign towards Middlesbrough, a sign of the increased confidence in the lads. In the red corner of our rented house, Gill was spitting fireworks. Years of living in Newcastle had taught her to despise anything black and white.

Revealing her love for football had instigated numerous conversations on nights out in the town (before meeting me), only to have them hastily cut short once her allegiance to the Boro had been revealed. Being branded a 'smogmonster' and asked how she fitted her gas mask into such a small bag hadn't endeared her to the supporters in her adopted home.

The silence between us in the days leading up to the game made the wait for the game fraught to say the least. I left her frantically searching for Century Radio, which broadcast all of the Boro's matches, and without the customary good luck message. In its place was a glare and a "don't think you're sleeping in this house tonight if you win" threat.

Reaching the ground was a breath of fresh (tinged with burger and essence of hot dog) air. In the battle that ensued, a fraught first half ended goal-less, a good result if I wanted to sleep in my own bed but hardly good for the Championship push.

When Ginola crossed perfectly for Ferdinand to head home, my joy was mixed with the knowledge that our front room would become a battleground and doubts raised about our future life together.

In the last few minutes, Boro's Mr `Not-So-Good-Looking' — Jamie Pollock was challenged by Darren 'Elle McPherson-look-a-like' Peacock. "Penalty!" screamed the away fans and the Century commentators, "Not so," replied the referee, decidedly uninterested.

What happened next probably saved my future marriage. Pollock's face as he chased angrily after the official resembled a cross between an award-winning gurne and Jimmy Hill's dream chin. The extra stubble that sprouted from it added extra distance to his chin and wiped all the anger Gill had bottled up at the defeat. Her not-so-silent sufferings as we watched the match highlights evaporated as the face to end all wars jutted from the television.

Normality returned to our relationship after that, as peace

descended upon Gosforth. That was, at least until the return match at the newly-built Riverside Stadium.

Sunday 1st October 1995 — Everton (a)

There it was, staring at me, like a slap in the face from a jilted girlfriend (not that you found many of those to the dozen) — on the front cover of the programme: FA Cup winners 1995.

They were rubbing my (and a few thousand other United fans) nose in it. It should have been our cup, if only Fox had hit the open net!

In total contrast to the FA Cup game the previous year, there was no problem getting a ticket thanks to the new computer system that gave away tickets to those people who went to the most games. If we'd had it working last year, perhaps cheering the lads from the away end instead of from amongst the Scousers (unsympathetic to my misery as they were), I might have been able to make a difference. I would now never know! Gill, unsurprisingly, doubted my theory on `ground positionality'.

The players must been as incensed as I was by Everton's affront the previous March and pounded the home goal. Although it was a case of bolting the stable door after the horse has fled, total humiliation would go some way to easing the pain.

Just for the Sky boys, Sir Les bolted between players before unleashing a venomous drive to put the Toffees firmly in their place. If only he could have done it here last season. Further strikes from Bobbie Lee and Paul (are you still here?) Kitson put the game beyond them.

A late blatantly-off-side Kanchelskis goal gave some respectability to the score from the home side's point of view, but there was no doubting our superiority.

It may not have been a coincidence that Fox, the man who could have earned a replay was sold to Spurs the very next week. Had he been Kevin's sacrificial lamb to ensure success?

It was a welcome win but cautiously greeted. Our placing, top of the league hadn't yet translated itself into a Championship challenge thanks to memories of last season's start and eventual decline being fresh in our minds.

Wednesday 25th October 1995 — CCC-3 Stoke (a)

A lasting memory of a deserted and rain soaked Boxing Day town in 1989 had hardly prepared me for the night ahead.

Losing to a Stoke side who were relegated in bottom spot from Division 2 but still managed to beat a high-flying Newcastle team 2-1 conjured up pictures of a dismal day all round.

Tonight the town was alive. I'd come up in the world as far as cars were concerned, being able to boast a G-registration Ford Escort Popular. Having clocked up over 126,000 miles in a Fiesta, I'd decided to quit while it was still in one piece.

The on-street parking was a nightmare and, wherever you looked, gangs of helpful eight and nine-year-olds were offering to "look after" fans' pride and joys — for a small consideration. It was a sure sign that something big was happening in the town's yearly calendar.

Life in the Premiership had turned us soft. Accustomed to large towns and cities and a more sedate attitude towards visiting fans (apart from some verbal abuse at Chelsea), the last thing we were expecting was football violence, but as we wandered towards the turnstiles, fighting broke out all around us. Individual Newcastle fans were being picked off by decidedly disgruntled youths.

The few police stationed nearby seemed to be too busy paying more attention to the various party costumes that seemed to be dragged out in an attempt to generate cup fever.

With 6,500 travelling fans descending on the Potteries, violence was always a possibility, but the proximity to the ground (and to the police) made the sight of a fan dressed in a nun's habit pouring with blood all the more surreal.

The venom from outside was transported inside as a sell-out crowd traded insults under the mild Autumn sky.

It was an occasion designed for Newcastle to trip up. Luton Town, Bradford City, Oxford United and Ronnie Radford all sprang to mind. Any worries there might have been were swept away as Beardsley provided us with a two-goal lead. Ginola had acquired a reputation as a member of the Jurgen Klinsmann school of diving and was duly abused by both home fans and players before Ian Clarkson earned himself first shot in the baths for two bookable offences.

You could bet your mortgage that Lou Macari, the one-time gambler responsible for Swindon Town's demise would have something to say and he towed the popular line of criticising the Frenchman.

At the time, Newcastle were threatening to run away with the game and gone would be the passionate atmosphere around us. The home fans (the ones not trying to attack us earlier) would lose heart and the game would lose its edge. The last thing I wanted was a sending off, contrary to the opinion of my peers about me.

I felt that Ginola's tendency to make a meal of some challenges put the back up referees and opposition alike. On this occasion an exciting game took a downward turn after that. The Stoke players seemed content to kick chunks out of the Premier League superstars and showed less inclination to attack.

Goals from Les and the long-haired Peacock finished off an easy victory. Victory had never been in doubt and despite previous mishaps in cup competitions most fans now expected victories against lesser opposition.

An unfortunate drawback to this complacency was that the need for a barrage of sound from the travelling army had been reduced. Les and the boys would do the business, so we didn't have to bother. Goals were expected and duly arrived, it was only when they were in short supply that their arrival generated ecstatic scenes.

Still a long way off "Only singing when we were winning", a slippery slide had started that might end with comparison to Man United's London mob. Defeats kept us on our toes and grateful for victories over the minnows. It was easy to see how regularly successful sides slipped into this lethargic state. Whether we followed them, only time (and success) would tell.

Leaving the ground, there were the tell-tale sounds of bother. Running fans could be seen up every street. Who was chasing who was hard to make out, but it was easier to blame the Stoke fraternity, rather than damage our own good record of late. Violent shouts were funnelled towards us by the rows of uniform terraced streets.

Reaching our car in one piece was only the first hazard overcome. Sitting in a traffic jam, we were sitting ducks, open to anybody who fancied smashing a window or setting upon us as we waited to make an escape. Covering our colours seemed wise in the circumstances.

Bodies raced past in search of unseen targets. Conflict remained out of sight, the occasional crash or shout serving to test our wits.

Released by the lights, tension ebbed away. Sleep for the others followed a brief discussion of tonight's action. As we headed Northwards through the dark with Radio I's Mark Radcliffe and the inanely nick-named Lard for company, I questioned the wisdom of being the only driver in the group.

Sunday 1st November 1995 — Tottenham (a)

The whole country suspected Ginola adored himself, but at White Hart Lane, he gave irrefutable proof of it.

The pre-match build-up had all surrounded Les Ferdinand and his attempt to set an all-time scoring record for consecutive games. In eight games he'd notched up 12 goals and a goal today would have set up a new all-time record.

An early Chris (I really wanted to come to Newcastle — honest) Armstrong effort had been cancelled out by a 'dancing' solo effort by the French genius. The stage was set for Ferdy to put his name in the record books.

With a break in play, the cameras happened to focus on 'Davide'. Faced with the sole attention of the nation, he resisted the obvious opportunity to wave and shout "Hello Mum." (the fact that his mum was probably tucked away in a French villa somewhere and unlikely to be watching may have held sway over this option).

Instead, he took the opportunity to give a knowing and seductive nod, before forming a kiss with his lips. The female fraternity might have loved it but at the expense of the traditional British male, can in hand, still digesting his Sunday dinner.

Faced with the added pressure to upstage him, Les bottled. Put clean through on goal he shot weakly at Ian Walker's legs and we were forced to suffer a year of repeats in the Match of the Day opening titles. A role model for Des Lymond was born in an instant, and didn't we know it.

The only consolation was that my journey from London after the game returned me back at 10pm, late enough to avoid any exposure to the Frenchman's charm. But it didn't last long.

Saturday 25th November 1995 — Leeds (h)

One defeat in the league, a three-point cushion over Man United in second place and a hundred percentage record at home — we were in heaven!

Freddie Fletcher was keeping a low profile after the Bonds crisis, the little but in the club car park which had sold a few Newcastle pencils and shirts had had a complete re-fit and was doing great business. Was everything in the garden rosy?

Not quite. The exorbitant cost of away travel (£23.50 to travel to Bristol City on official coaches compared to £16 on ex-supporters club buses Armstrong Galley) was being partly blamed on John Hall's dreams of a sporting club.

In addition to the football, United had bought ownership of the Durham Wasps ice hockey team and Newcastle Gosforth Rugby club. Worse was to follow when a new racing car was purchased and paraded before an unimpressed home crowd at St James'.

In the case of the rugby, millions of pounds were being spent to bring in the best talent around. Rob Andrew was signed to run them, while every new arrival was proudly announced in the match programme. My loathing of rugby stemmed from years spent from the age of seven standing on a freezing field in the middle of winter waiting for some gorilla to knock seven bells out of me — all in the name of sport.

As a fan of the Whitley Warriors in a former existence, my contempt for Durham had rivalled that for Sunderland and hearing of their continued success each fortnight was certainly bad for the indigestion.

I was happy to notice that the majority of fans shared my attitude towards the new venture. Articles and letters swamped fanzine pages. The fear was that money that should be spent on improving the team was being re-directed towards sports that currently only attracted a few thousand. If results took a turn for the worse would the attempts to emulate the likes of Barcelona and AC Milan backfire?
We hoped not, but it was still a cause for concern.

On the pitch, matters were still going well. After years of being kicked all over the field by successive Leeds teams, two goals in a minute had snatched victory out of defeat.

Sporting Club fears were dispatched for now and as long as we continued to strive forward on all fronts, supporters would be satisfied but if the unthinkable happened?

The shit would hit the fan.

Sunday 7th January 1996 — FA Cup 3 — Chelsea (a)

Football's ability to convert the most quiet and unassuming family man into a loudmouthed bigot was usually more evident on trips to Chelsea and today proved no exception.

The previous evening had been spent sampling the pubs in Soho with a Newcastle-supporting mate who had moved down to London to teach. As tradition dictated, wearing my shirt, Kelly (nicknamed Ned in honour of his namesake David) and I had been welcomed by every London supporter we met (mostly Arsenal). An evening packed with supporters of other London teams wishing us well demonstrated the feelings that existed towards Chelsea.

London teams disliked each other intensely, bar teams like Orient and Brentford who were constantly patronised with phrases such as "Good old..." or "It's nice to see the smaller London clubs doing well..." The fact that they rarely met on the football field enhanced the warmth towards them.

The reason for the disdain felt by other fans towards Chelsea was clear the moment I stepped onto the tube at Earl's Court. The drop in football violence, thanks to the new Premiership, meant I wasn't quite so worried about hiding my allegiance.

Although there was no danger of being physically attacked at this point, the sheer volume and quantity of comments intended to rile was astounding.

Seated in a carriage filled with warm sweaters and waterproof coats, I was forced to listen to various traditional tales of the North East, of whippets, cloth caps, closed mines, shipyards and unemployment.

If only the Jarrow marchers had thought about the number of Newcastle and Sunderland fans who would suffer ridicule at the hands of the smug Southern gentry, I'm sure they'd have thought twice.

Each conversation was projected at the small pockets of Newcastle fans dotted about and by the time we reached Fulham Broadway, it was nice to have some reasonably fresh air to replace the hot stuff in the train.

Leaving the station, the atmosphere took a turn for the worst. Gone was the joviality, replaced by intimidation. The well-off waterproof gang were now joined by shaven heads, bomber jackets and Union Jacks. The two groups, that would never have mixed so freely anywhere else combined to demonstrate the combined brains and brawn of Chelsea.

One of the waterproofs took one look at me before softly uttering "Geordie maggot" as he strolled past me, while one of the bomber boys crossed over the packed match-day street with the sole intention of calling me a "Caant".

A brief drinking session before stepping on the train had dulled my senses to their anger along with any sense of disbelief that they felt the need to do it in the first place.

I'd always looked forward to Chelsea matches because their fans' devotion to their team rivalled our own. Even their hooligan element "The Headhunters" represented dedicated fans who'd chosen "the dark side". It usually generated passionate atmospheres but so far, the mood was just sour and ugly.

The evening was slipping into darkness even as we wandered into the claustrophobic corridor that travelled the length of the monstrous East Stand.

A glance across to our right demonstrated Chelsea's commitment to building a great stadium. The two tiers behind the far goal contrasted sharply with the decrepit stand we presently sat in.

A temporary stand rose to the left in place of the old shed. Gone were the vast spaces behind each goal that had swallowed up so much of the ground's atmosphere, as were the crumbling terraces that had blighted Stamford Bridge.

Passion oozed from every corner of the ground and despite the tier above blocking out our view of anything over head height (the football equivalent of wide screen television) I was able to experience the type of atmosphere that had first made me fall in love with football and Newcastle.

A first half header from the annoying Mark Hughes looked to have settled the tie. We hadn't looked like scoring, the best the lads could muster a shot from Philippe Albert which was lucky to hit the post.

We desperately urged Newcastle on every time they crossed half way line and were drowned out every time Chelsea did the same.

Ten minutes from time, Sir Les knocked one in. I feigned delight because I'd heard the whistle for off-side the instant he'd touched the ball. It still didn't stop me showing my dissatisfaction, if only to show solidarity with my peers.

Full time slipped into injury time and despite camping out in the Chelsea half, Newcastle were creating little. That was until Sir Leslie again slipped through the defence, this time on-side, to slip in the equaliser.

Our hosts, who had been celebrating their progress to the next round since Hughes' header directed their displeasure at the referee and Sir Les. Once the players and officials had disappeared down the tunnel, their venom was directed at the 2,000 jubilant fans dancing, until then unnoticed, in one corner. I envisaged the biggest problem facing us was suppressing the broad grins that were now plastered on our faces.

Insults rained down as colours were covered up. In the cramped conditions below the East Stand the insults turned to jostles, with police nowhere to be seen.

Once into the open, within sight of cameras and recently-appeared constabulary, the aggression subsided. Ned and I trod silently towards the tube station, checking every now-and-again to see if my shirt was showing.

There were the familiar shouts of confrontation, followed by the nervous posturing of the few police horses positioned along the road.

The queue for Fulham Broadway was immense, so we opted to make tracks to West Kensington.

At first, the option to keep moving seemed the sensible one. Walking through a paved shopping area, taking in the opulent buildings that surrounded us, the absence of fans eased our worries only for the sounds of battle ahead of us to slow our steps.

There was no way we were going to turn back, especially because we couldn't actually see anything ahead. The only sound we could make out was the sound of horses' hooves on cobbles behind us. Without a second thought we dived for the nearest doorway as mounted police raced by.

Following the path the horses had taken we were relieved when the well-to-do houses of Chelsea ran out and the street market stalls and blocks of flats of West Kensington took over. We were able to blend into the down-at-heel surroundings. Nobody was bothered about Les or the goal here, they were too busy with their own lives to want to inflict any misery upon us.

We were able to smile for the first time since leaving the safety of our seats. Smiles widened when we thought about our detractors on the way here. How sweet it was to have the last laugh, it didn't happen very often so I was going to make the most of it.

Unfortunately it was Chelsea who had the last laugh, winning the replay on a penalty shoot-out after one of the most dramatic FA Cup matches I had ever seen.

My FA Cup dream was over but there wasn't the pain of the previous season. After all we were nine points clear at the top of the league, at least it wasn't going to be a dull end to the season!

Wednesday 10th January 1996 — CCCQF - Arsenal (a)

It was a Wednesday night and Newcastle were live on ITV. Runaway leaders of the Premiership against bloody Arsenal. We'd beaten Liverpool 1-0 in the last minute of the previous round and had beaten Arsenal in the last four league meetings, surely a place in the Semi-finals beckoned.

It was my fault, I know but I had to ring up Paul for the first time in two years. I realise now that it was the kiss of death for our whole season. Everything Kev and the boys had worked towards was to be blown away in spectacular fashion.

I hadn't even rung him to gloat. I was still philosophical about our cup chances (maybe a bit blasé about being nine points clear in the title race).

The old clichés about eleven against eleven etc were probably quoted but as it was nothing could have prepared me for the sheer blindness of the referee and the dirty tricks of the Arsenal team.

The writing was on the table when Ginola, after being hacked constantly by Nigel Winterburn and Lee Dixon, was brought down after another mazy run. "Free-kick, surely ref!" we shouted at the box in the corner of our sitting room, even the dome-headed Brian Moore agreed with us.

The referee had other ideas. A free-kick was duly awarded to Arsenal and Ginola booked for diving. There hadn't been a springboard in sight. Even Winterburn left the scene with a puzzled look. The type of look a gorilla must have when he stumbles across a banana plantation.

Matters took a turn for the worse when Ian Wright put Arsenal ahead. Fair enough I thought, we can still get back into it, we did at Chelsea.

This was new Newcastle.

The lads looked rattled but the score was still only 1-0 at half-time and Kev would sort them out, wouldn't he?

He seemed as if he had failed in this when Ginola, walking backwards 'accidentally' caught that nice Mr Dixon on the chin. The referee was even smiling when the linesman told him what Ginola had done.

That was effectively it. Ian Wright dived headlong to score another wonder-goal against us and all that was left to do was to switch off the television and avoid all thoughts of the game.

Why had I risked phoning Paul? I'd had no contact with him for nearly two years. Two years when they had gone from strength to strength.

As long as we beat them in the league, the score will be evened out. At least now we can concentrate on that. How many times had I heard that said to console losers? For now it made the utmost sense (but then it would do).

Saturday 10th February 1996 — Middlesbrough (a)

"I heard they are showing the game at the Lonsdale," Gill's friend Lisa remarked, so we went.

It was all very hush-hush. The pictures were being beamed from Scandinavia because British television wasn't allowed to broadcast matches live on a Saturday.

Considering it was so hush-hush, the bar was unusually packed with Newcastle fans for a Saturday afternoon.

With five minutes to kick-off the bar emptied. We followed the hordes up the stairs to a 'conference suite'. Making our drinks last the whole afternoon, we managed to ease ourselves into some seats by the side of the screen. We'd never be able to turn our heads again, but at least we'd get to see the match.

I'd forgotten how upset Gill had got after the match at St James' and maybe if I'd put an ounce of thought into it, we'd never have gone — but I didn't, so we did.

Although I wince to admit it now, I'd become a bit complacent about the title race. We were nine points ahead of Man United and had a game in hand. In the interests of an easy life and because Middlesbrough needed a boost after a run of poor form I had decided that it wouldn't be too bad if they won.

I was actually speaking heresy and if I'd uttered these thoughts outside of my home, would have been nailed to the nearest tree whilst magpies pecked casually and sadistically at my flesh. I didn't and so avoided a grizzly death.

John Beresford also felt some sympathy for our North East rivals when he slipped the ball past Pavel Srnicek to give Middlesbrough the lead. I was quite pleased to hear Gill's barely audible "Yes" and witness her smile for the first time when the words Middlesbrough and football were mentioned in the same breath.

Unsurprisingly, the rest of the room hadn't shared Beresford's generosity. Comments revolved around the words peroxide, ponce and the full range of expletive vocabulary. He was not popular.

With 23 minutes left, Newcastle were looking clueless. It was time for Kev to play his trump card. In the middle of the week, he had paid out £7.5 million for the Columbian Faustino Asprilla. He had arrived in a snow storm and still wanted to sign.

When he stepped onto the pitch, it took him seven minutes to set up the equaliser. After tying Steve Vickers in knots, he coolly crossed for Steve Watson to score.

The room exploded. Fans stormed the mini-stage that the screen had been stood on and danced to obscure our view. They were on the tables and on the floor. I smiled apologetically at Gill. Surely she'd be happy with a draw. Selfishly, she wasn't.

This was swiftly followed by a grass-cutter from Ferdinand that trickled between Steve Walsh's legs. The Lonsdale scene was repeated as Gill's head sank into her lap.

Driving away, it was hard to see how we could possibly not win the league. Boro, on the other hand were slipping closer to yet another speedy relegation. Our lead at the top had stretched to 11 points, still with a game in hand.

With only 13 games to play, surely even we couldn't blow it. It was to prove an unlucky 13.

Monday 4th March 1996 — Manchester United (h)

"I'd never despised Newcastle, in fact I quite liked them, until that season. It was then that they became a threat and I've never liked them since."

These immortal words have been constantly repeated to me by my present Manchester United-supporting colleague. The frequency of this admission has been helped by our constant disagreements on football along with the proximity of our classrooms: directly opposite.

Each time David White utters those immortal words he is convinced he has never uttered them before. Due to my reliance on him for lifts back from work I have kept quiet my feelings on the statement.

However, if he'd never hated Newcastle before that season and Manchester won the league — it's no surprise that he couldn't understand how I had felt after witnessing my one sniff of silverware thrown away in such a dramatic fashion?

In the week leading up to the game, Keegan had acted to add stability to the midfield by signing battling David Batty. Previously his reputation on Tyneside had been as a dirty player we loved to hate, but suddenly he became our battler, dedicated to our championship cause. Suspended for this game, he was the missing link with two championships already won with Leeds and Blackburn.

Batty's signing took the amount of money spent by Keegan in the last few weeks to £11.25 million pounds and allayed fans' fears that any available money was being piped into Rugby and Ice Hockey. Pages in the match programme had been dedicated to the two sports, while every big name that joined the rugby club was presented to the predominantly disinterested football faithful.

I wasn't alone in lacking any interest in either sport, especially after years freezing on a rugby field every week while I had hated being the poor relation of North East ice hockey to Durham as a Whitley fan. Why did I want them shoved in my face at the football? Man United didn't try to have their finger in every sporting pie so why did we?
The general feeling was round balls only, please!

The Sky cameras had come to town and as Newcastle ripped into the visitors, I eagerly anticipated receiving the video from my regular source at school the next day.

Twice, Sir Les was foiled by a sprawled Schmeichel at his feet while Philippe Albert (everyone knows his name) thumped his free-kick against the bar.

Half-time arrived without any score. Standing in the bar, looking out across a blackened Leazes Park, there was only the worry that Manchester's ability to score spawny goals would prove decisive. If the lads continued to pound away, surely the breakthrough would come.

Experience taught us to expect the worst and true to form, Philip Neville found Eric Cantona lurking at the far post to volley past Pavel Srnicek.

A record of thirteen home wins on the trot ended with that strike. The complacent belief that the league was Tyneside-bound disappeared in an instant. The Reds were only one point behind us with six wins on the trot.

The first time you win a trophy is special, especially since the last trophy had been won a few months before I was born. I'd waited 13 years to see any piece of silverware, what difference would it make to Man United if they didn't win this year? David used to get upset if they didn't win, for Newcastle losing was a way of life and the pain associated with it was dulled over the years.

Big games were there to be lost, but now a hope that the drought would soon be over had made the pain clearer. Defeat without pain could be laughed or drank off, but now in front of the nation, small groups of Newcastle fans were shamefully grieving.

Sky latched onto this group. We were portrayed as a club full of dreamers, prepared to cry if matters didn't go our way. The nation may have wanted us to win the title but they were also laughing at our sudden lack of resilience — we just couldn't take the heat.

The worst thing about it, was that Wearside was laughing louder than anybody else — and it hurt!

Saturday 23rd March 1996 — Arsenal (a)

If Manchester United had got the weaker members of the support crying into their cotton hankies, then the trip to Arsenal would have made them suicidal.

Arsenal's team and supporters showed just how sadistic they can be. There was to be no revenge for the cup exit in January as Newcastle struggled and Arsenal punished them for it.

With 17 minutes gone, it was all over. The unknown Scott Marshall, followed by the annoyingly sprightly Ian Wright, who never failed to score against us, set up a 2-0 lead.

In their wisdom, Arsenal had declared the section next to the away end "the singing corner". All the supporters who wanted to chime were encouraged to do so. The lack of atmosphere at St James' could easily have been avoided if they had let us loudmouths sit together.

It worked a treat. Having a large body singing together encouraged the rest of the ground to wake up and join in the dialogue with the away fans.

A tirade of increasingly humiliating chants bombarded us once Ian Wright had chipped them 2-0 up. It started with old favourite "Where were you were shit", sung to the tune of one of the ancient hymns I was forced to endure at school assemblies. It droned along the lines "bread of heaven..." and it was quite clear that God wasn't on our side today.

This was swiftly followed by "You're shit and you know you are." Various songs celebrated Arsenal's glory but they were cut short, due to the lack of reaction from our disconsolate support.

At the start of play, we had been above Manchester on goal difference alone. By losing 2-0 they leapfrogged into first place without playing a game. Once they had worked this out the final twenty minutes involved endless repetitions of "You lost the league at Highbury..." The most soul-destroying part of it all was that they had no interest in the title and had helped Manchester for the sheer hell of it.

Singing those words instead of the original hymn "When the saints..." Arsenal were demonstrating that our own failure had been not singing more variations on hymns ourselves. It was obviously the way to influence the one upstairs, who seemed to be wearing a red shirt.

You'd have thought that in a fight against the Red Devils, he might have been on our side, but he just mustn't have been interested.

At the final whistle, the fans who weren't hurling insults at our hosts or making use of king-sized hankies were stunned. Although having a game in hand, on present form it was of no consolation. We'd witnessed a complete capitulation. Ned, who had sat silently beside me was subjected to a libellous attack on his vocal inactivity — "...it's just not my way..." he pleaded.

In my fury, I'd lashed out at my closest ally. His refusal to react to the slanderous lies being thrown at us by the "singing corner" was tantamount to treason in my book. Even if it was a book written after a bitter and bloody battle.

Needless to say, Paul wouldn't be contacted until well after the season, when any wounds that need to heal have been healed.

Our last game in London, meant the end of my trips to The Smoke. I was glad to see the back of my ex-home. Six games there had been rewarded with a solitary victory and two draws.

There had also been cup defeats to two London teams. Without the capital's spectre hanging over us, surely we could turn the tables our way. What a way that would be to respond to the doubters down South.

Wednesday 1st April 1996 — Liverpool (a)

Away from football, matters with Gill were coming on apace. We were moving back to my roots by buying a house together in Whitley Bay. A wedding was being planned for August that had originally been arranged for early in the month but had to be put back to the Bank Holiday weekend. I was gambling on not missing a home game but had committed the cardinal crime of football supporting — never organise a wedding during the season.

Once the dust had settled after Arsenal, I had forgiven Ned enough to ask him to be my best man.

Today, however was the day we were moving into our new house. The rest of our Easter holiday had been spent on the home DIY front. Endless trips to the large superstores that were reserved for the days football had set aside for families and relationships — at one time Sundays but sadly not any more.

At lunchtime, I left my intended finishing off a last coat of paint to pick up her friend Lisa and a couple of mates.

One of whom, Peter, had travelled with us to previous games and had no inhibitions about singing and shouting — if Newcastle had set up a singing corner, he'd have been it. A real Geordie, he indulged in plenty of pre-match lubrication but still had an itemised memory of the match, despite his slurred speech.

I'd forgotten all about my poor spouse-to-be sitting with a pile of paint brushes and pots in a bare unfurnished house, thankful to be able to return to civilisation (admittedly with apple-white spattered hair). Two victories had already been achieved against Liverpool — both in the last minute and both by Steve Watson, perhaps we'd be shown the favour that had been missing in the last defeats.

Every pub was packed with Newcastle fans, determined not to let themselves down on Sky again. Memories of Derby County in 1992 (1-4 with 3 sendings off) and possible relegation to division 3, now that was worth crying about, not finishing second in the country. That was party time! Or would have been just four years earlier.

Described as the greatest match of all time by Andy 'camera angles' Gray, it had everything but a happy ending. An early goal from Fowler was cancelled out by Sir Les. Ginola raced from the halfway line to exquisitely finish past David James and at half-time we were gasping for breath.

No sooner had one attack broken down, another had been launched at the opposite end. To top it all off we were 2-1 up. I'd never known such action. We had achieved what we hadn't managed in our games against Arsenal and Manchester -to score.

In my greed, my thoughts even calculated a 4-1 win would put us level with Manchester on goal difference. The unrelenting pace and atmosphere continued but I was soon brought down to Earth by Robbie Fowler's equaliser.

We'd settle for a draw I decided but the lads had other ideas. Robert Lee curled an exquisite ball to the now-nick-named Tino Asprilla who repeated the curling trick around the advancing David James.

Liverpool weren't happy and for the rest of the match, they bombarded Pavel's goal. It was at this point in the match that the twilight zone that had cost Newcastle so dearly in the mid-80s returned with a vengeance.

With three minutes to go, we were still leading and hanging on by a thread. The mystical power of the zone added ten pound weights to the boots of the Newcastle players and deprived them of their ability to mark or pass.

Empowered by the mystical force, Collymore took advantage, not once but twice, scoring two for only the second time that season in the league. The final effort crossed the line in injury time.

It was hard to take, harder for some than others as more fans joined the growing ranks of the "blub club". Watching the match video later, Richard Keyes, the Sky presenter feigned compassion, using as many hard-luck clichés as he could muster to describe the poor sods whose dream was now slipping away. Andy Gray's enthusiasm for the game was lost on Tyneside. Arriving home at 2am I couldn't even bring on the comfort of sleep as my mind still whizzed about the evening's actions.

Wearside lapped every defeat up, fuelled by Sunderland's

domination of the 1st Division. The previous years of Newcastle domination had even resulted in pity towards them, and they didn't like.

I realised it was time to find a job closer to home, if only to avoid the amused looks and comments every morning after each weekend setback.

Saturday 6th April 1996 — QPR (h)

An easy home victory on paper, maybe but facing a 0-1 deficit, luck continued to elude us. Beardsley decided that it was up to him to put things right. A shot into a gaping net, followed by a shimmy past defenders to conjure up an unlikely winner.

The crowd had never been so desperate, screaming from start to finish. The title that had appeared improbable to lose, now looked possible to win.

Monday 8th April 1996 — Blackburn (a)

There was only the previous season's FA cup victory to give us hope of winning at a ground that had been unlucky since Liam O'Brien's last minute effort in 1990.

Chicken and beans were ceremoniously ridiculed as an ineffective and uninspiring pre-match meal but we all realised that it would make no difference to Blackburn's Mr Interesting what we or any of the other Newcastle fans travelling down that night said about him. He enjoyed making us suffer and he had had lots of practice at it.

A tight game looked to have been won when David Batty scored from long range, it was the perfect return to his old club, especially bearing in mind the number of shirts outside that had Batty printed on and either been removed or partially covered.

Shearer had been kept quiet (thrown the odd chicken bone) but yet again, the throwaway zone re-surfaced. Unknown Newcastle-fan-as-a-boy Graham Fenton struck twice in front of the massed hordes to prompt not only the predictable crying for Sky but over-the-top threats against his family in Newcastle.

A win would have put us level on points at the top still with a game in hand. Our own ability to shoot ourselves in the foot was now becoming legendary and Manchester were doing us no favours at all.

Monday 29th April 1996 — Leeds United (a)

My wife-to-be was having difficulty combining work, house decoration and marriage arrangement without her future husband. Having missed out on our first night together in our new home, a Bank Holiday Monday spent decorating along with numerous jaunts for home matches there was no way she was going to let me miss her birthday.

A lot of men might have left the "little lady" to amuse herself, after all it was nearly the end of the season and I could make it up to her later on. However, rather weak and pathetically, I decided to keep my internal organs internal.

Besides, I was going to Nottingham on the Thursday and I had to leave some time for the more mundane matters like sleeping.

A quiet meal in Newcastle's Chinatown was enjoyed without a mention of the evening's footballing feast, or within sight of a television set. It had been a strain not mentioning the "f'-word but I'd managed it.

Once out of the restaurant, that was it. Like a dog on heat. Straining at the leash-like hold Gill had of me, I could see the looming shape of Rosie's Bar and predictions were made and explained (by me) to pass the seconds before reaching the pub.

Once I had trod on the exposed floorboards, nerves were instantly calmed. Newcastle were leading 1-0, and it was half-time.

A second half of backs-to-the-wall defending proved we could still win games away from St James' but it was Keegan's outburst that made events so memorable.

I must have been walking about with my head in the clouds (or couldn't watch Sky) and had completely missed Alex Ferguson's comments about Notts Forest and Leeds but you could tell that Kev was agitated as he talked to Andy know-it-all Gray.

His answers were brief and then he launched into the now-famous tirade on Alex. When he came out with "...and he went down in my estimation..." the whole pub stopped.

Pints were gently set down and heads swivelled towards the tiny screens all around us. It was like Close Encounters of the Third Kind when the humans are all staring spellbound at the alien spacecraft opening before them.

Kev continued; "...and I would luv it if we beat them, luv it!" with that the atmosphere cracked and cheers whooped from every corner, followed by a medley of Keegan tunes —

"Walking in a Keegan wonderland", "Keegan, Keegan..." and finally "...Keegan is our king."

He had echoed the thoughts of Tyneside without uttering the words "miserable bastard" or any phrase which began with the word "Scottish...."

It reflected Tyneside protocol, we were unlikely to win the league, but at least we're going to let people know how we feel, months of frustration swept forth that night as we partied before the wake.

Thursday 2nd May 1996 — Notts Forest (a)

Three points behind Man United with a game in hand and a goal difference that was inferior by six. A win would have pulled us level with one game to play. There had been a brief hope of a red collapse when Southampton beat them at the Dell but it was only a blip on their otherwise faultless run-in.

While they had marched on we'd stuttered — great results ruined by late carelessness. They didn't make such mistakes, years of recent success had put an end to that. All we had left was hope of a miracle.

Beardsley worked his magic to score in the first half, Sir Les hit the bar in the second before a mistake by Batty gave Woan the chance to score from distance.

On the way home, there was only the consolation that we hadn't lost. A defeat for Man United coupled with a victory against Tottenham at St James' would give us the title.

Who had to do the business against them? Middlesbrough. The only hope was that the damage ex-fans of Newcastle in Graham Fenton and Frank Clark had done to us would by reciprocated by Manchester old boy Bryan Robson.

Sunday 5th May 1996 — Tottenham (h)

For the last time that season, I left Gill listening to the Boro on Century Radio. With the resigned air of a man anticipating the worst, I listened to the fans on the Metro talking about how Middlesbrough were going to let their opponents win, since Bryan Robson was one of

Man United's greatest players. Others talked of Boro's golden opportunity to deny their local rivals the title.

One had come in a borrowed Middlesbrough shirt, arguing that we should be supporting them for the day. This argument being met with ridicule and an interrogation of his true allegiance, "I'm no smoggie" he maintained throughout.

The chances of a shock home win on Teesside looked bleak, especially given Middlesbrough's effortless plummet towards relegation.

The Newcastle team sensed that they were on a hiding to nothing. Despite a first half full of effort, their hearts seemed to lack the belief and fervour of previous matches. When Jason Dozzell scored for Spurs, Manchester were already ahead after weathering a first half of Boro pressure. A further two goals on Teesside made Les's equaliser academic.

The helicopter, carrying the Premiership trophy, that had been hovering between the two North-East towns headed South, leaving Tyneside to reflect on missed chances.

The team lapped the pitch a few times to appreciative applause (and a few tears) before departing for undoubtedly sunnier climes. The streets of Newcastle embarked on one of the greatest scenes of drunken debauchery for many years.

Gill met up with me after the game for a drink. Not only had every member of St James' Park stayed in town, so had the rest of Newcastle. Bars were heaving with black and white bodies, toasting the coming of a new age. We'd missed out this time but we'd be back was the message.

The effects of all day drinking took effect early in the evening as fans spilled out onto the streets to sing the team's praises. Nobody had believed we'd be challenging for the title so soon and it was the shock of lasting the pace that had prompted the predominantly male party.

Unfortunately, getting drunk and slipping into a stupor in the gutter like everybody else, wasn't enough for some, as bravado took over.

Haymarket's antics started with individuals scaling drainpipes outside the Three Bulls' Heads pub, to balance precariously from first, second and third floor buildings. Once boredom with this achievement had crept in, and prompted by the crowds below, the brave (or mindless) ones leapt from their perches onto lamp-posts over 10 feet away.

Others scaled the outside of nearby multi-story car parks to demonstrate their own brand of daring on the sloping roofs of Eldon Garden shopping centre — 60 feet or more above the striped pavements.

Gill and I headed away from the scene which we expected to end in tragedy to try and find some food. As we neared the Bigg Market, police vans raced past us to deal with a rumoured outbreak of vandalism and violence. We decided to skip the impromptu street parties (and never-ending waits to get served) in favour of a curry and drink in the more sedate and hopefully calmer streets of Tynemouth. Had all the efforts of the previous year been for this? It was a sad way to see off a memorable season.

Although the shirts were evident at the coast, the mood was more sombre. Gill apologised on behalf of her Boro team and we left it at that. We'd be back.

Exile over

For the first five years of my working life I had been forced to find glory on the teaching front outside Tyneside; West London followed by Wearside.

The sporting glory of my first appointment had given way to the harsh reality of North-East football — it means everything to everybody. It was time to move on, if only to avoid the nightmare of the Tyne Tunnel and its unpredictable early morning chaos.

The job of a **PE** co-ordinator came up in North Shields and the lure of home (and the chance to lie in an extra half-hour) was strong.

The lean sporting years in Sunderland (bar winning a rugby league cup) meant I had to convince the head and assembled governors of my potential. I trumpeted my glorious past before them, comparing my former school to Southampton, where just staying up was considered an achievement. With a bigger school, the sky would be the limit!

They were convinced and my return home via Sunderland was complete.

On top of the new job, it was all steam ahead towards married life. Despite the warnings; "The bairns'll be half smoggy" (among others) I was blinded by love and the colour of her football shirt was not going to stop me marrying her (especially since she was paying half the mortgage!)

The wedding had been set for the 24th August — a Saturday. A date made long before the fixture lists were printed, I'd prayed for an away match against Southampton, (a ground that held only embarrassing defeat and therefore an advantageous match to avoid).

The summer had been spent decorating and revelling in the extra month of football on offer thanks to the European championships. St James' had been chosen to host three of the group matches and throughout the season the opportunity to witness the cream of Europe had us all salivating. That was, right up until they announced that the teams to play would be France (undoubtedly without Ginola and Kung Fu kid Cantona since they traitorously played outside of the mother country), uninspiring Bulgaria and Romania. Interest further dropped when the limited number of 'cheap' £15 tickets disappeared along with the £30 'bargain seats', leaving only the scandalous £45 one left.

The greed of the organisers resulted in a barely half-full stadium (though the massive big screen marquis nearby was packed).

For the first time since 1990 Gazza showed us what he could do as England raced through to the Semi-finals (albeit with a penalty shoot-out win against Spain) to lose out to Germany on penalties again.

Alan Shearer had impressed and his position as competition leading scorer had set the country buzzing. Every radio played Three Lions (the official England song), while a bald bloke called Fat Les (a name designed to attract football fans the country-wide who enjoyed hearing about other overweight individuals) sang about Vindaloo and cups of tea.

Once the fuss had settled down (and Gill and I had returned to our former past-time of decorating), Tyneside was set alight by the news that England's captain was going to be ours!

Mr Chicken and Beans, Mr Personality himself was to join Newcastle. This was way bigger than the humble pie we had been forced to eat when David Batty had joined. It was time to fall on the floor chanting "We're not worthy..." and half of Tyneside did just that as he stood before them outside St James' for the first time as a Newcastle player.

He arrived for £15 million, a record signing not just for Newcastle but the Premiership. It was a far cry from the days of allegedly 'being forced' to sell Gazza's for £2million. If we'd missed out on the Premiership last year — it was ours for the taking now, surely?

Sunday 11th August 1996 — Charity Shield — Manchester Utd

What more could you ask from a stag night weekend? An evening of drinking on foreign soil, followed by a few hours dancing to Indie hits of the

80's and 90's and the chance to witness vengeance exacted on Alex Ferguson and his annoyingly successful team.

Nearly everything went to plan. The first blip occurred when, despite clear and concise instructions that everyone in the party must be decked in black and white —only I, the groom-to-be, adhered to them. Arsenal Paul objected on grounds of allegiance (and allergy), Ned preferring to avoid drawing attention to himself and the others claiming it might affect their pulling power.

By 2am, the traffic in North London's Tufnell Park had never heard such poor renditions of Newcastle tunes from on top of one traffic island.

The rain that teemed down only added to the sense of occasion. All thoughts of my impending wedding were replaced by child-like dreams of Shearer hat-tricks.

The next morning, the drive through Central London was memorable for the numbers of Geordies cluttering the tourist-laden pavements. The groups that swarmed around the pubs on Baker Street added spice to our journey, especially since there wasn't a red shirt to be seen anywhere.

40,000 had made the trip and nobody envisaged defeat in any shape or form. The early sun beat down, declaring today to be the start of Newcastle's dominance.

Dropping the car at Hangar Lane, intending to get a quick getaway afterwards, Ned and I set off for Wembley Stadium (having lost the others the moment they spied a packed pub).

Wembley Way was everything I had dreamed of. Black and White merged with the odd clump of red as far as the eye could see.

Flags that had long since been banned from St James' proudly adorned every inch of the overpass coming out of Wembley station. The debris of modern football littered the concourse; burger and chip wrappers, cans of all sizes and cast-off newspapers that had provided brief distraction on the way down.

The sight of Wembley Stadium, after respective journeys from Manchester (?) and Newcastle brought clusters of be-shirted fans to song, "Who the fuck are Man United..." echoed around us, competing against the well-worn Mackem favourite "Cheer up Kevin Keegan..." Sunderland's adaptation of "Cheer up sleepy Jean".

The noise was constant as fans acclimatised themselves to another season of broken promises and hopes. The grassy verges to the side of the turnstile steps were filled with the most unlikely picnickers. To the left the grass had turned a grey-white, while the other resembled clumps of poppies, the variety that would thrive despite constant attempts to kill it off.

Face painters must have cleaned up, with vast numbers of professional, and not so professional, enthusiastic attempts.

The nuns were out in their habits while a black and white Pierrot who we recognised from matches the previous season was being half-carried up the steps and you had to question how much of the match she would recall.

The Honey Monster was about the only 'new fan' we didn't recognise that day as Tyneside must have emptied.

"Last one out switch off the lights!" had once been scrawled on a road sign just outside Sheffield when United and Wednesday had met in a Wembley FA Cup semi-final and you had to wonder how many had been left in Newcastle.

The sun beat down and every player's name rang out from the growing army. They applauded our efforts and in anticipation of theirs we replied in kind. John Hall's name was even chanted by the short-sleeved, striped end of Wembley. Everything was going great, Peter and Lisa who I had dropped off at Baker Street on the way here took their seats and hopes were high.

The only thing that could spoil our whole weekend was the team, and on cue they obliged with interest.

Like headless chickens they ran around after the streaking reds before the inevitable goal arrived. My recollection of the whole match was blotted out by my selective memory, the apathy of the collapse to the stunned murmurs once the fourth Manchester goal crashed in.

My frustration was taken out on the fans around us. I'd waited 13 years of my life to witness Wembley with a full contingent of Newcastle fans and I was desperate to show the spirit of the 80's hadn't died. Win, lose or draw we were still arguably the most loyal fans in the country... and still the noisiest.

We had watched worse defeats than this and carried our heads high — the team had given up, this was no reason for the supporters to do like-wise. But, we did.

Had we become too used to the high life? Our lofty position of 2nd softened us up? If the tears of the previous season had been anything to go by it had. A few devoted souls battled to rouse the sleeping giant but most had lost the heart to fight.

The second half passed with three goals and barely a murmur from the Tunnel End. Our £15million captain had sunk without a trace under the sea of red. His team trooped off after the presentation, leaving the Manchester players to parade the latest addition to their trophy cabinet.

This obviously displeased the Gods as the Heavens opened and we were treated to a Summer soaking. Sprinting for cover, we joked off the humiliation but another trophy-less season beckoned.

Memories of 1988's false dawn resurfaced to darken the mood further. Driving back, the roads were slow as Northerners evacuated the South. Flash floods caused by the rain slowed us down, as did the A1's inability to cope with the exodus.

The final kick in the teeth arrived once we met the Al. With home barely an hour away, traffic ground to a halt as roadworks closed off half the road. An extra hour was spent with the same depressed sets of supporters listening to Manchester's Oasis live on the radio. Their Manchester voices (although City supporters) reminded us of an afternoon best forgotten.

Returning from my stag weekend at 1 am (having driven everyone there and back myself) the one mistake we'd made was watching the match. It had been a buzz up until then!

Saturday 17th August 1996 — Everton (a)

The day before my birthday and at the ground that opened one of Newcastle's worst seasons. Cottee and his opening goal after 35 seconds — I could still see the spot he had stood and picture Beasant's face. Was lightning about to strike twice?

Of course it was! The same mild day, white clouds lolling across the sky lulling you into a false sense of security. The memories of Wembley the previous week put down to a bad dream, a practice — today was what mattered.

Only eight years ago we'd stood in the strip of terracing in the Park Stand at pitch level, watching Dave Beasant, Wimbledon's hero of the FA Cup final. Our hopes were of championships but relegation and in-house fighting were the order of the day.

Today's match seat in the same stand at £16 cost four times more than the same terrace spot had. The Newcastle fans were now pushed into a corner of the Bullens stand with its wood-backed benches (so beloved of Sheffield) and the match programme was twice as thick and similarly increased in priced. Gary Speed and Sir Les's determination had replaced the smiles of Pat Nevin, Tony Cottee, Spotty McDonald and Stuart McCall. Their combined valuation of £4.3 million hardly scratched Sir Les's.

Before Newcastle had settled, an Unsworth penalty and a Gary Speed strike had dumped them on their pants. 1988 and 4-0 beckoned.

By half time, the football had taken second stage. Amongst the Everton fans, a red and white striped shirt had been spotted and for the rest of the half, the incensed Newcastle contingent chanted good-natured ridicule towards him. Pleased to have been noticed, the otherwise anonymous body returned the compliment by leading occasional choruses of "Sun-der-land."

This wasn't unusual since Everton fans delighted in annoying us in this way. It was all part of their match-day routine. Sing their own team's praises before singing those of the opposition's greatest rivals.

Most took it in the spirit it was meant, pitying the unfortunate individual and his chosen devotion but there were those who considered this to be an extremely dangerous action.

Despite Sunderland's promotion to the Premiership, they were in a completely different world to Newcastle. Their struggles to stay in and eventually escape the First Division and our own meteoric rise had created an air of complacency.

On achieving promotion they'd refused to strengthen the team. Manager, ex-Evertonian, Peter Reid had nobly avoided spending outrageous Premiership prices for average talent.

As far as I was concerned they weren't a threat to us, just one of the teams we expected to beat and the lone fan in the Park Stand should be treated accordingly.

One individual sitting at the back of the stand didn't share my view. As the half time whistle blew he scuttled towards my seat at the end of the upper stand. Like a commando on a vital mission, he clambered over bodies and seats. His unshaven face and shaven head giving him the military undercover air. With a shove he was past Lisa and myself and had a clear view of the Mackem.

He proceeded to wave his arms to attract his prey's attention but when that failed he took to shouting "How, Mackem!" with increasing levels of delirium. His hands were hooked firmly on to the wooden stand like talons. His knuckles were now white with the pressure he was exerting on the wall.

"I'm going to fucking kill you, you fucking Mackem bastard scum!" he screamed, occasionally thumping the wall to vent his anger.

Bizarrely, every time a steward so much as looked at him, he immediately dropped onto the seat, still maintaining his maniacal fix; he wasn't going to let this one go. The ranting carried on throughout the interval but once the teams returned, he meekly returned to his seat, minus glaze and fervour.

Those who'd witnessed the scene only laughed, hollow nervous laughs after witnessing a most surreal experience. In previous years there were plenty who held similar levels of hatred not just for Sunderland but for anybody who wasn't a die-hard Newcastle fan. Their presence at football matches had thankfully become a rarity but there was still an endangering few who still clung to the bad old ways of small-minded thuggery.

At Newcastle home matches, in their desperation, there were a number of fans who insisted everybody should support them in hating Sunderland. Their insistence that we all "Stand up, if you hate Sunderland" was becoming a source of friction.

My visitor today reminded me of a similarly angry fan who shouted aimlessly at all around him, every time we refused to stand up when ordered. But was his frustration really about Sunderland or the lack of vocal support generally? Being able to vent his frustration in the positive support of the team was being denied him. How long would it be before his kind resorted to violence on being ostracised from his fellow supporters?

Saturday 24th August 1996 — Sheffield Wednesday (h)

I'd vowed this would never happen to me, I'd sneered at those who'd done it — how could they possibly be a true supporter? But here I was, Newcastle were at home and I was getting married. What sort of idiot would do that?
Me!

Gill's dad was a vicar and an extremely busy one at that, especially in the Summer when everybody was getting married. The only date he could marry us was the Bank Holiday weekend. Everything had been arranged for months and the only consolation for me was that I wasn't missing Man United or Liverpool.

For the first time in my life the match wasn't centre stage. Staying at my mum's after being turfed out of my own house by an extremely excitable future mother-in-law was weird enough and it was bizarre sitting reading the morning paper, knowing that I wasn't going to the match.

None of it had sunk in, missing the match or the wedding, despite having saved and planned for the last 18 months — even before last season's unbelievable start, even before I had heard of Ginola or thought of Les playing for the lads.

I'd been going out with Gill since April 1994 and we'd known each other since the previous September. That was an outstanding 68 wins 26 draws and 30 defeats with 215 goals scored and 125 conceded in the Premiership ago. Newcastle had appeared in two cup quarter-finals (losing both) and appeared at Wembley once.

On this basis I was convinced I wasn't rushing into marriage. Since first meeting her, Newcastle's seasons had been comparable to the Supermac days of the 70's and they looked like continuing, despite her allegiance to the Boro.

Instead of heading off at 1 o'clock for a pre-match bevy, I was having my last drink as a bachelor boy — just a few to steady the nerves. I was accompanied by Ned, who I had forgiven for not singing at Arsenal, as my Best Man. Arsenal Paul had come up the night before with his fiancée thanks to Arsenal's away pairing with Leicester that day.

All I could think about was whether the Shearer/Ferdinand partnership was going to be a success, so far, the (allegedly) greatest day of my life was passing me by in a haze.

Reaching the church, I still couldn't talk about anything but the match, the ramifications of missing it spun around me, aided by the alcohol in my system.

Once Gill walked up the aisle, Shearer, Sir Les, Sheffield Wednesday and their lack of form at St James' all slipped away. The huge rush of emotion was comparable to that experienced watching Gavin Peacock's opener against Leicester in '92. Seeing her, for once, I was speechless. Watching a beautiful move in a game, I knew exactly what to do, but confronted by beauty of the female variety I was dumbfounded.

I couldn't take my eyes off her and it was only the sound of Metro radio that returned me briefly to reality. Sitting in the hired Jaguar as we headed towards the reception, we listened to the cheer as Shearer rammed home his penalty to make the score 1-0 after only twelve minutes. I could relax even further, safe in the knowledge that Wednesday hadn't won at St James since 1989.

Lisa, who had also missed the game sat through the

reception with one ear tuned to the match as Gill's dad questioned the wisdom of having a Newcastle fan in the family.

Ned chose a particularly mellow moment to reveal that he'd become an Arsenal season ticket holder. By now, filled with life's joys, his admission didn't sink in and it was only after two days of the honeymoon that it dawned on me.

The wedding day was the party I'd always dreamed of holding. All my mates were there, I was able to drink, dance and talk football with each and every one of them, not one of them having the heart to tell of Sheffield's goals that had won the game 2-1.

We danced stupidly to The Jam, The Smiths' and Lou Reed (thanks to a mate doing the Djing), the perfect day.

Once at our Tynemouth sea-front hotel, the merriment gave way to our welcoming matrimonial bed, as unbeknown to me, in the background Guy Whittingham knocked in Wednesday's winner on Match of the Day.

Saturday September 21st — Leeds (a)

The shock of having to work with not only a smug Sheff Wed but an even more self-satisfied Man United fan, had subsided. A short honeymoon spent in a tent in extremely wet Derbyshire had been the only affordable break before I had to prepare for my new job.

Despite the wedding day defeat, there had been a great return of 15 points in 7 games. Away wins at Spurs and Sunderland had been gleefully accepted. The victory at Roker had been played out in front of a crowd devoid of away fans.

Those fans who had made it in and naively celebrated Newcastle's goals were able to listen to the match from Sunderland General Hospital as trouble marred the fixture (as usual).

My married life obviously agreed with Newcastle. Shearer and Sir Les looked to have clicked.

I had taken over my new school's football team from David, the Man United fan and he never missed an opportunity to remind me that he had emulated Alex Ferguson's achievement with the previous year's team — winning the league and cup.

My first game in charge had resulted in a 1-0 win over local rivals Waterville, with a strike from my own version of Sir Les. It was certainly a first for me — a winning start.

The match was ironically played on the pitch used by non-league North Shields, the team that had started my thirst for football with violent cup clashes and squandered 3-0 leads. The original ground of Appleby Park had been sold to property developers when the club had fallen on hard times.

On the site where I had once paid my £1, there was now the entrance to a cul-de-sac of rabbit hutches and where the Wallsall fans had been gleefully thrown over the wall, now stood someone's kitchen and living room.

The trip to Leeds was waylaid when we spotted a sign promising pub food. With time to kill, I was easily able to convince the others to have a pint while I tackled a spicy Cumberland sausage sarnie with all the trimmings.

The pub was packed with Newcastle fans, the majority of whom avoided the delights of a similar meal, preferring to set new records for downed pints, which, as sole driver (and owner of a car) in our group I was unable to partake in.

Leaving with three-quarters of an hour to kick-off, I hadn't banked on encountering the mother of all traffic jams approaching the ground.

With the game imminent, half the car unloaded while Lisa bravely
accompanied me (to remind me where I'd parked the car) and once a particularly dodgy spot in my favourite Leeds industrial estate had been secured we followed swiftly (or as swiftly as the sausage permitted).

With ten minutes gone, we re-joined Peter whose drawled speech had already picked out Ginola's lack of interest in the game and Leeds' decision to hack anything in a striped shirt.

The ungainly Carlton Palmer had already been booked when Shearer found himself on the floor and after what appeared like a discussion between Newcastle's No.9 and the referee, Palmer was duly dispatched to the dressing room.

As far as the Leeds fans (and indeed a good majority of the national press) were concerned Shearer had got Palmer dismissed and the circumstantial evidence didn't look good for our striker.

However, one thing I'd learnt to my cost as a referee, once I'd made up my mind, nobody would respect you for changing it and, at the same time, it was a mistake to listen to players' whinges. Shearer was accused of un-sporting conduct, but with my black and white contact glasses on I doubted whether he would have had any effect, unless there were tenners exchanged at half time.

Facing 10 men, Newcastle put in the worst display of attacking football witnessed in a long time. Ginola had carried on his lethargic contribution and was duly substituted. My frustration at his lack of interest in the game (and our own lack of success at taking the game to Leeds) boiled over.

I ranted for five minutes as he walked past Keegan in the bench and wandered down the tunnel to the dressing room. Memories of Lee Clarke's outburst at Southampton sprang to mind and I demanded his immediate transfer as punishment for his lack of commitment to the cause.

It might have been the Cumberland sausage talking but I had to be dragged down by an embarrassed Lisa and a blissfully unaware Peter after their initial pleas of "Si'doon man" were ignored.

For the first time in my life I'd started looking at footballers' wages enviously. I thought about how hard I had to work for the same amount of money they earned in a week or two. It had never been an issue before because I had always been so grateful that they had chosen to sign up for the lads.

Ginola's apparent indifference riled me, "If I was getting paid that much..." I started, only to be interrupted by Lisa's reply of;

"Well you're not, so shut up!" I looked to Peter for support but from behind eyes that reflected an unknown number of bottles of Newcastle Brown he simply added
"Aa think he's canny!" before slandering another Leeds player.

My mood changed completely when Shearer rammed home his fourth goal of the season to secure the win but my views had been in complete contrast to the others. What was happening to my blind allegiance?

I convinced myself it was only a temporary blip, before commencing the journey home.

Saturday 12th October 1996 — Derby (a)

My sister's 30th birthday bash in Chester was nicely combined with a small 'detour' to the Baseball ground and a meeting with ex-Newcastle manager Jim Smith. The Bald Eagle had valiantly attempted to keep us in the First Division before relying, unsuccessfully, on a team of oldies to achieve promotion.

His replacement, Ossie Ardiles failed to make his diamond formation win, never mind sparkle, leaving it up to Kev and £60 million to sort the club out.

How Jim and Ossie would have fared given that sort of money was anyone's guess but they'd have found it hard to be doing better than he was doing now.

With six league wins out of six, we were two points behind leaders Liverpool. The early defeats having been more than compensated for.

I'd convinced Gill that it was only a small detour to Derby from Chester, so she might as well join me at the match, thus living out my fantasy of taking a footie loving girl to the match.

Whilst searching for a pub which sold food, Man United took the lead in an early morning Sky match against Liverpool. The mixed emotions at having the 'new enemy' give us a helping hand was easily forgotten because it meant a Newcastle win would see us return to the top.

Sitting in what could only be described as a downtown Derby 'tropical' bar, Manchester's victory was greeted with reluctant cheers. Surrounded by brightly coloured walls and the odd Swiss cheese plant, I tucked into another sausage standard and, along with new arrivals Peter and Lisa, we discussed the prospect of reaching the league's summit.

When you're married to a Boro supporter, you don't expect to have the full support of your spouse when it comes to Newcastle but her hatred for Manchester outweighed the inbred dislike for stripes, so she was firmly behind our latest Championship challenge.

The last time I'd visited Derby, I'd brought Sarah to witness our promotion push and it was a nice touch to be welcomed back to the ground by a flooded toilet. Thankfully, it wasn't seeping down the converted terraces behind the goal.

The old ground generated a great atmosphere. It was sad to think that Derby would be moving to a modern one just outside of town at the end of the season.

The new breed of stadia were functional, protecting you from the elements, offering suitable toilet facilities and 'refreshment stands' (burger bars) but lacked individuality. Boro's Riverside stadium looked impressive but looked like St James', Sunderland's successor to Roker and now Derby's new home.

Modern construction had done to football grounds what it had done to houses — created large sheds instead of a club's 'home'. New houses all looked like identical rabbit hutches all crammed together in giant warrens.

Safety dictated that all entrances had to be a certain size, as did gangways. Pillars were a thing of the past to avoid giving any cheaper "restricted view" seats. Roofs now towered skywards, letting the noise drift away, rather than the low-pitched Veitch stands.

The floodlights that had identified the position of a ground in a town were disappearing to be replaced by miniature versions on the roof. The league had gone cantilever-crazy!

All the history around us was to be wiped away, all because of a few leaky toilets. First it was the terraces then the toilets, what other pleasures were football fans to be deprived of?

I wondered whether Shearer was a traditionalist as he chested the ball, before volleying in the goal that returned us to the top of the league. If he was, his limited, short-phrase interviews hadn't indicated as much. After all, he hadn't had to wade through a couple inches of unidentified and unwanted liquids, had he?

Sunday 20th October 1996 — Manchester United (h)

Nearly nine years after Glenn Roeder had sent a Boxing Day St James' Park, and an inadvisably-brought flask of tea, into the air we were still waiting to beat them. Equalisers had been scraped, title battles lost and, for the last two months of my job, I'd had to listen to David wittering on about how great Manchester was. Typically, he ignored my calls of "Do you come from Manchester?" He considered his hometown of Leeds to be a suburb of the North-Western city.

The school football team was struggling to live up to the previous year's brilliance. Mid-table security looked the odds-on favourite for them and every night on the way home I had to listen to the same red propaganda.

One day he'd pay — why not today?

The players obviously felt the same way as they chased, harried and battled like never before. Even Ginola with his wet look (thanks to the constant downpour) was putting himself about, obviously he had been stung into action by my comments at Leeds (and two appearances as substitute).

We hadn't scored against them since Paul Kitson's equaliser in January '95, so it was an unexpected surprise when Shearer headed on for the pony-tailed Peacock to score. The ball barely looked to have crossed the line and when referee Steve Dunn seemed to be working in slow motion, hopes of a favourable decision weren't high, but after glancing over to the Russian linesman the goal was given.

You could almost hear the totally impartial Andy Gray moaning "I'd like to have another look at that," but thankfully his opinion mattered not one bit.

A goal it was. If only you could have framed a picture of Alex Ferguson's face after that one, if they could have found a camera low enough.

The long-haired Poborsky, who had inspired Czechoslovakia in Euro '96, tried to get full marks from the diving judges for his salmon leap and succeeded but apart from his penalty appeal Manchester hardly threatened.

We taunted their fans that "Shearer had turned you down..." and the whole ground (bar one miserable corner) registered their dislike for the Reds by standing up.

When Ginola curled a cracker round Schmeichel, thoughts of a 1-2 defeat changed to 2-3 but the lads had other ideas.

Shearer walloped the post just before half time and after half time Sir Les hit the post, but for the first time it bounced in. Everything was going our way. A Les shot ended up at Shearer's feet and he crashed the shot in. To add a touch of glamour, Philippe Albert chipped Schmeichel from the edge of the penalty area.

The smile on my face broadened thinking of David White's face. The surprise on everybody's faces was a joy to behold. Even the usually docile fans beside me who rarely registered more than a cracked smile were leaping about for joy, extending five fingers towards the steadily thinning group of Man U fans.

The win returned us to the top spot, leaping over Arsenal and Wimbledon. It was a more satisfying feeling having beaten the Champions so convincingly. I couldn't wait to hear Whitey's excuses. Surely, a trophy wasn't far off now?

Saturday 30th November 1996 — Arsenal (h)

It had all looked so promising at one point. We'd survived Shearer's absence due to a groin injury and we were still top. Admittedly we'd been beaten by Middlesbrough in the Coca-Cola Cup but it was the league that counted (we kidded ourselves) and we'd beaten them in that. If anything, it had restored parity in our house after Boro's cup victory as we agreed Newcastle could win the league if Boro could win the cup, quite an amicable settlement that saved a potential marriage-threatening argument.

I should have known that resuming friendly relations with Arsenal-Paul was a recipe for on-pitch disaster.

At 1-1, Shearer's goal looked to have set us on the path to victory, especially when Tony Adams was sent off for annoying our £15 million man.

Unfortunately, I'd forgotten Ian Wright's ability to score from outside the stadium when Newcastle was concerned. His smile could have easily stretched across Leazes' Park as he scored the winner. Not content with knocking us off the top last season, he was up to his old tricks again.

"We only had ten men..." the little band of Londoners gloated as we shuffled out. Our month-long stay at the top was over, just when hopes were being raised again, a dangerous thing to do because as soon as you start believing in something, some bugger will always snatch it from after knocking you to the ground and kicking you a bit.

Gill met me at the Monument Metro station, having unsuccessfully tried to pre-empt the Christmas rush. She'd failed to follow my advice about doing all your shopping on Christmas Eve because there was hardly anyone around.

I couldn't even show a token interest in our Christmas list, defeat had hit me bad. I hadn't even contemplated defeat. Right from the moment when I'd tuned into the club's Radio station — Radio Magpie early (ish) that morning to find out how the grass had been cut and whether it was still green I'd expected to see off the upstarts from 'doon Sooth'.

Despite my lack of interest at her exploits, Gill was surprisingly understanding. Years of watching Boro had trained her not to get her hopes too high — a trap I far too easily fell into.

To distract me from my disappointment, we took a trip to the Newcastle Arena to watch John Hall's ice hockey team — the Newcastle Cobras. A change of name making it possible for me to step foot in the place.

Sitting reading the Pink's dissection of the United match and digesting some over-priced chips, we found it quite an enjoyable experience.

We were able to put our bitter footie feuds to one side and watch, as completely impartial visitors the battles below us. From the Newcastle fan who was thrown out for banging his drum, whilst sitting amongst the visiting Manchester fans to the scraps on the ice.

A whole sporting sub-culture I had no idea existed was alive in Newcastle, from replica shirts to away supporters. Big business was nowhere to be seen. The bare breeze block walls of the Arena reminded me of the corridors of St James'.

The fans were a combination of ex-Durham Wasps fans and new arrivals to the sport. Between the sets of rival supporters a surprisingly good atmosphere was maintained as Newcastle won 8-3, hardly a score you'd encounter in football.

More importantly we hadn't argued about Shearer's cynicism or John Hall's greed. We'd have to do this again we promised each other like a couple of pensioners discovering a new use for their bus pass. A cessation of hostilities for a few hours had made a welcome change.

It was an experience that we found ourselves repeating, eventually becoming regular visitors to the sport that introduced me to spectating.

Wednesday 3rd December 1996 — UEFA 3 (2nd leg) — Metz (h)
Newcastle's greatest European night since 1969; French visitors Metz standing between the Mags and their first UEFA Cup quarter-final in 27 years. Town was buzzing with expectation, a 0-0 draw, all that was required after a 1-1 game in the first leg in France.

Where was I? Sitting in a room full of 30 equally expectant 8 year-olds trying to get any sort of reception from the school's one battered television!

I was not happy. It was the second night of the school's annual Christmas pantomime — the whole school involved, my mob on stage for a total of about eight minutes and back-stage (in the classroom) 'keeping quiet' for an hour and a half.

It was enough to drive a man/woman insane, but to miss the match to boot —that was torture.

My evening had been spent suspending a portable aerial from various light fittings and children. The latter provided a decent reception, but only when they stood still... a major difficulty for this excited mob.

We sat through a fuzzy EastEnders. A whole class gradually whittled down to a desperate one child who hadn't brought anything to occupy the time. By the time the match started, it was down to just me, desperately trying to make out the blobs before me and maintain order.

The moments spent standing next to the stage grimacing encouragingly to my class as they performed proved agonising. One of the blobs might have scored while I was out of the room, I hope it was one of my blobs.

Like a frustrated junky, I raced back to get my fix. The snow did its best to disguise the 0-0 score-line. "Boring" chanted the slightly interested few before drifting back to play with various wrestling figures and Gameboys.

Pantomime over with, the delicate task of matching parents with children began. Tino Asprilla and company had to take a begrudging second stage.

By the end of half-time, the coast was clear. Gill, who had been watching the theatrical entertainment, rushed us to our local where the second half was but ten minutes old and the score-line still, thankfully, goal-less.

Joined by an exhausted David White, desperate for some Gaelic ingenuity to annoy me with the next day, we supped welcome pints.

Two pieces of Tino magic turned the tie. In celebration, he exposed his vest underneath to wave his number 11 shirt on a corner flag. His punishment was swift — a yellow card and a suspension for the first quarter-final match.

Like an excited gazelle, he tore around the park, a damaged hamstring his eventual reward. Lying on a stretcher, he was wheeled out to enthusiastic but disappointed applause, the second striker to join the injury list (Sir Les the other casualty).

Tonight, the lads had climbed the mountain. Glory beckoned us forward. After losing top spot on Saturday, the ignominy of a cup exit to accompany it had been avoided.

The thought of another night spent in the company of "the little angels" and their assorted plastic figures tomorrow would be slightly more bearable after this victory.

It made up for missing out on a night of Newcastle glory in some small way, at least I'd be able to witness the next round.

A future clash of football and evening school duties would have to be avoided, a family crisis or simply pleading insanity might do the trick, anything to avoid a repeat display.

Saturday 11th January 1997 — Aston Villa (a)

It was the end of an era and Tyneside was in shock. Kev had gone — resigned, the official line stated but who could believe that?

The club had decided to hold a share issue again. They were aiming at attracting the big city money. There was no talk of giving the club to the fans — it was all for big bucks. As far as they were concerned, Kev was a loose cannon.

His alleged attempts to resign and unwillingness to stay at the end of the season made him a destabilising factor on an otherwise booming proposition. Plenty of fans would have longed to have a piece of the club, but they were to be ignored in favour of dark-suited nobodies whose knowledge of the town started and ended with the Tyne Bridge.

The Evening Chronicle would have been discarded as a 'local rag' instead of the sporting bible it was. Its announcement of Keegan's 'decision' sent thousands into despair and hundreds on a pilgrimage to the ground hoping to catch their Messiah before he left town to convince him to change his mind.
Their search ended in vain and people were left to wonder why.

In the car on the way down to Villa that Saturday, Lisa and I sat in a substantial tailback on the M6. The radio bombarded us with everyone's views on Kev. Former players, managers, sporting 'experts' and unknowns from obscure city stock exchange companies all had their two-penny worth but what about us? The people who made the club what it was today?

Our views were conspicuous by their absence. It was hardly the best of days to be stuck between two articulated lorries staring down at Birmingham's sprawl.

This lack of consideration and the club's complete contempt for us was the subject of my ranting to Lisa. To top it all, they were asking the sum of £18.50 for the privilege of watching Charlton Athletic in the FA Cup. Lisa nodded unwittingly, trying desperately to find anything of interest out of the window before feigning sleep. My complaints eventually dried up and I fell silent.

Attaining near proximity to the ground, we avoided the street urchins who had obviously been taking lessons from their Liverpool counterparts in the art of persuasion. The big group that had virtually surrounded one hapless fan's vehicle seemed to have persuaded him of the need to take out that little bit of extra `insurance' when parking on these streets.

His misfortune proving our gain as we wandered unchallenged

up the featureless terraced street.

Terry McDermott, the 'loveable Scouse rogue' who'd leapt obediently around on the touch-line with Keegan was placed in charge. His relationship with the club had dated further back than Kev but he had only been the side-kick.

His new charges set about the task vigorously and duly handed him a 2-0 lead. This was in spite of Villa's complaints that Bosnich's untimely slip (that had handed Clark the chance to lob into an empty net) had been caused by a Shearer 'tug' on the poor lad's shirt.

Despite the score-line the away end remained noticeably downbeat. Attempts to cheer on the caretaker manager's charges fell like the proverbial lead balloon. The majority just didn't want to know.

My frustration grew with the inept attitude around me. The shock of losing Kev had obviously knocked the belief out of them. The team soon slipped into the old habit of giving away leads as first Dwight Yorke, then Savo Milosevic excited the home crowd.

It all looked over when Philippe Albert gave away a penalty. Yorke stepped up only for the re-installed Shaka Hislop to pull off a blinding save.

That would normally have prompted the fans of old to roar the lads on, but not today. The rest of the game seemed to be endured by the majority without much more than a whimper.

The return journey was completed in silence, after my longings for the 'good old days' of singing (unaffected by dire performances) lasted until we reached an untouched Ford Escort. "Why bother going if you're not going to get behind them?" I argued.

My efforts at releasing all my anger and frustration at the match had backfired. Not feeling the same way as the few angry souls dotted about the travelling army. Hadn't everybody shared our sense of injustice?

Keegan had ignited my passion for United thirteen years earlier and now his reign had ended in mysterious circumstances. We had seemed destined to grow old together, tending our allotments and reminiscing over past glories that had at last come our way.

There was to be no walking our greyhounds together or picking up our pensions. Newcastle and Kev were no more. The love affair was over, we'd been jilted after all the happy times together, but who had broken us up?

The men in London were not welcome in our house any more, for sure!

Saturday 22nd February 1997 — Middlesbrough (a)

This time last year, Tino Asprilla had gracefully changed the course of the Tyne —Tees derby to stretch our lead at the top of the Premiership.

Today, matters were a little different. The Messiah was no more. The mumbling Kenny Dalglish had taken over and Notts Forest had ended dreams of Wembley in the FA Cup.

Gill and her mum had taken up the offer of a seat in the Boro stands, while Lisa, Peter and I were seated in the front row of the away end, in their full view.

The large expanse of concrete in front of us would provide the perfect opportunity to charge madly at the fences in recognition of any game-winning strike, the modern equivalent of being moulded to the perimeter fence.

Not only did it avoid the previous pain and suffering, but it also allowed for free expression since it avoided the need to extract someone from your midriff. The more sedate sprint allowed a good deal more self-expression than its predecessor but this option was rarely (if ever) taken up due to the need for uniformity amongst fans.

When Sir Les's drive swept into the net for a likely winner I was presented with the dilemma — individuality (and instant cries of dickhead) or the popular sweep to the front. With both wife and mother-in-law cursing me anyway, I opted for the latter.

Lisa, Peter and I raced to the barrier, arms aloft to herald our hero, who had found the Boro fans at the opposite to us less appreciative of his efforts.

The entire stadium might have been watching our celebrations but I could feel two piercing sets of eyes stabbing at me. The post-match re-union promised to be strained to say the least. Controlling my smugness was going to prove to be the least of my worries.

The rest of the game was spent practising poker faces and repeating "I really hoped you'd get at least a point, dear" without bursting into infantile giggles.

Part of me wanted an equaliser to aid Boro in their fight against relegation, the last couple of trips had lacked the violence of the Ayresome Park days and it was another local derby to triumph in (and a cheap day out).

Juninho, Ravanelli and company failed to reply and after having three points deducted for not turning up at Blackburn (a sensible move if you ask me), they were rooted to the foot of the table.

Before the game, the mood had been relaxed (too relaxed), as shirts were proudly displayed and fans mingled amicably around the ground "Geordie git" and "dirty Smoggie" two of the conversational items bandied about.

Afterwards, as I waited for the inevitable cold shoulder and "night in the shed" routine the mood matched the dark and brooding sky overhead.

Shirts were covered up as much as possible as Newcastle fans set off along the windy banks of the Tees towards Middlesbrough station. Banter had been replaced by threats. The chill wind missing before kick-off acted as a warning.

Gill had expected defeat and prepared herself for it. However, her mum had the look of a wounded animal preparing to lash out at its attacker.

She naively shouted about "you Geordies", "thieving magpies" and "We saw you celebrating". This attracted more than casual glances from the passing Boro fans. Calls for her to calm down as she launched at me with a match programme fell upon deaf ears.

Once calm had been restored and the crowd that had semi-gathered had drifted away, we said our goodbyes and Gill and I wandered up the road. We avoided the jostling queues of Boro fans and a few lonely Mags being subjected to chants of "We hate Geordies..." while they waited to cross under the railway line.

With the Tees lapping to our right and derelict sites bordered by the railway lines there was only one direction to go. I was glad to have covered up as five young lads sprinted past being chased by an even larger group of Boro youth that outnumbered them five to one. Neither group showed any interest in us and the five harsh Geordie voices contrasted with the Boro mixture of Geordie and Yorkshire.

Silence had descended upon us the moment Gill's mum had started her tirade. Her disappointment combined with my natural state of preservation until we reached the car.

Football had been a wearing experience for us both. Boro's slide down the table had contrasted completely with their achievements of reaching the quarterfinals in the FA Cup and semi-finals of the Coca-Cola Cup. The manner of Keegan's exit and the end of an era had been hard to take. To be replaced by Kenny Dalglish who lacked Kev's charisma and used tactics instead of flair had confirmed the Cavalier days were over.

No longer would we be the darlings of the Premiership — results would be ground out instead. The Zetland multi-story car park where we found ourselves marooned for the next hour dragged us down even further — the darkness turning its featureless concrete and petrol stained walls into a backdrop of despair.

True we were now third, but today's display had been workmanlike. This would only be accepted by the fans if it delivered silverware.

Tuesday 4th March 1997 — UEFA QF (1) Monaco (h)

Oldham Athletic had started the rot. For the first time, I had seriously questioned the wisdom of forking out for a match. The instantly forgettable encounter with a lower league side, won by a penalty strike from Beardsley, hardly represented good value for £18.50.

The players, still on cloud nine after stuffing Man United 5-0 looked hungover and couldn't care less. There was such a gulf between the two teams that defeat still never looked possible and conversation with my two neighbours a distinctly unrewarding experience.

A similar price to watch Charlton Athletic had proved the breaking point. For the first time since starting my support in 1984, I was not going to a home match, despite being only nine miles away. Apathy had taken over, I no longer felt a part of the club.

For years I'd gone to games, home and away, whenever I could, witnessing dire performances and results, travelled hundreds of miles to watch last minute winners against us, a multitude of thrashings but all the time I knew I belonged and was proud to wear black and white.

The atmosphere had dropped, wins were expected and the fans sat back more and waited to be entertained. The constant calls to stand up and show your hatred for Sunderland from one bloke behind were always followed by a stream of abuse aimed at all around him.

His anger wasn't at Sunderland — it was the apathy and complacency that had set in. He and I were fans of the 70s (in spirit) and 80s. Joining in with songs from the back of the Leazes, a sorry few would find their voices isolated.

Was our time past? Home games were becoming increasingly frustrating occasions and at the gradually increased cost of £20.50, I decided it was time to vote with my feet. Enough was enough.

Newcastle's strike force of Shearer and Les were injured, Tino was suspended for his corner flag-waving and the unthinkable had happened, Pedro Beardsley had grown old and his best days seemed behind him.

It may have been the quarter-final but I wasn't going to be there. Watching at home, the whole affair seemed subdued and lacking the passion of old. A 0-1 defeat made matters worse for the second leg and in millionaire-land a 0-3 defeat disposed of the lads comfortably.

I felt no remorse at abandoning them in their hour of need. I felt like a throwback to a previous generation. The players would still be paid their ludicrous wages so why should I worry?

If nothing else, my neighbours at St James would have had a quieter night without me.

Saturday 13th April 1997 — Sheff Wed (a)

A day out to watch our respective teams compete seemed a great idea. My Wednesday-supporting colleague sat on the Kop while I took my place in the Leppings Lane Upper Tier.

A lacklustre display from both teams was brightened up by a goal from Newcastle's young left-back Robbie Elliott, his fourth in eleven games.

Wednesday equalised in the second half but the match and atmosphere lacked both passion and interest. The only thing worth watching was the half-time dancing girls and their pom-poms.

The contrast with previous encounters was made stark by the distinct lack of banging seats. It was tradition to repeatedly crash the wooden seats down whenever Newcastle threatened to score but sadly it was left to a few old hands to unsuccessfully fly this particular flag.

The biggest cheer that day came when the scoreboard announced the latest score from the FA Cup Semi-final between Middlesbrough and Chesterfield. A 2-0 score-line to the Yorkshire outfit went down well with both sets of fans desperate to find something to amuse themselves with.

My mind raced back to Gill, sitting in our front room listening to the match on Century Radio and the range of sharp implements available to her in the kitchen. If the score continued in the same manner, one of us would suffer — either me for deserting her in an hour of need, or her in a desperate state.

My mind was put at ease by a bloke at the empty urinals, who informed me that Boro were 3-2 up. Returning to the subdued stands — the score was confirmed, amid cries "Smoggy bastards" and "Jammy..."

A point earned, we listened to Chesterfield's equaliser sitting in a traffic jam up the hill from Hillsborough.

The match we'd witnessed had failed to satisfy us. Apart from the constant barrage from Sheffield's brass band, churning out the theme from "The Great Escape", atmosphere had been at a premium.

The tactics of Kenny Dalglish had drained the game of any excitement. Oh... to support Chesterfield!

Saturday 3t^d May 1997 — Arsenal (a)

Fatherhood was beckoning. This time next year I would, hopefully be the proud father of a five-month-old baby. Gill was going to go part-time after her maternity leave and that would mean less money coming in. Some pleasures would have to go.

This was to be my final away match. My resentment for the constantly increasing prices and diminishing entertainment under Kenny Dalglish had also been a factor but the baby news had kindled a dream I would never be able to realise.

The desire to take a son or daughter to the matches had been strong in me longer than I cared think about. As a teacher, I'd encouraged children to enjoy both playing and watching football. I despaired to see the generation that were growing up with Sky never thinking of journeying to their local ground.

Having been spoilt watching the riches of Arsenal, Man United and Newcastle on Sky each week, why would they want to leave the comfort of their living room? The joy of feeling a part of a club, standing or sitting in all conditions cheering on eleven hopeless misfits would pass them by, even if they could afford it.

It was all too easy to switch off the television and have a kick-about or play a computer game instead of enduring such dire performances.

Paying to watch them made you feel a part. You'd paid good money so it was in your interest to encourage them however you could.

My dad's lack of interest in football (or any sport) made my trips to St James' a solo affair or one with mates, but when I came home, my excitement would fall on deaf (but politely interested) ears.

Beating Liverpool for the first time thanks to Rambo Reilly was lost on them and attempts to re-enact the goal using old pieces of fruit went the same way.

It would be left to my trusty Subbuteo table to maintain my joy.

I needed to share my passion with my family and with the price of tickets and the number of season tickets, my days ahead would be a solo affair, while my family grew up in my absence.

If there could have been one game to sign off on, it was this one! My best mate from college would be sitting in the stand to my left, with my best man from my wedding to my right. The previous years of disappointment at Highbury needed to be avenged, along with two defeats that had lost us the top spot.

Arsenal was five points ahead of us in second place. Man United looked to have won the league again and a place in the Champion's League the prize for runners-up. We had two games in hand on the Londoners and were on a run of six games unbeaten.

There was none of the desperation of the previous season. Paul and Ned congratulated me about the baby and we parted amicably to our separate ends.

Kenny's team smothered the home team and apart from a few scares, Newcastle looked solid, if not inspiring.

The Jumbotron tried to encourage the singing corner, but apart from the odd chants of "You lost the league at Highburee" and "We only had ten men", both sets of fans soaked the fare on offer without putting much back in.

A minute before half-time Robbie Elliott woke our docile corner up by scoring our first goal at Highbury since 1994. Surprised by this unexpected gift the celebrations were restrained, perhaps by the previous lack of excitement.

The second half drifted on in a similar manner, only livening up when Keith Gillespie, coming on as a substitute received two yellow cards in four minutes.

For the final twelve minutes, North London reverberated to inspired choruses of "We only had ten men". This level of poetic justice hadn't occurred since Mirandinha made his debut at Norwich to be taunted with "You come all this way, and you lost", seconds before our equaliser.

The result had given us back some pride, but it would have been greeted more enthusiastically if it had been the previous year.

A bomb scare in Central London deprived me of my chance

to gloat, Paul being unable to reach the World's End pub in Camden. An unusually under-theweather Ned made little conversation and my last trip to London ended a damp and subdued affair.

Despite the catalogue of defeats and poor performances in away matches they provided my favourite memories. The most memorable occurred when they were least expected — Arsenal in 87 and Leicester in 92: both relegation battles.

Sunday 11th May 1997 — Nottingham Forest (h)

The new arrival had forced my hand, but football had taken a hefty toll on both credit cards and bank accounts. There was no way we could afford football and a baby, the baby getting the nod, since it was already on its way.

When the baby was old enough, I'd dreamt of that proud moment when father and son, or daughter, stepped over the threshold, clad in matching shirts to venture on another pilgrimage. Mother would be standing there waving us off with calls of "Hope you lose!" whilst vigorously waving two fingers.

This 'dream' would remain just that. With a waiting list of thousands and tickets costing considerably more than £10 a match for a child, I would have been destined to remain bankrupt (probably divorced) and on my own.

It was fitting that my last game should be a comprehensive victory. A 5-0 win, combined with a favourable result at Hillsborough, offered us second place and a shot at the Champions' League. Tino, Sir Les and Shearer had completed the scoring between them and the only regret was Peter Beardsley didn't get a look-in.

He had scored that first ever goal that had started my fever, fourteen years earlier. As it was he'd not played in the last eight games as a substitute and this was to be his final bow at St James'. His appearance as substitute completed our farewell performance.

The team started the traditional trek around the pitch, applauding the fans who returned the compliment. Next year, a play-off game would decide if Newcastle were to take part in UEFA's club money-spinner but at least they achieved something.

Shearer's name was hailed, but he'd never caught my imagination, not in the same way as Tino and Les had. He'd scored stonking goals that season but paying £15 million for anyone, never mind a local lad seemed bonkers. Every bad pass he made, I would think of his weekly wages and how earned in a week more than I earned in a couple of years.

The cost of getting into stadiums made me more desperate to enjoy myself, to the point that I would leave games more uptight and annoyed if the fans hadn't supported the players enough or if I hadn't had value for money. Had my expectations risen too high?

Football had stopped being fun... it was time to get out, while they were still at the top. I wasn't a rat leaving a sinking ship with glory just around the corner but it wasn't for me — I was never comfortable about success.

The ground was still packed with cheering and appreciative fans and players as I gradually climbed the Leazes steps to the exit.

Standing at the top of the steps, I could still imagine a heaving Gallowgate terrace complete with dotty scoreboard and jumping square hat-men. The barrel-roofed West Stand and paddock terrace below, a more civilised mass of raised arms offering their final farewells to the one player that had turned the club's fortunes around — Kevin Keegan.

Unnoticed, I slipped into the featureless concrete stairwell, then into the eerily empty streets.

Newcastle United had guided me from adolescence to fatherhood with a series of broken promises. If nothing else they had been consistent.

From now on I was no longer a part of the crowd. A combination of bitterness and melancholy surfaced, I'd been rejected because I could no longer afford to pay the asking price. But I wasn't an employee who had given years of service, only a fan who had devoted his time to following his team. They'd no idea I existed, somebody was already waiting in the wings to take my place, my seat only on loan to me.

I knew I'd sung my heart out for the lads and that I would still support them evermore — you can't give up that easily. They were part of me and always would be.

My priorities had changed. A wife and baby would be expecting me to look after them. I was ready to start the next stage in my life, the one of devoted father playing football in the park, telling ludicrous tales of journeys away whilst attempting to bend one in off the crossbar.

The first reluctant steps away from St James' gave way to the more familiar march, the party still carrying on in the background, a party now a part of my past.

A dream realised in my absence.

The reality of life without weekly doses of Newcastle United only sunk in when the new season started.

As a result of finishing second, they had to play off against Croatia Zagreb for the right to enter the Champions League. Seeing the Croat fans parading down Northumberland Street before the first leg set my pulse racing, not only because apart from a group of Oxford United fans who stumbled upon the Three Bulls Heads, I had never seen any away fans outside of the confines of the ground.

The thought of forking out £20+ proved a stumbling block — I couldn't bring myself to do it. One look at Gill's growing bump made me remember a cot, decorated room, clothes and a whole range of baby clart. It was a wrench not being a face in the crowd... but a necessary one.

From then on Metro Radio and the odd match on television was the closest I got. The thought of missing out on my Saturday's entertainment proved easier than expected. Under Dalglish, United struggled in the wrong half of the table.

Ferdinand had gone to Spurs along with Ginola (no real loss there) while in came bald nut-case Temuri Ketsbaia, Jon Dahl Tomasson and Andreas Andersson, a striker in the Mark Stimson mould, lacking in both skill and commitment.

My opinions had been formed from reading match reports and television but this was hardly a good basis to judge players from. The new lads were just names to me but only Ketsbaia had made an impression (thanks to his equalising goal against Croatia that earned Newcastle their place in the Champions' League). Sir Les and even the erratic Ginola would be sorely missed.

The players brought in failed to live up to the early hype - a far cry from the glorious performances of the previous years. Glory loomed in the Champions League when Spanish giants Barcelona were beaten 3-2 thanks to a Tino hat-trick but when he got injured the dream went pear-shaped.

In the last few days of 1997, the reason for my absence at St James' arrived after a visit to watch another Newcastle team — the Cobras ice hockey team. Our daughter was born hours after a labour-inducing match. The tiny little object in my arms was going to eat more money than Newcastle United could ever have dragged out of me. Days of TV football lay ahead.

I was now officially condemned to life as an armchair supporter.

Sunday 4th January 1998 — FA 3 — Everton (a)

My first duty in my new position was to take in the romance of the cup in the hours or so that the baby had given us to recuperate from nights of changing nappies and feeding.

By the turn of the year the FA Cup was the only chance of silverware. How many times had I heard that mentioned in joke before, only for Newcastle to end that dream at the first available opportunity?

An unbearably dull game was beamed live to the nation. I'd long since drifted away from the dirge on offer, preferring to read the Sunday papers when a scrappy scramble from old-timer Ian Rush (signed by Dalglish to add potency up front) secured the win. It was about the only goal he scored for Newcastle but the win it earned hardly indicated a trip to Wembley.

Sunday 25th January 1998 — FA 4 —Stevenage (a)

In the next round non-league Stevenage looked easy meat but Newcastle did their best to wind them up, complaining that the tie should be played at St James' in the interests of crowd safety'. The rest of the country translated this to mean that we were frightened of losing.

I'd become sufficiently removed from the club to realise what fools the board were making of themselves. Sky chose the clash to show live, hoping for embarrassment to follow.

Complacency must have set in because there was no way anyone thought the minnows stood a chance but when they took the lead, the stampings of the board looked to have backfired drastically. Alan Shearer earned a replay at St James' but even then they struggled, eventually winning 2-1. Hardly a score you'd expect from the moneybags in the Premiership.

Treacherously, if Stevenage had won, I wouldn't have batted an eyelid. The whole affair had tarnished Newcastle's name. The arrogance shown towards the minnows meant they had "gone down in my estimation".

Another easy fifth round draw saw them scrape past

Tranmere 1-0 at home. Why couldn't we have had an easy draw when I went regularly?

The good luck continued as Manchester United were beaten 3-1 by Barnsley to set up a quarter-final tie at Newcastle. The visitors were struggling to avoid relegation and Newcastle did what was expected of them, winning 3-1 in what was their best display of the run.

With the semi-final awaiting, two members of Newcastle's board did their best to drag the club into the gutter.

On a trip to Spain, Freddie Shepherd and Douglas Hall bragged about their amorous conquests to an undercover tabloid reporter who lapped it all up. They also branded Newcastle's women as "dogs" (not that they were great oil paintings themselves) and laughed at the fans who paid over-the-top prices for shirts they said cost peanuts to make.

As if the club's position just above the drop zone to the First Division wasn't enough, they now had the biggest public relations fiasco in the club's history. John Hall came to steady the reigns and the two miscreants were banished and told to stand quietly in the corner.

At least Newcastle was in the Semi-final for the first time since 1974 to take the fans' mind off the pair's views. I had waited fifteen years, hoping for this moment and was sick at missing out. Once again, luck had been on Newcastle's side with another easy draw — Sheffield United. Shearer came up with the goods to win 1-0 and a place in the final against Arsenal.

Before the cup final, however there was the little matter of Premiership survival and when Alan Shearer and Neil Lennon got into a tangle, the United striker looked to stamp on Lennon. Shearer maintained that he had lost his balance but the tabloids, desperate to run him down, started their witch-hunt against the England captain who understandably was having a hard time. Despite the FA taking his side and Lennon saying it was an accident, the nation (outside of Tyneside) were not convinced.

Shearer's surly style of play and character-less monotone voice eventually became his trademark in endless McDonalds adverts but didn't endear him to the wolves that were waiting for him to slip up.

At least Newcastle avoided relegation as a 0-0 draw in that game at Leicester combined with a 3-1 home win against Chelsea to lift spirits for the impending final.

Saturday 16th March 1997 — FA Cup Final — Arsenal

Newcastle had gone FA cup mad. Every shop window was filled with black and white crepe paper, while from every car aerial black and white ribbons flapped joyfully. Wandering around Newcastle put a lump in my throat. This was what football was all about, despite all the arguments, bickering and scraped results the town had pulled together for one big party.

The near 30,000 fans who had travelled down, combined with those dedicated souls who had started watching Sky's coverage at eight o'clock, gave the streets an eerie feel to them. You could sense the imminent match was gradually drawing people off the streets.

The town was bustling but not crowded, most busy preparing for the party of the decade. I felt duty bound to show my support. Last year this would have been the greatest day of my life. It was like a large chunk of me was missing.

My whole life had changed without me realising and I was quite put out that Newcastle had reached Wembley without me. My uncle from America came across with his son, getting tickets in a hospitality suite. My dislike for the whole 'business hospitality' ideal didn't stopped me from begging him to take me.

After all I'd been through for Newcastle, surely there had to be some justice in the world. But, I'd deserted them, hadn't I? The reason why I'd taken such drastic action was looking at me from a baby carrier, completely unaware of the events unfolding before her.

Using deviousness unseen since my days of sneaking off to book bus tickets to Norwich or Chelsea, I convinced Gill that I was just popping to the club shop to buy some ribbons.

Once inside, I took one look at the 70's-style shirts that had been introduced that season and carried out my devious plan. This was the same shirt that I'd berated the club for bringing out, since it carried a large black shield on the back that required a number to fill it (at an extra cost of £3).

The one player that represented the days before Newcastle and football in general had become so money-orientated was Robert Lee. He'd been there in the second division so I had his number 7 printed on the back of my shirt. The connection with Keegan's number as a player added extra weight to my decision.

Ignoring Gill's displeasure, I installed myself in the shirt and felt a part of the club again.

Our five-month old daughter seemed quite happy to be pressed against the club crest, finding great interest in the two seahorses embroidered on it.

I'd discovered the sense of regional pride that came from having a successful team. Everybody on Tyneside felt it when they watched the teams strolled out onto the turf for their pre-match wander.

The only disappointment was not having witnessed the team in the flesh. I couldn't associate myself with the majority of the team, a stranger looking in.

The pride and sense of occasion disappeared the moment Arsenal scored through Mark Overmars in the 23rd minute and Nicolas Anelka in the 69th. In between, Shearer and Dabizas hit the woodwork, but Newcastle was second best.

I thought of Ned — in his second season of owning an Arsenal season ticket and Paul, in his umpteenth, celebrating what turned out to be the league and cup double. How jammie could you get?

Watching all the Newcastle fans proudly cheering on another apathetic Wembley reminded me just how great Newcastle fans were, cheering on regardless. The day turned sour as the sun drifted behind the clouds and gloom descended on Tyneside.

The violence that had spoilt Keegan's attempt at the Championship again marred another defeat. The riots in the Bigg Market were threatening to become an annual event as defeat had become associated with vandalism and violence.

Newcastle's season had been a relative disaster (apart from the cup). From being the nations favourite other team under Keegan, they had narrowly avoided relegation in the penultimate league game; had its directors rubbish both the region and its fans; and their star striker had become public enemy number one. Not exactly what had been expected.

Sexy football?

The honest but dull Dalglish, despite ringing every fan after every game (according to British Telecom) to thank them for their contribution was on his way.

In came the flamboyant Dutchman, Ruud Gullit. He promised Sexy

Football and despite an early setback when Liverpool (and England's World Cup '98 star Michael Owen) handed out a 4-1 lesson in football, September was a bright month.

The lads reached the heights of 3rd before the season went pear-shaped. By December they had slipped to 15th and it looked like nothing had been achieved by sacking Dalglish, bar more comprehensible press conferences.

Gullit suffered from a tendency to shrug his shoulders a lot while his head lolled from one side to the other, as if he was trying to shake his brain into action.

Once again the FA Cup came to United's rescue with easy wins against Crystal Palace (2-1) and Bradford (3-0) earning a spot in the fifth round. A trip to Premiership strugglers Blackburn was won by a goal from the instantly recognisable but soon forgotten Saha. His black and white dreadlocks might have been intended as an offering to the home fans but after a few appearances and two goals he disappeared from the scene.

A noticeable difference was the number of British players in the team as the foreign invasion really took hold of the Premiership. Chelsea managed to field a team without a Brit (apart from Dennis Wise but he didn't count).

In the sixth round, the team notched up a 4-1 demolition of Everton as revenge for defeat at the same stage in 1995. A semi-final place against Tottenham meant Newcastle had avoided both Manchester United and Arsenal.

Sunday 11th April 1999 — FA SF — Tottenham

Arsenal Paul and his wife had come up to Whitley Bay for the weekend. A sedate Saturday was spent at Newcastle Arena watching a Concert for the Minimum Wage, this was followed by the obligatory curry, essential for any visitor to the region.

We sat watching the two Semi-finals on television starting with Arsenal against Manchester United.

Although Paul still had an Arsenal season ticket, his experiences the previous year at Villa Park had put him off the return journey. He was just not cut out for such occasions, I reminded him, a stay-at-home supporter, unwilling to endure the hardships of away travel that proved you were a true supporter. If the roles had been reversed, I would have been there like a shot — baby and all.

As Paul slipped into his match mode, I realised how mellow I'd become and unable to drop everything at the chance of a semi-final. The time spent away from St James' had calmed my aggressive nature. I no longer felt the need to shout obscenities at the screen, unlike Paul who became a figure of great fascination for my toddling daughter. She desperately wanted to empathise with him but couldn't understand what all the fuss was about.

Manchester taking the lead didn't go down well. I sat serenely enjoying seeing my mate so worked up as all the occasions when I had cursed him and his smug team flooded back to me.

Ginola's sending off in the Coca-Cola Cup; Alan Smith's last minute overhead kick and losing the league at Highbury — all moments of the utmost depression on my behalf and smugness on his. He hadn't even had the courtesy to gloat it meant so little to him.

Arsenal's equaliser ended his torment but a missed late penalty brought a smile to my face.

Since Newcastle were playing his local rivals, Paul gladly cheered them on and in contrast to last year's dominance of Sheffield United both teams produced a well-matched display that eventually went to extra time.

I found myself being drawn into the match atmosphere as once more the travelling support did us proud. My language reflected the closeness of the situation. Luck was with us when the referee missed a handball by Greek defender Dabizas while Shearer tucked away a penalty at the other end.

The celebrations woke up my daughter but it was worth the cries that lasted until milk was duly given. Shearer's second was the kind of goal I wanted to see settle a place at Wembley — top corner screamer. Tap-ins or spawny penalties had no place settling matches — I wanted to be entertained, and Shearer had done just that. He may well advertise Big Mac's but there was nothing dull about that strike.

Arsenal's defeat in the replay of the other semi-final to Ryan Giggs' solo run denied Newcastle the chance for revenge against Arsenal. Watching Shearer's 89th minute overhead kick win the cup would have been the ultimate put-down for years of Arsenal supremacy.

It was all now just a dream. At least we'd have the satisfaction of beating Man United instead.

Saturday 22nd May — FA Final — Manchester United

So sure was I that lightning couldn't strike twice that I splashed out on all manner of bets, Shearer and Ketsbaia to score first (in separate bets) among others. I ignored the fact that Newcastle had failed to win any of their games after that Semi-final. The common excuse was that they were saving themselves for the final but later developments pointed elsewhere.

Rumours had surfaced of a rift between Gullit and Shearer and also German mid-fielder Hamann. Tales abounded of Gullit's arrogant streak and his dislike of anybody that had as big an ego as his.

Newcastle's performance against the newly-crowned Champions hardly justified the wonderful support that the travelling army gave them. Sheringham scored after 10 minutes to ruin all my bets and Scholes wrapped things up just after half time. The score could have been 4-0.

The second Wembley visit in two years avoided some of the fever that had struck the previous year. Newcastle wasn't as decorated but there was still the same anticipation.

The starting line-up between the two games reflected a 50% drop in British players from eight to four — David Batty and Stuart Pearce had left the club while Steve Howey was injured and Warren Barton out of favour.

The feeling I had for the team lessened every time one of the recognised players I'd loved to watch left. There were only Shearer and Robert Lee left from two seasons before. If Gullit stayed... how long would they?

I couldn't feel the same way for the foreign players and it was easier to turn off at the final whistle, if only to avoid the crowing Manchester fans.

At least the police were prepared for trouble in the Bigg Market and the evening in town passed relatively peacefully.

Monday 3rd January 2000 — West Ham United (h)

In two short years, Newcastle United had reached two FA Cup finals, fought two successful relegation battles, sacked two managers, managed to alienate the female population of Tyneside along with any fan who had bought a replica strip. Share prices that had started at about £1.30 had plummeted to less than half of that.

In the wake of this, season ticket prices had continued to rise along with players' wages.

The club's public relations record, already at an all-time low after Douglas Hall and Freddie Shepherd's comments sank to new depths.

The club was half-way through extending the Leazes and Milburn stands to raise the capacity to 51,000. A cause for celebration had turned into a courtroom battle between a group of bond-holders and the club. The directors wanted to move them to make way for new corporate bars at three times the price.

The fans objected because they had been led to believe that their seats would be guaranteed for 10 years when they had bought them. The SOS (Save our Seats) campaign was set up to fight back. This was the backdrop to my return to St James'.

Using Lisa's ticket, I set off for the first time in three years. I quickened my steps in the same way I'd done countless times before, never once knowing the Metro times. That knowledge would have taken away the sense of urgency and tension that was such a part of match-day.

The journey dragged in the same way it always had, the increasing numbers of fans pushing up the volume in the carriage and my heart rate. The buzz was still there!

Stepping through the turnstile at the Gallowgate end, it was like I'd never been away. Although at the opposite end of the ground, the layout was identical, even down to the bars and food bars.

The PA blazed out a repetitive mix of adverts and music: gone, thankfully, were the days of Alan Robson screaming for us to "Make some noise!"

Adverts for Virgin radio's rock'n roll football and computer games attacked your ears every few minutes.

The only distraction from the din was a pair of large magpie characters cavorting around the pitch to AC/DC. A male and a female... they didn't care what they danced to, as long as it was loud.

The extension rose above the opposite end of the ground. A structure that now dominated the Newcastle skyline from every direction failed to look as impressive from the inside as from the outside.

Ruud Gullit had been replaced by Bobby Robson, from dour Scot to flamboyant, but arrogant Dutchman to old-time

Geordie. Newcastle fans had seen it all in the previous years.

In Robson, they seemed to have found the man that should have replaced Keegan but was never available. He'd turned a side that had collected just one point in the first seven games into one that had lost just three in thirteen league games.

Alan Shearer's form had dramatically returned under Robson with a five-goal blast in Bobby's first home game against fellow strugglers Sheff Wed, a game that finished 8-0.

After two years of struggle, the winning expectancy had returned to the club. This was confirmed when Dabizas (in the style of countless home-grown centre-backs) scored.

Half-time was greeted early by some desperate souls, dashing to get the drinks in and by the time the break did arrive a good proportion of the crowd were imbibing.

Following the crowd, stationary bodies ahead forced me to stop as the halftime scores were read out. A familiar anticipatory hush fell upon the ground as Sunderland's score at Wimbledon was read out. Their 1-0 adverse position was greeted with a cheer, before the hubbub, annoying adverts and activity resumed.

In the days of terrace, that result would have been celebrated long after the teams had emerged for the second half, but the lack of highly-charged teenagers with nothing better to do accounted for that.

I made my way into the glass-fronted middle bar of the stand, with the spectacular view across the city and river that had been lost to spectators by the building of the stand.

Groups of young men and the occasional girl chattered in ever-expanding circles. What children there were running in and out of the groups annoying just about everybody by knocking pint-laden hands and demanding more food from already financially-challenged parents.

The rail in front of the glass front was occupied by the lonely souls who enjoyed their own company every week — the anoraks, ridiculed by their peers. They stood surveying the Gallowgate car park and bus station below, the view along the newly widened Blenheim Street, the Newcastle Weather Centre and the imposing Newcastle Breweries complex. The buildings stood for a century of change - a mix of early precision and 70's ugliness that had become so familiar to thousands of fans over the years.

Even the starlings were still 'swarming' about the skyline

inventing ever more complex patterns.

Despite all this familiarity, it didn't feel like home any more. Three years restricted to passive armchair viewing had taken the passion away. I was a stranger, uncomfortable in once accustomed territory.

Returning to my seat I was reminded that ginger presenter Chris Evans' football show featured a team of football experts and Terry Venables "the godfather of football". He'd certainly proved to be that, as supporters of Crystal Palace and Portsmouth were finding out to their cost.

I was sitting behind one of Lisa's friends Chris, who responded to my opening line of "Last time I was here..." with "...all you could see was green fields...". He had no time for my reminiscences as the second half began, preferring to continue his ritualistic abuse of the officials and players.

A half-volleyed goal from Speed calmed Chris's nervous chatter as the crowd woke up for five minutes to sing the team's praises before a studious murmur descended.

Complacency set in as West Ham responded with goal five minutes before time. The half-empty away end woke from their slumber and when an injury-time equaliser secured an extremely lucky point, they positively crowed.

The home fans trooped home to the blare of the PA, arguing amongst themselves as to who was to blame for this slip.

As an Newcastle old boy looking in, it was good to see that even with all the expensive imports that made up the bulk of the team, they still had the ability to shoot themselves in the foot. A rare talent that Manchester United weren't able to match.

Life away from St James'

I'd never imagined not watching Newcastle. When I started watching them in 1984, I thought our lives would be inextricably linked. I hadn't bargained on the rise in Football's popularity that resulted in the price rises.

As I learnt in my Economics O-level it was simple supply and demand. When nobody wanted to watch it, the price stayed relatively low, but once demand shot up so did the price to compensate for the limited numbers of seats.

There would always be part of me devoted to Newcastle,

could I ever support any other football team in the same way? They'd taught me to be proud of my region in a way that I could never have expected. I took a pride in the Geordie accent (much to mum's annoyance), learnt to love the Metro and appreciate the North Sea because they were a symbol of what is great about our region.

I loved the cold, dark nights and the sight of people's breath hanging in them. Memories of winter night matches sprang to mind and the glare of the floodlights. I sated smoking but whenever I smelt cigarette smoke in the air, found myself drawing t in, recalling the Gallowgate terrace and its combination of dodgy burgers, cups of 3ovril and `ciggies'.

The homeliness of the ground had gone, the lived-in look 'spring-cleaned' to leave the sterile but impressively functional ground. Each piece that disappeared: book memories with it. The loss of the scoreboard, the corner, even the bloke we sarcastically cheered when he stood up to create his shrill, warbling 'bird-call' had disappeared.

My first visit to St James' cost me £1.50 (many remember it cheaper) but now that wouldn't even buy you a match programme. I wouldn't be able to do the same now, a whole generation had lost the chance to follow in my footsteps. There may be places in the family enclosure but the lads who wanted to visit with their mates — how could they visit now? St James' has become a closed shop. Not being able to share the match ritual with my family diminished its appeal.

The ones who remained are under threat from new initiatives as United introduce more new bars and members' schemes, each requiring initial expenditure on the part of fans wanting to join.

Wearing the shirt has been banned in some of the bars, making the thousands who spend money on the merchandise second class citizens.

The ground now rises impressively above the city centre and can be seen from nearly every bit of the city, a cathedral to football.

The amazing fact is that a 51,000-seat stadium is being built for a team that hasn't won a major trophy in over 30 years. I was convinced that the days of 50,000+ crowds had gone with terracing but now Sunderland are looking to expand beyond 40,000 while Man United pack 60,000 into each game.

Unfortunately, the rest of the league has been forgotten. First Division clubs invariably return straight down, unable to match transfer fees or wages. Clubs (including Newcastle) are even further in debt and paying out exorbitant wages for average players.

What will happen in fifteen years' time when banks start getting tough on overdrafts? Will the youth that has been deprived of live football be able to pull themselves away from computer or television screens?

I have been retired to the sofa… and the bitterness of my first few months have gone. The atmosphere at away matches has picked up again and although Sunderland has surprisingly turned the tables on Newcastle, under Bobby Robson, we have the manager who understands the town and the people.

Like an old man, I moan about the state of the modern game but one thing is certain…

Newcastle will always be a part of me no matter what the board does…but everyone has their breaking point.

Printed in Great Britain
by Amazon